2012-2015:

The

SEASON OF
RETURN?

COMPELLING NEW SIGNS THAT POINT TO
AN IMMINENT SECOND COMING

2012-2015:

The
SEASON OF
RETURN?

COMPELLING NEW SIGNS THAT POINT TO
AN IMMINENT SECOND COMING

T.W. TRAMM

Now learn a parable of the fig tree; When her branch is yet tender, and putteth forth leaves, ye know that summer is near: So ye in like manner, when ye shall see these things come to pass, know that it is nigh, even at the doors. Verily I say unto you, that this generation shall not pass, till all these things be done.

—Mark 13:28-30

For those who sense that summer is near.

PREFACE

It goes without saying that Bible prophecy, particularly as it relates to the Second Coming, can be a contentious topic. So, before we begin, I would like to establish a few key things: First and fore mostly, this book should not be construed as an attempt at "setting a date" for the return of Jesus Christ. As indicated by the title, we are merely looking at a specified window of time and asking the question, "Is this the season of return?" While I will demonstrate that we pose this question with overwhelming justification, the important thing to keep in mind is that we are ultimately only posing the question. Thus, any hypotheticals or speculation regarding events or timeframes should be viewed only as *possibilities* and treated as such. The Apostle Paul tells us to "test everything" and to "hold on to the good." (1 Thessalonians 5:21). It is in the spirit of this biblical precept that this book was written, and it is in this spirit that I hope it will be received.

Secondly, under the heading of "I know this sounds crazy but..." some fantastic things will be discussed in this book. These include events that took place in the days before Noah's flood, as well as some more, shall we say, "contemporary" supernatural activity that is manifesting in our world today. I bring this up because in an age of skepticism some have a difficult time with a *literal* interpretation of the Bible and therefore struggle with certain claims that it makes; for instance, the week-long timeframe given for the creation of the world, or the notion that the entire globe was once flooded, destroying all life except for one family and an ark full of animals. Still others have a difficult time reconciling certain biblical assertions about the reality of demons or demonic possession. On this topic in particular it is evident that, despite man's tendency to discount what he cannot see, we are dealing with a literal reality here. The fact is that these malevolent beings are as real as the book you are holding in your hands, and their stepped-up efforts account for virtually all of the so-called "paranormal" activity—as well as the startling upsurge in evil—that we are seeing in the world today.

The point to be made is that the Bible is not a book of mere allegory, or poetry. The histories it chronicles, the figures it portrays, and the as of yet future events it describes are all very real indeed. Once this simple fact is acknowledged, the world around us begins to make a lot more sense. Still, I urge the skeptic to not merely take my word on these things, but to do his or her own research. Fortunately, for those who care to seek, the evidences for many of the Holy Book's most fantastic claims are more accessible than ever.

And lastly, several chapters of this book will focus on topics that many would consider "Jewish" centric, such as certain holy days or traditions. Many feel that these applied only to the ancient Hebrews who lived under the Old Testament "Law" and therefore have no bearing on the modern Church. Some even feel that Israel has been *replaced* by the Christian Church and is somehow no longer relevant to God's plans for the end of the age. The fact remains, however, that God entered into an everlasting covenant with Abraham and his descendants that must be completely fulfilled or Bible prophecy will be proven to be in error. So while all "believers," Jew and Gentile alike, will indeed be heir to God's promises, it must be understood that the Jews, the holy land of Israel, and its capital, Jerusalem—the place where Hebrew legend claims that God stood when He created the world—all have yet to play a special role in the culmination of the end-times prophecies. A basic grasp of this is crucial to understanding both the current and forthcoming fulfillment of these prophecies.

These things noted, regardless of your background in prophecy, or lack thereof, I am confident that you will find in this book some surprising revelations, some interesting food for thought, and some invaluable insights, all of which, in light of the hour we are living in, will serve you well in the days and years ahead.

—T.W. Tramm

CONTENTS

INTRODUCTION

Speaking to the "climate change" debacle set off by scientists' alleged suppressing of temperature data, the U.N. Secretary-General, Ban Ki-moon, asserted recently:

"Nothing that has come out in the public as a result of the recent email hackings has cast doubt on the basic scientific message on climate change, and that message is [still] quite clear...*climate change is happening much, much faster than we realized and we human beings are the primary cause.*"[1]

While personally not a proponent of *man made* global warming, I would have to say that to a certain extent I actually agree with this statement, but only in the sense that the planet is indeed going to experience a major change in "climate" in the near future. This change, however, will not be a consequence of the actions of human beings but due to a miraculous reconfiguration in the natural order of things. This reconfiguration was spoken of millennia ago by the prophets of the Bible; untold multitudes have lived their entire lives longing to see it; and today, many scoff at the notion—but not for much longer.

The fact is, change *is* coming to planet Earth. It is not the type of change envisioned by anxious climatologists, but an actual shift in *reality* that can only be brought about by the creator of matter Himself. The aftermath of this shift is described in the Book of Isaiah as an era of peace and harmony in which the proverbial lion will lie down with the lamb—a state of being that has eluded humanity since the fall at Eden.

How can one be so sure of all of this? Most believers would cite certain prophetic passages and then point to their present-day fulfillment, i.e., Matthew's predictions of escalating natural disasters, pandemics, famine, and war (Matthew 24); Timothy's description of rampant moral decay (2 Timothy), or Daniel's foretelling of a great proliferation of knowledge and travel as we enter into the last days (Daniel 12). There is also the rebirth of Israel in '48 and the Jewish recapture of Jerusalem in '67—both events believed to be critical benchmarks in the countdown to Christ's return. All of these signs, according to Christians, tell us that the time is near.

But how near? Twenty years? Ten years? Five—or less?

In searching for clues, many today watch and wait for some very specific events to unfold. For some, this includes the rebuilding of the Jewish Temple in Jerusalem and the signing of a "seven year peace treaty"; for others, the rise of a "one-world government" and the implementation of a global currency that will herald the "mark of the beast." Still others believe that the "rapture" will occur well before any of these things.*

What we as believers sometimes forget, however, is that while Scripture will indeed be fulfilled as promised, there is no guarantee that these fulfillments will look exactly like the scenarios we have imagined, or even those set forth by today's best-selling authors. The truth of the matter is that for even the most astute prophecy scholar much about how the last days will unfold remains a mystery. For now, as Paul put it, we only "know in part" and "prophesy in part" (1 Corinthians 13:9). This begs a provocative question: What if, due to a prevailing lack of insight and an abundance of erroneous teachings,

---

* Please note that I am not proposing that any or all of these things are not going to happen, only that it is advisable to keep an open mind in regard to all matters prophetic. For details on my perspective on a "one-world government" and "the mark of the beast," please see my other book, *From Abraham to Armageddon.*

the Church is largely oblivious to some clear "signs," as their collective gaze remains doggedly fixed on the anticipated fulfillment of this prophecy or that?

This book is not like most other "end-times" books you may have read. We will not be reviewing what you already know about the signs of the times, nor will we needlessly map out a particular prophetic scenario which may or may not resemble what the actual fulfillment will look like. To the contrary, the idea here is to look beyond these well-worn themes and expand our end-times repertoire of things to watch for by taking note of some *other* signs, some of which are manifesting before our eyes yet remain unnoticed or are discounted because they do not fit the criteria or timelines that we or our favorite authors or teachers may have set. These signs consist of a collection of unique, diverse, and, dare I say, *time specific* indicators that seem to point to the soon return of Jesus Christ:

For instance, we will note how some special "holy day" observances given directly to Moses by God actually reveal the Hebrew calendar day (to the exclusion of the year) on which the Second Coming will occur. We will also delve into the recently rediscovered writings of preeminent genius, Isaac Newton. A little-known fact is that Newton, who wrote extensively on Bible prophecy, believed that chapter 9 of Daniel pointed not only to the precise year of Christ's first coming (as is widely acknowledged) but also to the year of His *second* coming.

Next, we will note how both of these seem to be linked via a recent discovery of some extremely rare solar and lunar activity. Could these "signs in the heavens" be a message from God that confirms Newton's interpretation and thus the fact that the time is nearly upon us?

There are also other indicators to consider: While these are still largely unrecognized as being related to Bible prophecy, each, I believe, is a direct corollary of biblical events and therefore sheds a corroborative light on our proximity to the last days; these include the current "Mayan-2012 phenomenon," the ever-burgeoning New Age

Movement and, believe it or not, the increasingly conspicuous incursions of UFOs and their supposed extraterrestrial pilots into our earthly airspace.

Thus, in the following pages, we are going to examine some ancient Hebrew traditions, some long-regarded prophecies, some celestial signs, some fascinating ancient myths—and even some apparent modern-day supernatural activity—an eclectic and compelling array of data, all of which seems to point to the timing of the most anticipated events in the history of mankind: the resurrection, or "rapture," of the Church and the bodily return of Jesus Christ to earth. Each chapter will touch on a unique yet profoundly intertwined piece of the end-times tapestry, ultimately leading to a common thread that binds all of them together: a specific timeframe, a year even, that repeatedly emerges as one of perhaps great prophetic significance—2015.

Could it be that we are that close? Only God knows for certain, but many today are asking, might the Lord be sending some signs in these last days that reveal much more about the timing of His return than most had previously dared to imagine?

This, for many believers, is the question of the day, and the question that this book will endeavor to answer.

PART I

PREPARATIONS

Call unto me, and I will answer thee, and show thee great and mighty things, which thou knowest not.

—Jeremiah 33:3

Can We Know?

When is Jesus coming back? For nearly two millennia the question has been posed by countless believers.

But why bother posing the question when the Lord Himself has made it clear that neither man nor angel can know the answer?

> But of that day and hour knoweth no man, no, not the angels of Heaven, but my Father only.
>
> —Matthew 24:36

Indeed, most Christians have taken this verse, or at least their understanding of it, to heart. In fact, many today, perhaps having been disappointed by past failed predictions, frown upon those who make it a practice to speculate.

A prime illustration of this sentiment is cited below in the "Rules & Doctrinal Statements" of a popular website that hosts chat on various end-times topics. Rule number eleven makes it clear that even "suggesting" a timeframe for the Second Coming is not only taboo, but is *outlawed* on this particular website:

> **Rule [11]** "No End Times Date Setting, Date Speculating, Date Framing, Date Suggesting, Date Alerts, or designating specific [events as preceding] the main event of the Rapture or Second Coming…No quoting from others on date setting

future events…This includes linking to sites and books that also speculate and throw out dates…"

Needless to say, the owner of this site seems to have adopted a "zero tolerance" policy toward those who wish to indulge in this type of speculation. But is this the mind-set that the Bible prescribes—one of utter resignation to a state of unknowingness?

IT'S NOT A SIN TO SEEK

In this brief chapter, we are going to cite numerous passages of Scripture that demonstrate not only does God give us the means to find what He has hidden, but that He is, in fact, in the business of revealing these things to those who seek them.

As for speculation, one must simply keep in mind that it is what it is: man's best, albeit *imperfect*, attempt to discern the as of yet unknown. Any failed prediction is, of course, not to be looked upon as undermining the prophetically divine nature of Scripture, but as merely a reflection on the interpreter's lack of understanding. It is consequently up to us, as believers, each imbued with his or her own measure of God-given common sense, to make these distinctions. Therefore, speculation, assuming that it is *grounded in Scripture* and presented as "speculation," would seem to be a valuable exercise for those seeking the answers to the Bible's most intriguing mysteries— including the timing of Jesus' return. In fact, while this statement is also ultimately somewhat speculative, it seems certain that the very act of searching, in and of itself, would be pleasing to God.

Now, all talk of speculation aside, let us take a look at a few verses that highlight God's willingness to reveal His mysteries:

Surely the Sovereign LORD does nothing without revealing his plan to his servants the prophets.

—Amos 3:7

Here, Amos tells us that God does "nothing" without first "revealing His plan" to His prophets, the very prophets who—inspired by the Lord Himself—penned the Bible.

> I make known the end from the beginning, from ancient
> times, what is still to come…
> —Isaiah 46:10

Here, in Isaiah, the Lord relates that He has "from ancient times" chosen to "make known" what is to come. Make known to whom, you ask? To you and me, in the Scriptures.

> I have even from the beginning declared it to thee; before it
> came to pass I shewed it thee…
> —Isaiah 48:5

And here, Isaiah declares that "before it came to pass," God has shown it to us.

These verses make it clear: God has revealed the future in the Bible. And judging from the frequency of statements like these, He wants it known.

Still, the core question remains: Does He reveal the *timing* of future events?

DOES GOD REVEAL THE SPECIFICS?

Those familiar with Bible prophecy are almost certainly well-acquainted with the Book of Daniel. In Daniel, we find several examples of God revealing not only specific future events, but the *timing* of these events. A case in point is Daniel 9:2; here, we find that the Prophet, through his study of Scripture, was able to determine that the time of Israel's captivity in Babylon was about to end. A stunning and no doubt welcome revelation to Daniel, but this divine demonstration of foreknowledge is dwarfed by what we find later in verses 25 and 26 wherein God reveals, centuries in advance, the year of Messiah's arrival, as well as the year of His death and resurrection!

What this means, of course, is that the people who lived in Christ's era, had they understood the prophecies, could have, at least in theory, determined from Scripture *exactly* when these future events would take place. Unfortunately, most of the Jewish leaders did not understand the prophecies and as a consequence did not recognize that Christ was fulfilling them before their eyes. This being the case, it is interesting to note Jesus' less-than-glowing appraisal of this prevailing state of blindness:

> "…O ye hypocrites, ye can discern the face of the sky; but can ye not discern the signs of the times?"
>
> —Matthew 16:3

Another famous instance of God revealing the timing of coming events is found in Genesis, wherein He tells Noah *exactly* when the rains of the great flood would begin—seven days before the fact:

> The LORD then said to Noah, "Go into the ark, you and your whole family, because I have found you righteous in this generation. *Seven days from now I will send rain on the earth* for forty days and forty nights, and I will wipe from the face of the earth every living creature I have made."
>
> —Genesis 7:1, 4

In yet another example, God revealed to the prophets the very day on which Elijah would be "raptured," or taken up to heaven:

> And the sons of the prophets that were at Bethel came forth to Elisha, and said unto him, *Knowest thou that the LORD will take away thy master from thy head to day?* And he said, Yea, I know it; hold ye your peace. And it came to pass, as

they still went on, and talked, that, behold, there appeared a
chariot of fire, and horses of fire, and parted them both
asunder; and Elijah went up by a whirlwind into heaven.

—2 Kings 2:3, 11

The obvious lesson to be taken from these examples is that in
addition to revealing future events God has, on numerous occasions,
revealed such details as the *timing* of said events.

"MY PEOPLE ARE DESTROYED FOR LACK OF KNOWLEDGE."

Now, as we delve even further into the question of "can we know
the timing?" let us revisit the verse that was cited at the beginning of
this chapter:

But of that day and hour knoweth no man, no, not the angels of Heaven, but my Father only.

—Matthew 24:36

At first glance, this statement would seem discouraging to those
who might seek to know the timing of the Lord's return. Yet, if we
take Jesus' words here at face value, we note that He is merely telling
us that we will not know the "day" or the "hour" of His coming.
Thus, knowing the "season," the month, the week—even the timing
to within a couple of days—is not precluded. In fact, concerning this
particular verse, many feel that rather than the meaning typically
ascribed to it (that the timing is unknowable), Jesus was actually
employing a very specific phraseology with the intention of directing
us toward a certain day of holy observance on the Hebrew
Calendar—an observance that provides a *major* clue concerning the
timing of His return![1]

This remarkable link, among many others, will be explored in depth in a later chapter. For now, aside from baiting the reader, the point to be made is that often times the most important clues to the end-times puzzle go unrecognized due to an underappreciation of things perhaps taken for granted by the Early Church.

Now, having dropped an ever-so-subtle hint as to some of what lies ahead, let us take a look at a few other examples that support the notion that we might know the time, or "season," of return.

THE PARABLE OF THE TEN VIRGINS

In Matthew 25, we find another passage that speaks to the time of Christ's return. Here, using the Jewish wedding tradition to draw an analogy, Jesus likens the coming "kingdom of heaven" to ten virgins who are awaiting the return of their bridegroom. As you read this passage, pay special attention to the actions of the "foolish" virgins:

> Then shall the kingdom of heaven be likened unto ten virgins, which took their lamps, and went forth to meet the bridegroom. And five of them were wise, and five were foolish. They that were foolish took their lamps, and took no oil with them: But the wise took oil in their vessels with their lamps. While the bridegroom tarried, they all slumbered and slept. And at midnight there was a cry made, Behold, the bridegroom cometh; go ye out to meet him. Then all those virgins arose, and trimmed their lamps. And the foolish said unto the wise, Give us of your oil; for our lamps are gone out. But the wise answered, saying, Not so; lest there be not enough for us and you: but go ye rather to them that sell, and buy for yourselves. And while they went to buy, the bridegroom came; and they that were ready went in with him to the marriage: and the door was shut. Afterward came

also the other virgins, saying, Lord, Lord, open to us. But he answered and said, Verily I say unto you, I know you not. Watch therefore, for ye know neither the day nor the hour wherein the Son of man cometh.

—Matthew 25: 1-13

Decidedly cautionary in tone, Jesus' message here centers on the fact that some of the brides, or virgins, are caught completely by surprise at His coming and are therefore left out of the "marriage" ceremony. These are referenced as the "foolish virgins" because they did not fill their lamps with oil, as did their wise counterparts. (The "oil" is thought to be symbolic of the presence of the "Holy Spirit" within the believer, signifying a relationship with Christ.) Jesus goes on to explain that while the bridegroom (representing Himself) "tarried" (was away in heaven), all of the virgins "slept" until, suddenly, the cry is made, "Behold, the bridegroom cometh." The wise virgins, whose lamps were filled with oil, rush to meet the groom (at the resurrection or rapture) and go off to the marriage (in heaven). Behind them, the door is shut. The foolish virgins frantically search for some oil for their own lamps, but it is too late. They are left behind and will not take part in the wedding.

The difficult lesson learned by the foolish virgins is that the oil, which, again, represents a relationship with Christ, is not something that can be had at the last minute. In essence, their asking to share of the wise virgins' oil is akin to asking to borrow of another's personal relationship with the Lord. This, of course, is not something that can be borrowed of, or lent to another, as it is a product of one's own direct communication with God.

Nonetheless, more specific to our question of knowing the *timing*, we note that at the very end of the passage, in verse 13, a phrase very similar to the one referenced earlier from Matthew 24 appears: "ye know neither the day nor the hour wherein the son of man cometh." Most of us skim over this line, assuming that it applies to all who read it—but a careful examination of the two verses just prior

11

reveals something crucial: This statement is directed specifically at the foolish virgins! Christ speaks to the foolish virgins saying, "I know you not." This is because they have failed to fill their lamps with the knowledge of God. For this reason, they were left in the dark and caught unawares at His appearing, knowing "neither the day nor the hour." It is thus implied that the wise virgins, unlike their foolish counterparts, are definitely *not* among those caught off guard at the Lord's return.

Let us look at another parable often cited by those who insist that the Church will be utterly surprised at Christ's appearance.

A Thief in the Night

In the Bible, the return of Christ is likened to a "thief in the night," seeming to suggest a state of utter surprise on the part of all. But is this the intended message?

Again, the answer seems to lie in to whom the statement is being directed. To illustrate, we look to a well-known instance of the "thief" analogy, as found in the Book of Revelation. Here, we note that Jesus is speaking to the *sleeping,* or "dead," church, which, many would contend, is an apt description of today's state of affairs:

> And unto the angel of the church in Sardis write; These things saith he that hath the seven Spirits of God, and the seven stars; I know thy works, that thou hast a name that *thou livest, and art dead. Be watchful,* and strengthen the things which remain, that are ready to die: for I have not found thy works perfect before God. Remember therefore how thou hast received and heard, and hold fast, and re- pent. *If therefore thou shalt not watch, I will come on thee as a thief, and thou shalt not know what hour I will come upon thee.*
>
> —Revelation 3:1-3

Notice that Jesus says "If...thou shalt not watch" He will come upon them "as a thief." A plain but careful reading of the verse reveals that the statement is conditional: Only those who are *not* watching will "not know what hour"—once again implying that those who *are* watching *will* in fact know, perhaps not the literal hour but nevertheless the "hour" in a more general sense.

Utilizing the same (thief) analogy, the Apostle Paul reinforces this notion in 1 Thessalonians:

> But of the times and the seasons, brethren, ye have no need that I write unto you. For yourselves know perfectly that the day of the Lord so cometh as a thief in the night. For when they shall say, Peace and safety; then sudden destruction cometh upon them, as travail upon a woman with child; and they shall not escape. *But ye, brethren, are not in darkness, that that day should overtake you as a thief. Ye are all the children of light, and the children of the day: we are not of the night, nor of darkness. Therefore let us not sleep, as do others; but let us watch and be sober.*
>
> —1 Thessalonians 5:1-6

Here, Paul is referring to the fact that his brethren, the believers who are diligently watching and waiting, are *not* in the dark as to the "times and the seasons" and will therefore not be caught off guard, as so many will be.

The consistent theme, then, in all three of these passages is that the Lord draws a distinction between those who are watching and those who are not. In the cases where He says you do *not* know "the day nor the hour" He is by no means speaking to the *entire* Church, or to *every* believer, but to those who are not watching. By drawing this distinction between those who sleep and those who watch, He, again, seems to be emphasizing the fact that while many will not know the timing—some, in fact, *will*.

CONCLUSION

Having addressed the question that is central to the thesis of this book, we note that while knowledge of the literal or precise hour may be out of the question, it is apparent that Jesus does indeed expect His flock to be ready and watching at His return.

Of course, one could argue that this same message has resonated with virtually every prior generation, many of whom expected the return of the Lord in their own lifetimes but were ultimately disappointed. The fact is, however, unlike previous generations, those currently living have every reason to take this message to heart and to watch, as *all* of the signs that are to herald His return are present as never before. Moreover, as we proceed, it will become increasingly clear that some of these signs may be much more time-specific than most had previously imagined.

TWO

Then God blessed the seventh day and sanctified it, because in it He rested from all His work which God had created and made.

—Genesis 2:3

GOD'S SEVENS

Of all the written expressions that give tribute to God's magnificence, one would be hard pressed to find a more beautiful collection of hymns and musings than that which is found in the Book of Psalms. For instance, in Psalm 19 we read:

> The heavens declare the glory of God; and the firmament sheweth his handywork.
>
> —Psalm 19:1

As we gaze up at the seemingly endless masses of twinkling stars, or ponder our own blazing sun as it sinks slowly behind the horizon, this verse resonates in the hearts and minds of those who hold to the biblical account of creation. Indeed, when one begins to consider the magnitude of what lies beyond our own earthly atmosphere—the planets, the stars, The Sun, and the Moon—it is difficult not to be filled with a sense of awe.

Yet, in addition to inspiring wonder in the hearts of men, anyone who uses a calendar or a clock will recognize that the celestial bodies also serve another, albeit somewhat less romantic, purpose: They provide a precise and practical means of tracking the various cycles and seasons as we journey through time. This reckoning of time is first described in the beginning verses of the Book of Genesis. It is here that we find the most basic and fundamental unit of measure, known as the day:

...and God divided the light from the darkness. And God called the light Day, and the darkness he called Night And the evening and the morning were the first day.

—Genesis 1:4, 5

Later, on the fourth day of creation, God set the Sun, the Moon, and the stars in the heavens as a means to "divide the day from the night." He would then declare them to be for "signs and for seasons, and for days, and years" (Genesis 1:14).

Thus, God would define the length of one day as a complete rotation of the Earth on its axis.

He would then complete His work by creating fish, birds, and animals to populate the earth; all of this leading up to the crowning act of creation on the sixth day, the formation of man from the dust of the ground.

And then, on the seventh day, The Lord rested from His work, blessing and sanctifying it as a "Sabbath." In this manner, He established a type of a pattern based on seven units of time, representing both completion and perfection. This same pattern, known to us today as the "week," or in the Hebrew as a "shabua," is, as we are about to discover, a pattern that God would repeatedly employ in the course of His dealings with man, from the very beginning—to the very end—of time.

THE SABBATH AND THE SABBATICAL

Thousands of years after His initial creative act, as the Lord led the Israelites out of bondage in Egypt and into the Promised Land, He instructed them to observe a Sabbath day of rest on the seventh day, thus repeating the pattern He had established at creation week.

Later, expanding on this model, He applied the same principle to a period of *years*. His instructions to Moses were as follows:

Six years thou shalt sow thy field, and six years thou shalt prune thy vineyard, and gather in the fruit thereof; But in the seventh year shall be a sabbath of rest unto the land, a sabbath for the LORD: thou shalt neither sow thy field, nor prune thy vineyard.

—Leviticus 25:3, 4

Again, we see the familiar pattern emerge: six units of time dedicated to work (planting and harvesting), followed by one unit of time reserved for rest. Absolutely no sowing or reaping was to take place during the seventh or "sabbatical" year. Hence, the owner of the land, his servants and any strangers, and also any animals, were to sustain themselves on only the natural, or spontaneous, yield of the soil.

Other sabbatical regulations included the cancellation of monetary obligations between Israelites, legally barring anyone from attempting to collect debt. And so, like the weekly Sabbath, the sabbatical year would serve as a respite from mundane toil, as well as any associated financial dealings. After six long years of labor, both land and people were allowed a full year in which to physically and spiritually recuperate.

In noting all of the above, then, we see how God long ago ordained two distinct "weeks," or "shabuas," for the Jewish people: one based on seven *days* and one based on seven *years*. But these were only a shadow, a preview if you will, of what was in all reality a much broader plan.

THE SEVEN THOUSAND YEAR PLAN

In 2 Peter 3:8 we are told that "one day is with the Lord as a thousand years, and a thousand years as one day." This verse forms the basis of a long-held understanding that has been consistent with Jewish thought for millennia: the notion that God has mapped out a period of seven thousand years in which to accomplish His plans for mankind. According to this tradition, which is still embraced today, the first six thousand years of human history represents the work of Satan and his attempts to make mankind ignorant of his true destiny. The last thousand years is to be a period of Sabbath rest, at which time God will revoke Satan's dominion over the earth and Jesus will reign as King.

While the Bible does not explicitly state that God's plans for the present world will be completed within a period of seven thousand years, we find substantial support for this belief in the early Jewish and Christian writings, including the Talmud. The Talmud, in fact (considered to be the most authoritative source of ancient Jewish customs and understandings concerning biblical teachings), states quite clearly that based on Psalm 90:4 "the world is to exist six thousand years" (San Hedrin 97b).

Another frequently cited source for belief in God's seven thousand year plan was Irenaeus. Irenaeus, born in AD 140, worked intensely against powerful Gnostic heresies (perverted teachings concerning the Gospel) and wrote a treatise on the virtues of the Christian faith. Among his writings was found this statement:

> "For in so many days as this world was made, in so many thousand years shall it be concluded...and God brought to a conclusion upon the sixth day the works He made...This is an account of the things formerly created, as also it is a prophecy of what is to come...in six days created things were completed: it is evident, therefore, that they will come to an end after six thousand years."[1]

Yet another proponent of the seven thousand year plan is the disciple Barnabas. Barnabas was one of the seventy disciples that Christ sent out to spread the gospel. In the early days of the Church he distinguished himself as a prominent Christian servant by selling his land and laying the proceeds at the Apostles' feet (Acts 4:36).

Barnabas's teachings concerning God's seven thousand year plan are clearly communicated in "The Epistle of Barnabas," excerpted below. These writings are not considered canon (official Scripture) but nevertheless demonstrate that the Early Church understood the seven thousand year concept and its symbolism in relation to the seven-day creation week and Sabbath, as well as the seventh-year sabbatical:

> ...And God made in six days the works of his hands; and he finished them on the seventh day, and he rested the seventh day, and sanctified it. Consider, my children, what that signifies, he finished them in six days. The meaning of it is this; that in six thousand years the Lord God will bring all things to an end. For with him one day is a thousand years; as himself testifieth, saying, Behold this day shall be as a thousand years. Therefore, children, in six days, that is, in six thousands years, shall all things be accomplished. And what is that he saith, And he rested the seventh day; he meaneth this; that when his Son shall come, and abolish the season of the Wicked One, and judge the ungodly; and shall change the sun and the moon, and the stars; then he shall gloriously rest in the seventh day.
>
> —The Epistle of Barnabas 13:3-6

Moreover, this teaching from Barnabas has found its way into many millenarian books, often in a condensed form and stated as follows:

> "As there had been two thousand years from Adam to Abraham, and two thousand from Abraham to Christ, so there will be two thousand years for the Christian era and then would come the Millennium."[2]

Here, the major biblical epochs are divided into three periods of two thousand years each, totaling six thousand years, or six "days" of earth history. The remaining thousand years is, again, relegated to Christ's millennial reign.

In light of these "two thousand year" periods, it is interesting to note the following verse from Hosea, which speaks of the revival and raising up of the Jews at the Lord's appearance in the last days:

> After two days will he revive us: in the third day he will raise
> us up, and we shall live in his sight.
>
> —Hosea 6:2

According to Hosea, God has promised to "revive" the scattered and decimated Jews after two days (two thousand years) and raise them up to "live in his sight" during the Millennium.

Here, then, is where things begin to get interesting: Considering that this scattering took place two thousand years ago, we can only conclude that the time for this predicted revival is *now*, as we today are living in the days these prophets and apostles spoke of—the six thousand year mark from creation!* This is supported by the work of respected Bible chronologists like D. Petavius who has calculated creation to have occurred in 3983 BC. Moreover, the Hebrew calen-

---

* As it would require a book in and of itself, we will not be addressing the scientific claims that the Earth is many billions of years old as opposed to the biblical narrative that indicates a much younger planet. For those who reject a literal interpretation of biblical creation based on the current opinion of evolutionary scientists, however, it should be noted that there are many in the scientific community who, based on such evidence as geomagnetic field decay, quantized redshift, Moon recession, etc., believe that the Earth, the solar system, and indeed the Universe are very young. For more information on the surprisingly overwhelming evidence for a young Earth, there are many books available on the topic. The argument, of course, essentially boils down to this: Evolutionists, who require vast amounts of time for their theory to be viable, assert that the scarred and marred Earth is the result of many eons of erosion and other natural processes, whereas creationists attribute the current appearance of the planet to a catastrophic flood. Significantly, evolution, a theory that relies on the existence of "transitional" forms that can demonstrate how one species has evolved into another, has yet to provide any such fossil evidence.

dar corroborates this approximate age: Though the Jews record the current year (2009) as being just the year 5769 from the creation of Adam, it is acknowledged that this number was arrived at in the eighth or ninth century in response to modern dating methods. When one adds the approximately 250 years that were not accounted for during the period in which the Jews were taken captive in Babylon, we find that the Hebrew calendar—sometimes referred to as "God's calendar"—indicates that we are indeed living at the six thousand year mark from creation—the very end of the age.[3]

SUMMARY

As we bring to a close this brief chapter, we note that we have only begun to touch on one of the most intriguing aspects of Scripture, which is the immense symbolic significance that God has ascribed to the number seven. From the seven days of creation to the seven seals of Revelation, the Bible is literally saturated with this mystical number: Beginning in Genesis, the Lord introduced the number seven as a symbol of completion related to His initial creative act. Thousands of years later, He designated a seventh-day Sabbath for the Israelites and also established seven year "sabbatical cycles" whereby the people would work the land for six years and rest during the seventh.

We also, in this chapter, began to acknowledge God's use of foreshadowing in the Bible, noting that both the week and the sabbatical cycle are, in essence, a type of template, or model, for His overall plan for the world. This plan consists of a six thousand year period in its current fallen state, to be followed by a seventh and final thousand year period under Christ's kingship, thus fulfilling the *ultimate* Sabbath.

And lastly, we learned that, according to both the Gregorian (Western) and Hebrew calendars—though the exact date cannot be determined—we today are living at the very end of this first six thousand year period!

Now, with this fundamental understanding of "God's sevens" and how they relate to His overall designs for mankind, we are prepared to move on to the next chapter wherein we will explore an additional aspect of God's reckoning of human history—a measure of time that—as you may or may not have already guessed—is also rooted in the number seven.

THREE

Blessed is the people that know the joyful sound: they shall walk, O LORD, in the light of thy countenance.

—Psalm 89:15

THE JUBILEE

Previously, we learned how, based on the pattern established at creation, God instituted both the seven-day week and the seven-year sabbatical cycle. What we did not discuss, however, is the fact that soon after giving Moses His instructions regarding these cycles and Sabbaths, the Lord began to detail yet another repeating cycle:

> You shall count seven Sabbaths of years for yourself, *seven times seven years; and the time of the seven Sabbaths of years shall be to you forty-nine years.* Then you shall cause the trumpet of the Jubilee to sound on the tenth day of the seventh month; on the Day of Atonement you shall make the trumpet to sound throughout all your land. *And you shall consecrate the fiftieth year, and proclaim liberty throughout all the land to all its inhabitants. It shall be a Jubilee for you.*
>
> —Leviticus 25:8-11

Here, God commands Moses and the Israelites to "count seven Sabbaths of years," or *seven sabbatical cycles*, totaling forty-nine years. Then, at the beginning of the fiftieth year, on a holy day known as "the Day of Atonement," they are to sound the trumpet of "jubilee," proclaiming a year of "liberty" throughout the land. This jubilee year was to be a very special Sabbath. In addition to no planting or harvesting, it was ordered that all land be returned to its original owner and personal property returned to persons who had lost their inheritance through sale, confiscation, or some other misfortune. Similarly, those who had been delivered into voluntary or involuntary slavery were to be released from all prior commitments and set free. Thus, the once every fiftieth year Jubilee provided a built-in safeguard within "the Law" to prevent long-term conditions of impoverishment, as well as inequities in the distribution of land or wealth among the Jewish people.

THE SPIRITUAL MEANING OF THE JUBILEE

In our last chapter, we noted how the Sabbaths foreshadow a future millennial period of rest for the earth and its inhabitants under Christ, thereby revealing the underlying *spiritual* meaning of the seventh-day and seventh-year observances. The Jubilee, also a type of Sabbath, likewise foreshadows the Millennium. Yet the Bible teaches that there is something special about this once every fiftieth year Sabbath. Chapter 61 of Isaiah gives us a major clue as to what this is:

> The Spirit of the Lord GOD is upon me; because the LORD hath anointed me to preach good tidings unto the meek; he hath sent me to bind up the brokenhearted, *to proclaim liberty to the captives*, and the opening of the prison to them that are bound;
>
> —Isaiah 61:1

The first thing to note about this verse is that it speaks of Christ's earthly mission, which is to "preach good tidings unto the meek," to "bind up the brokenhearted," and to "proclaim liberty to the captives." Here, though, we are primarily interested in a specific aspect of this mission—the italicized portion. As you will notice, the phraseology used here, "to proclaim liberty," echoes precisely that used in Leviticus 25 (previous page) to define the Jubilee. Thus, interpreters view this reference in Isaiah as being an obvious allusion to the Jubilee and, therefore, the Jubilee as being directly linked to Christ's earthly mission. As we read on in Isaiah, we find out in what respect:

> To proclaim the acceptable year of the LORD, and the day of vengeance of our God; to comfort all that mourn; To appoint unto them that mourn in Zion, to give unto them beauty for ashes, the oil of joy for mourning, the garment of praise for the spirit of heaviness; that they might be called trees of righteousness, the planting of the LORD, that he might be glorified.
>
> —Isaiah 61:2, 3

Here, the reference to "the day of vengeance of our God," reveals that these lines speak of Christ's return at the end of the age. And so verses 2 and 3 (here) combine with verse 1 (previous page), in effect tying Jesus' charge to "proclaim liberty" (or declare jubilee) to His prophesied return in the last days. The Jubilee, then, is seen not only as a foreshadowing but as being synonymous with the Second Coming. Thus, it is believed that in some future year, a jubilee year, Christ will return to fulfill in the *ultimate* sense what He has promised in Isaiah: He will at that time relegate the current world system to the dust bin; He will release the captives from their bondage and liberate a planet that has been ravaged by the influence of Satan for six thousand years. In other words, He will proclaim a Jubilee!

WHAT CAN THE JUBILEE CYCLE TELL US?

Now, in light of the notion that Jesus will return in a jubilee year to begin His millennial reign, and keeping in mind that this special year of liberty is declared only once every forty-nine years, it stands to reason that knowing where we currently sit in relation to the jubilee cycle could go a long way toward narrowing a possible timeframe for the Second Coming. Nailing down the jubilee cycle, however, turns out to be a much more formidable task than it would seem, as it is no longer observed in the manner it once was, nor has it been for a very long time.

But has this seemingly invaluable knowledge truly been lost?

LOST—AND FOUND?

The Bible tells us that the first Jubilee was to be observed after the Israelites entered the Promise Land. Not too far beyond this, though, things become somewhat murky. Due to a variety of circumstances, including calendar changes, uncertain dating of historical events, the fact that jubilee cycles have been counted differently throughout the years (some have counted fifty rather than forty-nine year cycles), and also the fact that Jubilees have gone unobserved for long periods (due to the absence of the Jews from the Land), the *original* cycle has, for all intents and purposes, been lost to antiquity. Today, a simple web-search will yield a multitude of theories based on a complex array of factors and historical benchmarks that claim to have rediscovered this lost knowledge. Yet many rabbinical authorities seem resigned to the fact that this information is essentially beyond retrieval.

In spite of the general uncertainty surrounding the *true* jubilee cycle, however, it seems a limited level of consensus can be found. In fact, during the course of researching the topic, several sources were found to agree on a particular cycle—one that results in a forthcoming 2015-16 jubilee year. For this reason and others that will be explored later in this chapter we are going to focus on 2015 (equivalent to the Hebrew year 5776) in our endeavor to rediscover what has been lost.

Again, because opinions vary so widely on this topic, even among respected scholars and rabbis, a thorough validation of any particular proposed cycle will not be attempted here. We will instead simply post the data as gathered from our cited sources to reveal the rationale each has employed in identifying 2015-16 as a jubilee year.

The first of the three proposed cycles comes from a widely read author on biblical topics, Bonnie Gaunt. Gaunt's proposal tracks the jubilee years beginning with a *second* cycle that presumably began in 535-534 BC.[1]

Sabbath Year 575 - 574 B.C.
17th Jubilee   574 - 573
- - - - - - - - - -   Zero Year   535 - 534 B.C.
Sabbath Year 526 - 525   Sabbath Year 486 - 485
18th Jubilee   525 - 524   1st Jubilee   485 - 484

2nd Jubilee

3rd Jubilee

4th Jubilee

5th Jubilee

6th Jubilee

7th Jubilee

8th Jubilee

9th Jubilee

10th Jubilee

(Absence of a 0 year
is compensated for here)

11th Jubilee

	54 - 55
12th Jubilee	**55 - 56**
	103 - 104
13th Jubilee	**104 - 105**
	152 - 153
14th Jubilee	**153 - 154**
	201 - 202
15th Jubilee	**202 - 203**
	250 - 251
16th Jubilee	**251 - 252**
	299 - 300
17th Jubilee	**300 - 301**
	348 - 349
18th Jubilee	**349 - 350**
	397 - 398
19th Jubilee	**398 - 399**
	446 - 447
20th Jubilee	**447 - 448**
	495 - 496
21st Jubilee	**496 - 497**
	544 - 545
22nd Jubilee	**545 - 546**
	593 - 594
23rd Jubilee	**594 - 595**
	642 - 643
24th Jubilee	**643 - 644**
	691 - 692
25th Jubilee	**692 - 693**
	740 - 741
26th Jubilee	**741 - 742**
	789 - 790
27th Jubilee	**790 - 791**

	838 - 939
28th Jubilee	**839 - 840**
	887 - 888
29th Jubilee	**888 - 889**
	936 - 937
30th Jubilee	**937 - 938**
	985 - 986
31st Jubilee	**986 - 987**
	1034 - 1035
32nd Jubilee	**1035 - 1036**
	1083 - 1084
33rd Jubilee	**1084 - 1085**
	1132 - 1133
34th Jubilee	**1133 - 1134**
	1181 - 1182
35th Jubilee	**1182 - 1183**
	1230 - 1231
36th Jubilee	**1231 - 1232**
	1279 - 1280
37th Jubilee	**1280 - 1281**
	1328 - 1329
38th Jubilee	**1329 - 1330**
	1377 - 1378
39th Jubilee	**1378 - 1379**
	1426 - 1427
40th Jubilee	**1427 - 1428**
	1475 - 1476
41st Jubilee	**1476 - 1477**
	1524 - 1525
42nd Jubilee	**1525 - 1526**
	1573 - 1574
43rd Jubilee	**1574 - 1575**

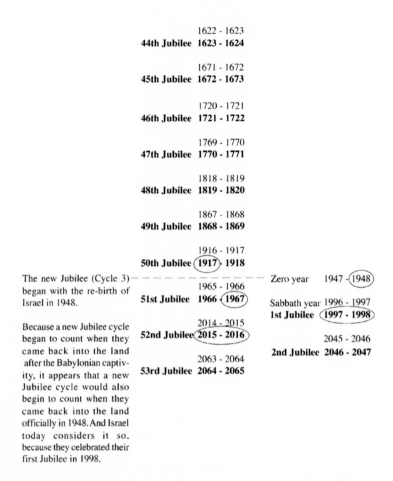

In determining the start date for the original jubilee cycle, Gaunt takes into account various factors. A partial explanation, as posted by the author on her website, reads as follows:

"The Talmud states that Josiah's Great Passover was in the 16th Jubilee. This would have been 623-622 BC (Tishri to Tishri). The fact that it was a jubilee year probably gave him cause to celebrate this Great Passover...The Talmud also states that Ezekiel received his Temple vision in the year of the 17th Jubilee. This would have been 49 years after Josiah's Great Passover. Thus 623-622 BC minus 49 years would put us in the year 574-573 BC for the 17th Jubilee year."[2]

Gaunt goes on to note that the cycle was interrupted and then restarted in 535-534 BC. She writes:

"However, when the exiles returned to the Land of Israel from the Babylonian captivity, and began the resettlement of Jerusalem, they began to count a new Sabbath and Jubilee cycle, beginning with the building of the Altar in 535 BC (Ezra 3:1-2). Zero year for this new cycle...was 535-534 BC (Tishri to Tishri). During that year the foundation of the Temple was laid."[3]

Lastly, she proposes that yet another cycle began in 1948 with the rebirth of the Nation of Israel. Thus, the modern state of Israel celebrated their "first" Jubilee in 1997-98. However, it is interesting to note that if one holds to the *ancient* cycle that began in 535-534 BC rather than resetting it in observance of Israel's reclaimed statehood in 1948, the cycle continues on to result in a 2015-16 Jubilee.

This being noted, let us look at another proposed cycle: This take on jubilee calculation comes from those who combine the opinion of Jewish sages Rabbanan and Rabbi Yehudah.[4] The theory suggests that one should count fifty years for each Jubilee up until the destruction of the Temple; then, for the period after the destruction of the Temple, it is proposed that one should revert to counting forty-nine year periods, with the first year of the subsequent jubilee period being counted as the jubilee year:

Jubilee Years	Rabbanan + Rabbi Yehudah 50 till 3415 then 49 — 3816 was the year after the last Yovel counted of the 2nd Beit HaMikdash — Jewish Calendar	Rabbanan + Rabbi Yehudah 50 till 3415 then 49 — 3816 was the year after the last Yovel counted of the 2nd Beit HaMikdash — Gregorian Calendar
1		
2		
3		
4		
5		
6		
7		
8		
9		
10		
11		
12		
13		
14		
15		
16		
17		
18		
19	3416	-344
20	3466	-294
21	3516	-244
22	3566	-194
23	3616	-144
24	3666	-94
25	3716	-44
26	3766	6
27	3816	56
28	3865	105
29	3914	154
30	3963	203
31	4012	252
32	4061	301
33	4110	350
34	4159	399
35	4208	448
36	4257	497
37	4306	546
38	4355	595
39	4404	644
40	4453	693
41	4502	742

42	4551	791
43	4600	840
44	4649	889
45	4698	938
46	4747	987
47	4796	1036
48	4845	1085
49	4894	1134
50	4943	1183
51	4992	1232
52	5041	1281
53	5090	1330
54	5139	1379
55	5188	1428
56	5237	1477
57	5286	1526
58	5335	1575
59	5384	1624
60	5433	1673
61	5482	1722
62	5531	1771
63	5580	1820
64	5629	1869
65	5678	1918
66	5727	1967
67	5776	2016
68	5825	2065
69	5874	2114
70	5923	2163

In this case, though the rationale applied differs from Gaunt's, we find the same end result—a 2015-16 Jubilee. We should point out here that due to the design of the Jewish calendar, as opposed to the Western calendar, a Hebrew year spans two Gregorian (Western) calendar years. Hence, while this chart displays only the year 2016, the Hebrew year 5776 actually extends into both 2015 and 2016.

Our third and last proposal comes from a comprehensive website put together by Bible researcher Nora Roth. Roth's theory is based on an assumption that Christ died in 31 AD in the *middle* of a jubilee cycle that spanned the years 6 AD through 55 AD. She also validates her jubilee cycle by calculating the date of the very first jubilee observance based on a presumed Exodus date of 1456 BC. This date for the Exodus seems plausible as it falls in line with the range given by Bible chronologists James Ussher and Edwin R. Thiele who proposed 1491 BC and 1446 BC respectively.

Based on her proposed Exodus date of 1456 BC, then, Roth concludes that the Israelites entered the Promised Land, or Canaan, forty years later in 1416 BC, and so observed the first Jubilee forty-nine years after that in 1367 BC.[5]

Dates of the 70 Jubilees

	Year - BC		Year - BC		Year - AD		Year - AD		Year - AD
1	1367	15	681	29	6	43	692	57	1378
2	1318	16	632	30	55	44	741	58	1427
3	1269	17	583	31	104	45	790	59	1476
4	1220	18	534	32	153	46	839	60	1525
5	1171	19	485	33	202	47	888	61	1574
6	1122	20	436	34	251	48	937	62	1623
7	1073	21	387	35	300	49	986	63	1672
8	1024	22	338	36	349	50	1035	64	1721
9	975	23	289	37	398	51	1084	65	1770
10	926	24	240	38	447	52	1133	66	1819
11	877	25	191	39	496	53	1182	67	1868
12	828	26	142	40	545	54	1231	68	1917
13	779	27	93	41	594	55	1280	69	1966
14	730	28	44	42	643	56	1329	70	2015

Once more, while the rationale varies, the end result is the same—a 2015-16 jubilee. Again, while theories abound, this proposed cycle is the most frequently encountered in the course of this author's research.

In addition to this limited consensus however, it seems that, as alluded to earlier, there is another factor that might be considered as corroborating evidence in support of this particular cycle. It goes beyond the mathematical benchmarking of various historical events and is grounded more so in the *prophetic* significance of the Jubilee itself.

"Proclaim liberty to the land and all its inhabitants"

As noted earlier, the jubilee year was essentially ordained by God as a time to proclaim "liberty," to free slaves from bondage, and to return property and land to its original owners. Therefore, in summing up the theme of Jubilee, it could be said that it is all about the freedom of God's people and their land.

With this in mind, it is interesting, beginning with a presumed 2015-16 Jubilee, to count backward in blocks of forty-nine years to identify what would have been previous jubilee years. In doing so, we arrive at 1966-67 and 1917-18 respectively. These two dates, then, assuming that the cycle proposed here is correct, would represent the only two jubilees to have occurred in the twentieth century. This is not the interesting part however. What we find so compelling here are the particular years involved (1917-18 and 1966-67). For those not steeped in Jewish History, the reason is this: In looking back at the twentieth century, it could be argued that two events stand alone as absolutely epitomizing the theme of "liberation" for the very capital of the land that God gave to Abraham and his descendents over three millennia ago. The years of these events are, strangely enough, 1917-18 and 1966-67! Let us take a look at what transpired during these years, beginning with the events of 1917:

History records that in November of 1917 the British issued the Balfour Declaration, which read in part as follows:

"His Majesty's government view with favour the establishment in Palestine of a national home for the Jewish

2012-2015: THE SEASON OF RETURN?

people, and will use their best endeavors to facilitate the achievement of this object…"[6]

This decree of support marked a pivotal step toward gaining international recognition for the return of the Land of Israel to the Jews; this after nearly two thousand years of desolation. Later, in December of that same year, British General Allenby captured the Holy City of Jerusalem, "liberating" it from four long centuries of Muslim Turkish rule.[7] Thus, within a single year, Jerusalem was liberated from Muslim rule, and determining steps toward the return of the Land to the Jewish people had been taken.[8]

Then, in June of 1967, forty-nine years, or the span of one Jubilee, later, something astonishing happened: Israel fought the Six Day War in which they recaptured East Jerusalem, containing the holiest sites in all of Judaism (including the all-important Temple Mount), from Jordan.[9] And so, for the first time in roughly two thousand years, God's Holy City, the location that repeatedly emerges in Scripture as the geographic epicenter of prophetic fulfillment, would be under the control of the Jews—the people through whom the Lord has chosen to disseminate His Word and thus bring to fruition His plan of redemption for all of humanity.

Again, the point to be emphasized here is that unlike any other pivotal historical events involving the Jews, the events of these years not only embody the theme of Jubilee in the fullest sense but happen to be separated by forty-nine years, the span of a Jubilee![10]

Of course, having noted all of this, in ascribing some connection between the two liberations of Jerusalem and a possible jubilee cycle, we are assuming that this is not mere coincidence but that God is perhaps trying to tell us something via the events surrounding the Holy City. Thus, we pose the question: Is it possible that these two liberations were divinely ordained to occur in these particular years as a means to reestablish the lost jubilee cycle, thereby serving as a type of "sign" that points forward to 2015-16 as the next Jubilee?

This, for now, must remain a question mark. Yet, even in the absence of utter certainty, it is stunning to consider the fact that these two liberations of Jerusalem could have just as easily taken place at any other moment during the course of the twentieth century (or any other century for that matter). They could have occurred forty-seven years apart, or perhaps fifty-one years apart—but they did not. They transpired exactly *forty-nine* years apart—the span of a biblical jubilee cycle.

HOW MANY JUBILEES?

As we bring to a close our brief look at the Jubilee and the uncanny way in which the two modern liberations of Jerusalem are separated by the span of this God-ordained observance, we note yet another intriguing aspect of the cycle proposed here: A jubilee year of 2015-16, notwithstanding any halting or restarting of the cycle due to lack of observance, would result in a total count of seventy Jubilees. While the Bible does not draw any obvious correlation between the number of Jubilees and the timing of the end of the age, it is nevertheless interesting to contemplate the number seventy and its significance elsewhere in Scripture. For example, God allowed Israel to violate seventy of the Sabbaths before sending them into exile in Babylon for seventy years (2 Chronicles 36:21). Some theorize that since the Lord allowed the Jews to ignore seventy Sabbaths that *seventy* is the key to the whole system of Sabbaths.[11] In other words, if seventy completes the system of the seven-year sabbatical cycles (Leviticus 25:1-7) then, similarly, seventy will complete the system of the forty-nine year jubilee cycles. According to this school of thought, by simply counting seventy blocks of forty-nine years from the first Jubilee, one should arrive at the year of Christ's Second Coming—in our case, 2015-16.

Again, while decidedly speculative, this notion is an interesting one to consider. Is it possible that just as the Jews spent seventy years in Babylon, God's people are to spend seventy *jubilee periods* in this *earthly* Babylon before being freed by Christ's declaration of Jubilee at the end of the age?

SUMMARY AND CONCLUSION

Here we have learned that the Jubilee is a special type of Sabbath proclaimed every fiftieth year on the Jewish holy day known as the Day of Atonement. During the Jubilee, debts were cancelled, land was returned, and slaves were given their freedom. These themes exemplify the underlying spiritual meaning that God intended for this observance. The historical jubilee celebration was thus a foreshadowing in which *temporary* freedom was realized whereas the ultimate fulfillment of Jubilee at Christ's return will grant *permanent* liberty.

We have also learned that, due to various factors, there are inherent difficulties associated with pinning down an authoritatively acknowledged jubilee cycle and count. Nevertheless, we have identified several sources that agree on a particular cycle—one that points to 2015-16 as the next Jubilee and, accordingly, 1966-67 and 1917-18 as previous Jubilees.

While admittedly speculative, our look at the seemingly *liberation*-themed events of 1917-18 and 1966-67 seems to bolster the notion that God might be employing this convergence of dates and events to reestablish a cycle that points forward to 2015-16.

Could the "rediscovery" of the Jubilee be a sign intended for those watching? Will the next Jubilee be *the* Jubilee—the one that believers have longed for millennia to see?

These questions, for now, must also go unanswered. Perhaps, though, some additional light will be shed in the first chapter of our next section, as we investigate a well-known prophecy that, like the Jubilee, is also tied to God's "sevens."

PART II

REVELATIONS

FOUR

---·◆·---

"*To believe that the facts and figures here detailed amount to nothing more than happy coincidences involves a greater exercise of faith than that of the Christian who accepts the book of Daniel as Divine.*"

—Sir Robert Anderson speaking to the
accuracy of the prophecies of Daniel

DANIEL'S SEVENTY WEEKS

As evening closes in, Daniel continues to pray. Dressed in a crudely fashioned garment made of sackcloth, his skin covered in ashes, he has been pouring his heart out in contrition and repentance for the sins of his people, pleading with God to turn His anger from Israel and restore them to the Land.

Then, all at once, he feels himself surrounded by a presence: ethereal, emanating light and warmth but at the same time great power and authority.

Daniel is frightened, but nonetheless lifts his head to find what appears to be a man standing before him. This man, though, has a countenance unlike that of any ordinary man. He touches Daniel, so as to console, and then begins to speak to him with an assuredness and serenity that is not of this world, but could only come from one of God's holy angels:

"Daniel, I have now come to give you insight and understanding…"

THE BOOK OF DANIEL

The Book of Daniel contains some of the most amazing passages that we find in the Bible. In chapter 9, verses 24 through 27, for instance, we find the central components of God's plan of redemption revealed. Here, in a brief, compact, and elegant manner, the Lord delivers through His angel Gabriel a sweeping prophetic message containing details—even *time-specific* details—concerning the future of the Jews, their holy city (Jerusalem), and the coming of Messiah.

Throughout the centuries, many volumes have been written about verses 24 through 27, also known as Daniel's "prophecy of seventy weeks," and, for various reasons, this passage is still among the most contentiously debated in prophecy circles. Much of this debate centers on the question of which elements of the prophecy have already been fulfilled and which elements await fulfillment at the end of the age.

By far the most popular teaching today is the latter (futurist) view, which holds that key parts of Daniel's prophecy are yet to be fulfilled. However, even among futurists, there is still much room for disagreement, namely concerning *which* events await fulfillment, *how* they will be fulfilled, and which, if any, might be fulfilled *twice*.

DUAL FULFILLMENTS IN THE BIBLE

Among students of the Bible, it is common knowledge that some prophecies are destined for dual fulfillment. This is known as "the law of double reference;" it refers to the fact that a partial fulfillment of a given prophecy may have been realized in the past, while the *complete* fulfillment is yet to be in the future. Thus, there is a significant gap of time between the preliminary and the *ultimate* fulfillment. An excellent example of this is found in the Old Testament prediction made by Joel concerning the Lord's pouring out of the Holy Spirit:

And it shall come to pass afterward, that I will pour out my spirit upon all flesh; and your sons and your daughters shall prophesy, your old men shall dream dreams, your young men shall see visions: And also upon the servants and upon the handmaids in those days will I pour out my spirit. And I will shew wonders in the heavens and in the earth, blood, and fire, and pillars of smoke. The sun shall be turned into darkness, and the moon into blood, before the great and terrible day of the LORD come. And it shall come to pass, that whosoever shall call on the name of the LORD shall be delivered...

—Joel 2:28-32

In the New Testament (Acts 2:14-21), God inspired the Apostle Peter to quote from the above passage to describe the events on the Day of Pentecost, which was, of course, the day the Lord fulfilled His promise to send the "Holy Spirit" to dwell in the hearts of the first believers. As those present would attest to, supernatural manifestations of God's power did indeed occur on that day (see verses 1 through 15). Also, as a result of being filled with God's Spirit, the "sons" and "daughters," would begin to "prophesy," thereby saving those who would "call on the name of the LORD." But these manifestations would represent only a *partial* fulfillment of Joel's prophecy. Obviously, the great "wonders in the heavens," such as the Sun being "turned into darkness, and the Moon into blood," did not transpire then but were destined for future fulfillment at the "great and terrible day of the Lord." Therefore, part of Joel's prophecy was fulfilled in the first century AD, while the complete fulfillment will not be realized until the days just prior to Christ's return.

A SNEAK PREVIEW?

Another aspect of dual fulfillment is that, often times, the partial, or historical, fulfillment can also serve as a prophetic picture of what the fullness of fulfillment will look like at the end of the age. For example, most scholars today agree that Matthew 24 speaks primarily of the great "tribulation" slated to occur just prior to the Second Coming. But in verse 2, Jesus, in referencing the manner of destruction wrought by the Romans, is obviously speaking of the siege of Jerusalem that would take place in 70 AD:

> And Jesus said unto them, See ye not all these things? Verily I say unto you, There shall not be left here one stone upon another, that shall not be thrown down.
>
> —Matthew 24:2

And so here we have not only a perfect description of what happened in 70 AD, but a foreshadowing of the *future* siege of Jerusalem that will take place just before the Second Coming.

Both of the above examples, then, illustrate how a single prophecy may apply to multiple events: one already fulfilled in the distant past and one that will be fulfilled in the future.[1]

NEWTON: A SCHOLAR AMONG SCHOLARS

One well-known proponent of the dual nature of prophecy was a man named Sir Isaac Newton. Newton (1642-1727) is perhaps the most famed scientific mind the world has ever known. He is called the "father of modern science" and the "father of the industrial revolution." He also made revolutionary advances in mathematics, optics, physics, and astronomy.

Possessing unequaled mental ability throughout his entire adult life, until his death at age eighty five, Newton's powers are legendary. It is often told, for example, how later in his life a problem in mathematical physics posed by the great mathematician, Bernoulli, was forwarded to the Royal Society, of which Newton was President.

The problem, which involved *determining the curve of minimum time for a heavy particle to move downward between two given points*, had baffled the famous eighteenth century mathematicians of Europe for over six months. Receiving the problem in the afternoon, Newton solved it before going to bed![2]

In addition to his scientific work (Newton would have said as a "part" of his scientific work) he was also an ardent student of the Bible. In fact, it is noted that only twelve percent of his vast library contained books related to the various disciplines on which his fame rests, the majority of them being on the subject of theology.

Newton believed that the Bible, which he was known to study and translate from the original Hebrew, was literally true in every respect. He thus viewed his own scientific work as merely a means by which to validate his belief in the infallibility of Scripture. In the course his efforts, Newton continually tested biblical claims against the physical truths of experimental and theoretical science. He never observed a contradiction.[3]

It is no surprise, then, that in Newton's view the prophecies found in the Bible literally contained "histories of things to come"; these histories, however—set out in symbolic and metaphorical language—demanded exacting interpretative skills. This was the challenge that Newton took up with unflagging enthusiasm for the last fifty-five years of his life.

Today, in spite of all of Newton's scientific accomplishments, some would say that his keen insight into certain aspects of the prophecies may be one of the greatest contributions he ever made, and it is likely that Newton, if he could weigh in on the matter, would agree.

NEWTON AND DANIEL

Newton was particularly drawn to the Books of Daniel and Revelation and wrote extensively on them. In 1733, six years after his death, J. Darby and T. Browne published his writings in a commentary entitled *Observations upon the Prophecies of Daniel, and the Apocalypse of St. John.* In his writings, Newton contended that based on Scripture, namely the angel Gabriel's statement that Daniel's book was to be "sealed till the time of the end" (Daniel 12:9), that the prophecies contained therein would not be fully understood until at or very near the end of the age. He writes:

> "The prophecies of Daniel and John should not be understood till the time of the end: but that some should prophesy out of it in an afflicted and mournful state for a long time, and that but darkly, so as to convert but few. But in the very end, the Prophecy should be so far interpreted so as to convince many."[4]

Here, Newton alludes to the fact that unfulfilled prophecy is always viewed as "through a glass, darkly" (1 Corinthians 13:12). This, of course, would hold even truer in the case of Daniel's book, being "sealed" as it were. Nonetheless, he did feel that his understanding of a crucial aspect of a certain prophecy—the prophecy of seventy weeks—would prove a worthy contribution to the effort of deciphering Daniel.

Indeed, among the common interpretations of the so-called prophecy of seventy weeks, Newton's take, particularly in regard to one key verse, is fundamentally unique and in the eyes of a growing number makes absolute sense of an aspect that many have struggled with throughout the years. In fact, it is Newton's unique interpretation that makes the prophecy of seventy weeks so relevant to our central topic, which is, of course, the timing of Christ's return. For this reason, the bulk of this chapter will be devoted exclusively to exploring this mysterious passage through Newton's eyes. What is revealed,

---

* Interestingly, it was only twenty years ago in 1991 that Newton's writings on Daniel were "rediscovered" at the Library of Congress and reprinted by Arthur B. Robinson of Cave Junction, Oregon.

I believe the reader will agree, is of vast implication for the current generation.

Before we get to that, however, in order to establish some context and thus maximize our understanding of the prophecy, it will be helpful to orient ourselves with a little background on Daniel, including the times and circumstances under which this Prophet lived and which, in turn, led to the amazing passage we are about to study.

SETTING THE SCENE

It is the year 539 BC and the Jewish people, including a now aged Prophet named Daniel, have been held captive in the city of Babylon for nearly seventy years. This captivity was, in all actuality, a punishment from God. The Jews had failed to observe the Lord's statutes, which included honoring the Sabbaticals and Jubilees, thereby depriving the Land of its allotted time of rest (Ezekiel 20:10-13). Though God repeatedly sent Prophets to warn that they would be removed from the Land if they persisted in their ways, they continued to rebel. Finally, as there was no other remedy than to dispense justice, God allowed the Jews to be taken into captivity by the Babylonians. In the process, Jerusalem was burned and ruined, the Holy Temple was destroyed, and countless numbers of Daniel's people were massacred.

The Jews had neglected the Sabbaticals and Jubilees for 430 years (Ezekiel 4:1-6). During this time, the Land had missed a total of seventy (year-long) Sabbaths. So, to make restitution, the Land was to be allowed to lay desolate for seventy years, enjoying its allotted time of rest, while Daniel's people would be held captive in Babylon (2 Chronicles 36:15-21).

THE FAITHFUL SERVANT

Throughout all of his decades spent in Babylon, Daniel remained a faithful servant and a follower of God's Word. At some point, through his study of the Book of Jeremiah, presumably the two verses below, Daniel came to understand the length of Israel's sentence in Babylon and thus the fact that their time of captivity was almost over:

And this whole land shall be a desolation, and an astonishment; and these nations shall serve the king of Babylon *seventy years*.

—Jeremiah 25:11

For thus saith the LORD, That after *seventy years* be accomplished at Babylon I will visit you, and perform my good word toward you, in causing you to return to this place.

—Jeremiah 29:10

Because the Lord did not wish to leave the Jews in a state of perpetual uncertainty, He had revealed in Jeremiah the exact length of their term, giving them an "expected end" (Jeremiah 29:11). Daniel, of course, knowing the year in which their captivity had begun, must have simply done the math to determine that freedom was at hand!

Reading beyond verse 10, as Daniel surely must have done, Jeremiah describes how the Israelites would seek guidance from the Lord and how He would show mercy by bringing them back into the Land:

Then shall ye call upon me, and ye shall go and pray unto me, and I will hearken unto you. And ye shall seek me, and find me, when ye shall search for me with all your heart. And I will be found of you, saith the LORD: and I will turn away your captivity, and I will gather you from all the nations, and from all the places whither I have driven you, saith the LORD; and I will bring you again into the place whence I caused you to be carried away captive.

—Jeremiah 29:12-14

Realizing that a return to the Promised Land was imminent, and perhaps taking a queue from the above passage, Daniel submits himself in prayer and fasting as he petitions the Lord to end the desolation of Jerusalem:

…We have been wicked and have rebelled; we have turned away from your commands and laws. All Israel has transgressed your law and turned away, refusing to obey you…O Lord, in keeping with all your righteous acts, turn away your anger and your wrath from Jerusalem, your city, your holy hill…hear the prayers and petitions of your servant. For your sake, O Lord, look with favour on your desolate sanctuary [in Jerusalem] Give ear, O God, and hear; open your eyes and see the desolation of the city that bears your Name…

—Daniel 9:5, 11, 16-18

God, of course, hears Daniel's prayer and sends the angel Gabriel with a message. He is about to go one better on His promise to give His people an expected end by revealing what the future holds for Israel—not only in the short term but right up to the end of the age:

…Daniel, I have now come to give you insight and understanding. As soon as you began to pray, an answer was given, which I have come to tell you, for you are highly esteemed. Therefore, consider the message and understand the vision:

—Daniel 9:22, 23

Gabriel then proceeds to deliver what is one of the most widely studied and debated Bible passages of all time, Daniel's "prophecy of seventy weeks":

> [24]Seventy sevens are decreed for your people and your holy city to finish transgression, to put an end to sin, to atone for wickedness, to bring in everlasting righteousness, to seal up vision and prophecy and to anoint the most holy. [25]Know and understand this: From the issuing of the decree to restore and rebuild Jerusalem until the Anointed One, the ruler, comes, there will be seven sevens, and sixty-two sevens. It will be rebuilt with streets and a trench, but in times of trouble. [26]After the sixty-two sevens, the Anointed One will be cut off and will have nothing. The people of the ruler who will come will destroy the city and the sanctuary. The end will come like a flood; war will continue until the end, and desolations have been decreed. [27]He will confirm a covenant with many for one seven. In the middle of a seven, he will put an end to sacrifice and offering. And on a wing of the temple he will set up an abomination that causes desolation, until the end that is decreed is poured out on him.
>
> —Daniel 9:24-27

Needless to say, for those unacquainted with this passage, Gabriel's message may seem rather cryptic, but with some help from Isaac Newton, we will begin to shed some light on what has just been revealed to Daniel, or, perhaps more accurately, what has been revealed to us.

BREAKING IT DOWN

Firstly, we should reemphasize that this message from Gabriel is in essence a response to Daniel's prayerful request that God show mercy and restore His people to the Land (specifically the Holy Sanctuary) so that they may serve Him and thus be heir to His promises regarding Israel. Therefore, this prophecy deals specifically with the two elements that lie at the center of God's promises to Israel and which, in turn, form the basis of the Jewish faith: the coming of Messiah and the state of the Holy Sanctuary in Jerusalem.

Now, in order to understand the finer elements of the prophecy, we must, rather than try and take it in as a whole as we just have, break it down into smaller and therefore much easier to digest pieces.

Let us begin to do so, then, by taking a look at just the first part of Gabriel's message—verse 24:*

> Seventy sevens are decreed for your people and your holy city to finish transgression, to put an end to sin, to atone for wickedness, to bring in everlasting righteousness, to seal up vision and prophecy and to anoint the most holy.
> —Daniel 9:24

In Newton's own words, Daniel 9:24-27, like all of the rest of Daniel, consists of two parts, "an introductory prophecy and an explanation thereof" (Newton, 52). Verse 24, above, is our introduction; it speaks in overall terms of a set period of time, "seventy sevens," that is decreed upon Daniel's "people" (the Jews) and their "holy city" (Jerusalem) to complete the ministry that God has appointed them, all of this being part and parcel of God's redemptive plan which, again, centers on Jerusalem and the coming Messiah.

Per Newton, as well as virtually all other scholars, in accordance with the "day for a year" theme as established in Numbers 14:34 and Ezekiel 4:6, the "seventy sevens" mentioned here are to be interpreted as seventy "weeks" of years, or seventy *sabbatical cycles*. Therefore, the

---

* Since Newtown held a primarily *historicist* view of this prophecy we will, for the sake of added perspective, be acknowledging a couple of alternative (futurist) interpretations along the way. Yet, for the sake of clarity and continuity, the scope of our examination here is constrained primarily to Newton's viewpoints.

"seventy sevens" actually refer to a period of time totaling 490 years (70 x 7 = 490) (52, 53). This 490-year span is the time allotted by God for the key components of His redemptive plan to be fulfilled, namely to: "finish transgression," to "put an end to sin," to "atone for wickedness," to "bring in everlasting righteousness," to "seal up" or complete the "vision and prophecy," and to "anoint the most holy."

Newton's interpretation holds that all of these things were accomplished by Christ at His death on the cross, at which time He atoned for the transgressions and sins of man, thereby sealing up the vision and prophecy by bringing everlasting life to those who believe in His name (53). Thus, according to Newton, the crucifixion of Christ marks the end point of the "seventy sevens" or 490-year span of time.

But what about the start point? Something significant must have happened 490 years prior to the crucifixion to set the "prophetic clock" ticking. To find out what it was, we must jump ahead for a moment to verse 25. Here we find that the 490-year clock was set in motion by the "issuing of the decree to restore and rebuild" Jerusalem (Daniel 9:25). The fulfillment of this specific event, as per Newton, is found in Chapter 7 of the Book of Ezra:* History records that in the seventh year of the reign of Artaxerxes Longimanus, a group of Jews led by Ezra returned from Babylonian captivity, revived the Jewish temple worship, and established judges to govern the Jewish people under God's laws. While the various historical calendars may be confusing, it has been determined by historians that Ezra and the Babylonian exiles returned to Jerusalem around 457-458 BC.

Thus, verse 24 finds its fulfillment in the 490-year span between

---

* Though the Jews (led by Zerubbabal) were freed to return to Jerusalem in Daniel's time (539 BC), Newton notes that this does not qualify as the time marker because "they only had commission to build the Temple," whereas during the time of the later return led by Ezra, the Jews actually "became a polity or city by a government of their own" and "revived the Jewish worship; and by the King's commission created magistrates in all the land, to judge and govern the people according to the laws of God and the King" (53).

the time the dispersed Jews were reincorporated into a people and a holy city in Jerusalem in 457-458 BC, and Christ's crucifixion in 32-34 AD. In other words, this verse, verified to have been written centuries before the birth of Jesus, predicts the precise year of His death on the cross!

Incidentally, the liberal scholars and critics who have tried to "late date" the entire Book of Daniel in an effort to negate the supernatural quality of its predictions do not even attempt to deny the fact that this prophecy was, by all accounts, recorded well before the time of Christ. But even if one chooses to ignore this fact and allow for the possibility that the prophecy was written or manipulated *after* Christ's crucifixion, there is no getting around the fact that in order to do so one would need to have a thorough understanding of this highly enigmatic prophecy and the specific historical events that it references, which no one did at the time!

And with that, we are prepared to move on to our primary area of focus, the first part of verse 25, which, if Newton was correct, may hold some critical if not earthshaking information for those seeking the timing of Christ's return.

> Know and understand this: From the issuing of the decree
> to restore and rebuild Jerusalem until the Anointed One,
> the ruler, comes, there will be seven sevens...
> —Daniel 9:25

The first thing we note in verse 25 is the mention of the time marker that was just discussed in regard to verse 24, which is the "decree to restore and rebuild" Jerusalem. This decree to restore Jerusalem also comes into play here in verse 25, albeit, as we will see, in a slightly different sense.

The second thing to note is the fact that we are no longer speaking of the period of "seventy sevens," or 490 years, mentioned in verse 24, but of a much shorter period of "seven sevens." Gabriel tells Daniel to "Know and understand" what this timespan of "seven sevens" signifies.

We also notice that the focus of this period of seven sevens is on an "Anointed One" who comes as a "ruler." According to Gabriel, this ruler will come "seven sevens" or forty-nine years (the span of one Jubilee) after a "decree" is issued to "restore and rebuild" Jerusalem.

Obviously, the "Anointed One," or "ruler," mentioned here is a reference to Christ. So, in essence, Gabriel is telling Daniel that Jesus will come forty-nine years after this particular decree to restore Jerusalem. But which restoration? Clearly it cannot be the same call to return and rebuild the city in 457-458 BC that started the aforementioned 490 year "clock" ticking, nor could it have been the later call to rebuild the wall around Jerusalem recorded in Nehemiah chapter 2, as both of these occurred *centuries* before Christ's arrival, far out of range of this span of only forty-nine years. Faced with this, Newton reasoned, quite logically, that the forty-nine years must refer to the prophesied future, or *end-times*, restoration of Jerusalem and therefore the *Second* Coming of Christ.

As we learned earlier, the dual nature of Bible prophecy was a concept not lost on Newton. In fact, He recognized that virtually every prophecy in the Old Testament concerning the First Advent of Christ, in some way or another, also related to the Second Advent. Yet Newton had even further justification for pinning this verse to the Second Coming: In his writings, he notes that there is an obvious distinction drawn between the Jesus we find here in verse 25, who is referred to as a "ruler," and the Jesus who is described elsewhere in the passage simply as the "Anointed One," or, as Newton puts it, a "Prophet." In Newton's own words:

> "The former part of the prophecy related to the first coming of Christ, being dated to his coming as a Prophet; this being dated to his coming to be a Prince or King, seems to relate to his second coming. There the Prophet was consummate, and the most holy anointed: here he that was anointed

comes to be Prince [ruler] and to reign" (53).

Here, Newton keys in on an aspect of verse 25 often overlooked and concludes that the period of "seven sevens," or forty-nine years, *must* relate to the Second Coming because it refers specifically to Jesus appearing as a "ruler." Obviously, at Christ's first appearance He came not to rule but to willfully lay his life down as the "sacrificial lamb." Thus, Jesus would not assume His role as "ruler" until His return at the end of the age.

To sum up, then, based on the fact that Jesus is here referred to as a "ruler" and also the fact that the span of forty-nine years does not fit the timeline of the First Coming, Newton concluded that this part of verse 25 must refer to the Second Coming. This event, he maintains, will take place exactly forty-nine years after a *future* return to "restore and rebuild" Jerusalem.*

Of course, the fact that this period of "seven sevens," or forty-nine years, is equivalent to the span of a jubilee cycle was not lost on Newton either. Here, he notes that this particular cycle would likely begin and end with actions that comport to the "highest nature" of jubilee:

"As the seventy and the sixty-two weeks were Jewish weeks,
    ending with sabbatical years; so the seven weeks are the

---

* Most interpreters do not seize on the idea that this "seven sevens" refers to a *future* restoration of Jerusalem but instead simply add this forty-nine year period to the period of sixty-two sevens, or 434 years, mentioned later in verse 25. This results in an entirely different interpretation that is based on a period of *sixty-nine* weeks, thereby limiting the scope of this passage in predicting the arrival of Messiah to His first coming only. Newton held that since the prophesied final restoration of Jerusalem was such a principal expectation on the part of the Jews, it would make no sense for the timing of said restoration, and thus the Second Coming of Christ, to be excluded from Daniel's prophecy. In affirming the rationale behind his interpretation, Newton further notes that for one to create one number (sixty-nine weeks) by adding the sixty-two weeks and seven weeks, "as interpreters usually do," does "violence" to the language of Daniel (Newton, 55).

compass of a jubilee, and begin and end with actions proper for a jubilee and of the highest nature for which a jubilee can be kept" (54).

Again, Newton's insight is astounding. Roughly three hundred years ago, when the idea that Israel might someday be reborn as a sovereign Nation was thought preposterous, he predicted—based on verse 25—that immediately following a *future* Jewish return to and restoration of Jerusalem, God's prophetic clock would begin ticking off a forty-nine year jubilee cycle that would culminate in the long-awaited return of Jesus Christ!

Needless to say, Newton must have been thrilled to have been allowed this insight. Moreover, considering his desire to unlock the secrets of the prophecies, he would have likely given anything to see the missing piece of the puzzle fall into place, which was, of course, the *date* that this final restoration of Jerusalem would take place. Thus, the current generation, had Newton been capable of seeing into the future, would have been the focus of his envy. The reason, for those not familiar with modern Jewish history, is a historical event that took place a little more than four decades ago at the conclusion of the 1967 Six day War: the Jewish recapture and restoration of the Holy City of Jerusalem![5] Indeed, history records that on June 7, 1967 the Jews recaptured East Jerusalem, liberating it from the Jordanians and reuniting the Holy City under Jewish rule for the first time in roughly two thousand years. Soon after, on June 28, Israel's parliament (The Knesset) promulgated and adopted a law that stated:

> "The Government is empowered by a decree to apply the law, the jurisdiction and administration of the State to any part of Eretz Israel (Land of Israel-Palestine), as stated in that decree."[6]

On the basis of this law, the government of Israel decreed in July of 1967 that Jerusalem is one city indivisible, the capital of the State of Israel.

Might this 1967 restoration and "decree" of sovereign Jewish rule over Jerusalem have been *the* latter-day decree that verse 25 of Daniel was referring to? Could this event therefore have marked the starting point of the "seven sevens" of Daniel, and thus the commencement of the very jubilee cycle (ending in 2015-16) that will herald the return of Christ?[7, 8]

Though the answers to these two questions are ultimately only known to God, it would be difficult, in light of Newton's thesis, for one to interpret the events of 1967 in any other way.

As for Newton, had he been alive to witness it, he would have most likely agreed that this twentieth century liberation and restoration of Jerusalem qualifies as being "of the highest nature for which a Jubilee can be kept." In fact, if Isaac Newton were alive to see all of this come together as it seems to be, he might be found on his front lawn doing cartwheels and back flips!

Nonetheless, even as we continue to ponder the enormity of this revelation, we move on to the remainder of verse 25 and part of verse 26, where we find some perhaps less timely but no less astounding predictions:

> …and sixty-two sevens. It will be rebuilt with streets and a
> trench, but in times of trouble. After the sixty-two sevens,
> the Anointed One will be cut off and will have nothing…
> —Daniel 9:25, 26

Here we notice yet another group of sevens, "sixty-two sevens." Once more, this period of time relates to the Messiah, but there is a subtle difference. Note that in reference to the "sixty-two sevens," or 434 years, Jesus is referred to as the "Anointed One," *not* a "ruler," as He had been previously in regard to the "seven sevens." This, combined with the fact that there is reference to Him being "cut off," or killed, tells us that the sixty-two sevens relate to Christ's *first* coming.

Secondly, we note that, similar to the case of the seven sevens, the sixty-two sevens are said to be counted from the beginning of the rebuilding of Jerusalem. However, in this case it is specified that Jerusalem "will be rebuilt with streets and a trench, but in times of trouble." According to Newton, this refers to the aforementioned *ancient* rebuilding of the wall around the city as detailed in Nehemia chapter 6: History records that the wall around Jerusalem was successfully completed in the twenty-eighth year of the reign of Artaxerxes, or the 4,278th year of the Julian Period. From this point, counting in Hebrew years from the month of September, exactly sixty-two sevens, or 434 years, would elapse until September of the year 4712. Per Newton, this year was acknowledged by numerous ancient historians, including Clemens Alexandrinus, Irenaeus, Eusebius, and others as the birth year of Jesus (54). Therefore, this prophesied period of sixty-two sevens finds its fulfillment in the span of time between the completion of Jerusalem's wall by Nehemia (4,278th year of the Julian Period) and the birth of Jesus Christ, or the First Coming.

Reading on, the next line predicts the subsequent death of Jesus by stating that "the Anointed One will be cut off." Once again, as proposed by Newton, despite His virgin birth and the many miracles that accompanied His ministry, the "Anointed One" was rejected by the Jewish leadership and "cut off," or killed.

Thus, we find in the compass of these few lines an accurate prediction of the timing of Christ's birth—to the year—and also a prediction that He will be killed, or "cut off." The actual year of His death, as we recall, was revealed earlier in the prophecy as taking place 490 years after the 457-458 BC return to Jerusalem.

Again, in light of Newton's interpretation so far, it is amazing to consider that the exact years of both Jesus' first and, quite possibly, His *second* entrance into the world are revealed in the span of only a few lines. Perhaps this passage, then, is the perfect example of "the law of double reference" as it speaks to both the First and the Second Advent of Christ.*

---

* Yet this timing is contingent upon Jerusalem's restorations, and thereby hidden or "sealed" until the time that these restorations occur.

Moving on, let us take a look at the second half of verse 26:

…The people of the ruler who will come will destroy the city and the sanctuary. The end will come like a flood; war will continue until the end, and desolations have been decreed.

—Daniel 9:26

According to Newton, the "ruler who will come" refers to Prince Titus, the son of Roman Caesar Vespasian, whose "people," or forces, would destroy the Jewish Temple in 70 AD. This battle, which is likened to a "flood," resulted in a massive loss of Jewish life via starvation, crucifixion, and the sword. Subsequently, both Jews and Christians were forbidden by the Romans to re-enter Jerusalem, which was later plowed under with salt.

Then, around 130 AD, the emperor Hadrian built a new Roman colony in Jerusalem and erected a temple to the god "Jupiter Capitolinus" on the Holy Hill, or "Temple Mount." As prophesied, Israel was broken up and the remaining Jews were dispersed into the Roman Empire, causing the "desolation" of the land. Per Newton, strife and "war" over Jerusalem and the Holy Land would then "continue until the end" when the twelve tribes of the Nation of Israel returned to the Land for the final time (55). Newton, therefore, believed that this part of the prophecy was fulfilled long before his own lifetime.

Incidentally, many interpreters today believe that this verse is yet another destined for dual fulfillment. This popular teaching holds that verse 26, in addition to describing the destruction of Jerusalem in 70 AD, also foreshadows the end-times invasion of the Holy City by the Antichrist and his forces.[7]

He will confirm a covenant with many for one seven…

—Daniel 9:27

Newton proposes a simple interpretation for this line: Seven years after the death and resurrection of Christ, the calling and conversion of Cornelius occurred, at which time a covenant was established between the "Anointed One" (Christ) and "many" peoples, referring to the Gentiles (55).

As in the case of verse 26, many prophecy teachers today ascribe an end-times fulfillment to this part of the prophecy. According to this teaching, the "He" in this verse does not refer to Jesus, but to the "Antichrist," who will confirm some type of covenant with the Jews. Therefore, the "seven" mentioned here is not considered to be a reference to Christ's first century timeframe but to a future "week," or period of seven years, most likely a sabbatical cycle, which will culminate in the end of the age.

While this author tends toward the latter theory of an end-times fulfillment, it is interesting, in the spirit of keeping an open mind, to consider the possibility of Newton being one hundred percent correct in his interpretation that this verse is already completely fulfilled. Today, millions await the signing of a "seven year peace treaty" as the definitive event in confirming the identity of the Antichrist. Once the Antichrist is revealed, it is believed that the return of Christ is but a few years in the offing. This precise scenario has been detailed in countless books that presumably map out the events of the last days as the majority expects them to unfold. In light of this, it is further interesting to play devil's advocate for a moment and pose the following: What if this "treaty" were not to materialize in the manner or at the time expected? Might this, for those who have dogmatically staked everything on a particular interpretation of one or two lines, hamper their ability to discern other possibilities and perhaps the larger unfolding of end-times events? The simple point to be made is the same one alluded to earlier by Newton: Until at or very near the time of fulfillment, we continue to look at these prophecies—perhaps some more than others—as through a dark piece of glass. So while some of the larger, more general, aspects may indeed be understood before the fact, it is likely that the end-times will hold many surprises for all.

...In the middle of a seven, he will put an end to sacrifice and offering. And on a wing of the temple he will set up an abomination that causes desolation, until the end that is decreed is poured out on him.

—Daniel 9:27

Again, Newton proposes a historical fulfillment: in speaking to the "middle of a seven," he notes that the Jewish war against the Romans lasted three and a half years, from 66 AD until 70 AD, when, contrary to the direct orders of Prince Titus, the Temple in Jerusalem was destroyed by fire, thus ending the daily "sacrifice and offering" (55).

In addressing the "abomination that causes desolation," which is rendered in the King James Version simply as "the overspreading of abominations," Newton proposes that after the Roman destruction of Jerusalem in 70 AD, the Holy City and surrounding lands were overspread by a successive army of false idols, gods, and religious abominations, resulting in the fulfillment of this verse (55).*

Other interpreters propose that the "Dome of the Rock," a Muslim temple built circa 688 AD on the Temple Mount, fulfills this prophecy.

Still others reason that since this is a continuance of the first line of verse 27, which refers to a "covenant with many," these actions should also be attributed to the Antichrist who will break said cove-

---

* Newton summarized the whole of Daniel's seventy weeks as follows: "Thus have we in this short Prophecy, a prediction of all the main periods relating to the coming of the Messiah; the time of his birth, that of his death, that of the rejection of the Jews, the duration of the Jewish war whereby he caused the city and the sanctuary to be destroyed, *and the time of his second coming*: and so the interpretation here is given more full and complete and adequate to the design, than if we should restrain it to his first coming only, as interpreters usually do. We avoid also the doing violence to the language of Daniel, by taking the seven weeks and sixty-two weeks for one number. Had that been Daniel's meaning, we would have said sixty and nine weeks, and not seven weeks and sixty-two weeks, a way of numbering using by no nation" (55).

2012-2015: THE SEASON OF RETURN?

nant with the Jews at mid-point, "in the middle of a seven," and place some type of "abomination" on a "wing" of a newly rebuilt Jewish Temple. This end-times interpretation is, again, predominant today.

Considering verse 27 in its entirety, this author, once more, tends to lean toward an end-times fulfillment but would stop far short of being dogmatic in this view. Already completely fulfilled? A possible future or dual fulfillment? As Newton once wrote, "Let time be the interpreter."

SUMMARY AND CONCLUSION

As we wrap up our look at Daniel's "prophecy of seventy weeks" we note that while questions remain regarding past or future fulfillment of certain portions of the prophecy, some key events can be convincingly shown to have been fulfilled. In fact, the accuracy of the prediction of the First Coming and also the death of the Messiah—both foretold to the very year—provide irrefutable evidence that the Bible could only have been inspired by God, who alone knows the future. Indeed, Newton went so far as to say that one could stake the truth of Christianity on these predictions alone.

Of course, considering the wide range of events covered in verses 24-27, not to mention the fact that Daniel's Book has been "sealed till the time of the end," it seems unlikely that anyone, even a genius of Newton's caliber, has flawlessly interpreted this passage. Nonetheless, differing viewpoints aside, perhaps all can agree that if Newton was correct in only one aspect of his interpretation (that relating to verse 25 and the Second Coming) that the current generation, as incredible as it may seem, is destined to witness what will no doubt be the most awesome event in all of human history: the return of Jesus Christ in Glory and the establishment of His millennial kingdom on Earth!

Did the final countdown of Daniel's "seven sevens" begin in

1967 with the Jewish recapture of Jerusalem? Has God accordingly marked the year 2015-16 (Hebrew year 5776) in His prophetic appointment book as the final Jubilee and thus the year of Christ's return?

As we ponder the notion of predetermined times, we are afforded perhaps the ideal segue into our next chapter, wherein the topic of "divine appointments" will be discussed in regard to some very special observances—observances that are most definitely marked on God's calendar.

FIVE

Ye worship ye know not what: we know what we worship: for salvation is of the Jews.

—John 4:22

THE FEASTS OF THE LORD

It is approaching the third hour of the day on Nisan 14, 33 AD. His back torn open and bleeding, Jesus stumbles forward under the heat of the almost midday sun. Staggering up the rugged heights of Golgotha, He finally reaches the appointed place of execution, where His hands and feet will be nailed to a cross.

The crossbar that Simon of Cyrene has carried for Him is placed on the ground. Jesus is abruptly thrown backward against the timber and held in position while a Roman legionnaire drives a heavy, square, wrought-iron nail through His wrist and deep into the wood. Quickly, he moves to the other side and repeats the action, being careful not to pull the arms too tightly, so as to allow for some flexion and movement. The crossbar is then lifted into place, and a small sign reading "Jesus of Nazareth, King of the Jews" is nailed above His head.

The left foot is then pressed backward against the right, and with both feet extended, toes down, a nail is driven through the arches, leaving the knees moderately flexed.

Jesus is now crucified. As His body sags downward from the force of gravity, exerting pressure on the nails that have pierced the median nerves in the wrists, excruciating pain shoots along the fingers and up the arms to explode in the brain. As He pushes Himself upward to avoid this stretching torment, He places His full weight on the nail through His feet. Again, there is the searing agony of the nail tearing through the nerves between the metatarsal bones of the feet.

He will hang like this for hours, the pitiless rays of the sun beating down on His thorn-crowned head, enduring limitless waves of pain, joint rending cramps, bouts of intermittent partial asphyxiation, and, of course, the vicious mockery of those present at the scene.

Afternoon arrives, bringing darkness—and a new agony: a terrible crushing pain deep in the chest as the pericardium slowly fills with serum and begins to compress the heart. A sponge soaked in cheap, sour wine is lifted to His lips, but He refuses the liquid.

It is now approaching the ninth hour of the day and the body of Jesus is in extremes; He cries out in a loud voice, "My God, my God, why hast thou forsaken me?" Immediately thereafter, He begins to sense the chill of death creeping through His tissues. This final realization brings an unexpected air of calm to His battered features—and a final utterance to his lips: "It is finished."

A BLIND REHEARSAL

The crucifixion of Jesus Christ is unquestionably the most important event in all of human history. It was, in essence, the ultimate sacrifice; the ransom of all ransoms in which one man would suffer unspeakable agonies as He bore the brunt of mankind's sin.

The above description of this event, written nearly twenty centuries after the fact, captures the basic details of what happened that day: the piercing of His hands and feet; the excruciating pain and near asphyxiation He suffered as the force of gravity literally pulled His bones out of joint; the terrible thirst that went unquenched; the mockery He endured at the hands of the Romans and priests gathered at the scene, and finally, the words that He uttered just before giving up the ghost. But did you know these same details were also spelled out in the ancient Scriptures many centuries *before* the crucifixion of Christ took place, in fact—long before the practice of crucifixion had been invented? (Psalm 22:1, 7, 14-18, 69:21).

Of course, the Jews who witnessed the event did not understand this, and even the Apostles and other disciples could not completely comprehend it at first, even though Jesus had spoken about it many times. Only later did things become clear, after the Lord in His resurrected state explained it to them.

SHADOWS AND TYPES

While most who know the Bible well are familiar with the prophecies that prefigured this ultimate sacrifice, many are not aware of another decidedly prophetic element of the crucifixion: Unbeknownst to the Jews, who rejected Jesus as Messiah and called for His execution nearly two thousand years ago, they themselves had been ritualistically rehearsing for and acting out this particular sacrifice to the very calendar day—and even the *hour* that it would take place—for well over a millennia before Christ was born.

The fact that Christ's crucifixion was ritualistically foreshadowed by the Jews long before the Messiah came into the world underscores one of the most common themes in the Bible: God gives us the natural to explain the spiritual (1 Corinthians 15:46, 47). Indeed, all throughout Scripture we find the Lord revealing His plan of redemption in the form of various earthly rituals and observances that He has given to man. For instance, we learned earlier how the seven-day week and the seven-year sabbatical cycles foreshadow God's larger seven thousand year timeline for the world. Also, we noted how the jubilee celebration prefigures the joyous return of Christ.

In this chapter, we are going to take a look at some additional types and shadows of things to come, specifically some special observances that God handed down to Moses and the Israelites as they wandered the wilderness en route to the Promised Land. Similar to the Sabbaths and Jubilees, these observances also prefigure key elements of God's plan. They are known as the "Feasts of the Lord," and, as you may or may not have guessed, there are seven of them.

THE FEASTS OF THE LORD

The seven Feasts of the Lord are first described to Moses by the Lord Himself in the Book of Leviticus, chapter 23:

> Speak unto the children of Israel, and say unto them, Concerning the feasts of the LORD, which ye shall proclaim to be holy convocations, even these are my feasts.
>   —Leviticus 23:2

In subsequent verses (3 through 44), God proceeds to lay out a series of dates on which the Israelites were to observe some very specific rituals, Sabbaths, and offerings. Beginning with the Feast of Passover and ending with the Feast of Tabernacles, He describes all seven, designating them as "holy convocations."

But what exactly was the Lord's purpose in highlighting these particular dates, and why does He designate them as "holy?"

LOST IN THE TRANSLATION?

To begin to understand what the feasts are really all about, it will be helpful to take a closer look at the two key words God uses to describe them in verse 2, which are, of course, "feast" and "convocation."

As we consider these words, the first thing to keep in mind is that they are an English translation derived from a Hebrew text. We note this because due to the inherent difficulties associated with translating any given text from one language to another, it is not always possible to convey the most accurate meaning of a particular word. In this case, for instance, when most of us hear the word "feast" we think food, perhaps relating to the Thanksgiving holiday. Yet if we look to the original Hebrew we find that the word translated as "feast" is actually *mo'ed*, which means "*a fixed time or season; an appointed time; a set time or exact time.*" Consequently, rather than necessarily denoting a gathering that involves food, as implied by the English translation, the Hebrew reveals that God was actually speaking more in terms of an "appointed" or "fixed" time.

The other word in question, "convocation," is in the English language normally associated with an "*assembly*" or "*ceremony.*" The original Hebrew word, however, which is *miqra*, denotes a meaning more specific to "*a rehearsal.*"

And so, as the added insight provided by the Hebrew meanings reveals, the feasts detailed in Leviticus were not merely to be celebratory gatherings, but were intended as holy "rehearsals" that were to be observed at "an appointed time" on God's calendar. Therefore, in keeping and observing the Feasts of the Lord, the Jews were essentially rehearsing and preparing for some very special "fixed" or "appointed" moments in time that God had pre-identified. These times, as will be demonstrated in this chapter, are those in which He has chosen to intersect human history through His Son, Jesus Christ (Chumney, 7).

THE FORGOTTEN FEASTS

Many Christians today do not understand the importance of the feasts and more or less view them as merely "Jewish" Holy Days that celebrate the ancient aspects of Hebrew culture. It should be pointed out, however, for those who hold this view, that the feasts are not called the "Feasts of the Jews" but the "Feasts of the Lord," thereby implying a universal relevance. Furthermore, Scripture tells us that these observances were not to be limited solely to the Jews but to be shared in equally by the foreigner or stranger in the land (Deuteronomy 16:11, 14).

Another reason the feasts are ignored by many Christians is the belief that when Christ died on the cross these ceremonies became irrelevant because they were part of the Old Testament Law and sacrificial system, which, of course, gave way to "salvation by Grace." This sentiment is somewhat understandable in view of Christ's teaching that salvation is not *earned* by upholding "the Law." Yet we must keep in mind that He also said, "Do not think that I came to abolish the Law or the Prophets; I did not come to abolish but to fulfill" (Matthew 5:17). The fact is that the early Christians continued to observe the feasts. Even the Apostle Paul in his ministry made it a point to observe the holy days with both Jewish believers and Gentile Christians alike (Colossians 2:16).

The point to be taken from all of this is that the primary role of the feasts, which, again, was to foreshadow what is yet to come, is just as important now as it was before the time of Christ. And so if we as believers want to fully understand what God has done in the past and even more importantly what His plans are for the future, we must ourselves begin to learn about the feasts and the rich symbolic meaning embedded therein.

Thus is described our objective for this chapter. In the following pages, we are going to begin to peel back the layers, revealing the remarkably prophetic nature of the feasts, thereby gaining access to some of the Bible's most incredibly detailed foreshadowings of the future.

Before we get into the details of each feast, however, let us first take a moment to note some general themes and characteristics that are common to all of them.

AN AGRICULTURAL THEME

The feasts observances are organized around the spring and fall sowing and harvesting cycles and therefore include many *agriculturally themed* rituals and activities.

AN APPOINTED PLACE

The Bible teaches that in addition to being observed at God's appointed "times," certain feasts, namely Passover, Pentecost, and the Feast of Tabernacles were to be observed at God's appointed *place*: a place that He shall "choose to place His name in" (Deuteronomy 16:2, 6, 9-11, 13-16).

As highlighted previously, God's chosen place is, of course, Jerusalem.

MULTIPLE MEANINGS

Unlike the ancient Jews who practiced them, we can, from our vantage point in time, clearly see how each of the feasts has not only a rich historical significance but also an instructive prophetic meaning. For instance, to the ancient Jews a certain feast may have served to commemorate a significant event in their relatively recent history, such as the handing down of the Ten Commandments at Sinai, but lost on them was the fact that the same set of rituals also pointed forward to a *future* event that would eventually be fulfilled by the Messiah.

AN APPOINTED TIME

Another obvious yet nonetheless amazing aspect of the feasts is that they prefigure much more than just the prophetic events themselves, but also reveal the exact day on which these events will occur. For example, let us consider once again the crucifixion: God predetermined Nisan 14 as the day on which the sacrificial "Lamb," or Jesus, would be put to death, roughly 1,400 years before Christ's birth!

SEASONS

Now, with our basic understanding of what the feasts are all about, we are prepared to take a look at each individually. The first four observances are known as the "spring feasts." These were fulfilled by Jesus Christ at His first coming. As history confirms, all of the key events in Christ's life, namely His death, burial, and resurrection occurred on particular feast days in the spring.

The remaining three feasts, which are yet to be fulfilled, are known as the fall feasts. Secure in the knowledge that God "does not change" (Malachi 3:6) and is eternal in His nature, we can be confident that just as Christ fulfilled crucial aspects of His redemptive plan on the appointed days in the spring, He will likewise return to fulfill the events foreshadowed by the fall feasts.

These important points noted, let us begin our look at the already fulfilled spring feasts, noting first how each was historically observed and then how each was ultimately fulfilled:

THE SPRING FEASTS: FULFILLED BY CHRIST AT HIS FIRST COMING.

1) THE FEAST OF PASSOVER (PESACH)

HISTORICAL OBSERVANCE:

As instructed by God, the Nation of Israel was to keep the Passover Feast by sacrificing a lamb "without blemish" on the Hebrew calendar date of Nisan 14 (Exodus 12:5, 6). For the Jews, this feast was a memorial of the night they put the blood of a lamb upon their doorposts and were spared by the Angel of Death that killed the firstborn of Egypt—the plague that finally convinced Pharaoh to release the Hebrew slaves from bondage.

Subsequent Passovers were observed by Jewish families as follows: The head of each household was to take a lamb of the first year on the tenth day of Nisan and set it aside until the fourteenth day (Exodus 12:3-6).* In the evening of the fourteenth day, at exactly 3:00 pm, the lamb was to be killed (Exodus 12:6). Then, just as on the very first Passover in Egypt, its blood was to be sprinkled on the lintel and two side posts of the household door. The lamb was to be roasted with fire, with bitter herbs, and with unleavened bread—then feasted upon by the entire household.

The Temple version of the sacrifice was observed in similar fashion: At the third hour of the day, or 9:00 am, the Jewish high priest would take the lamb and ascend the altar to tie it in place, where it would remain throughout the day. At the time of the evening sacrifice, which was the ninth hour of the day, or 3:00 pm, the high priest would ascend the altar and cut the throat of the lamb with a knife, afterword uttering the phrase, "It is finished."

SYMBOLOGY AND FULFILLMENT:

Spiritually, the ritual involving the blood of the lamb on the doorpost, which, again, memorialized the deliverance from Egypt, is a picture of the Messiah and the freedom He offers from the bondage of sin via His sacrifice as "the Lamb of God" (John 1:29). Here, sin is represented by the Jewish captivity in Egypt (14). Egypt represents a type of the world, or "world system," and its ruler, Pharaoh, represents a type of "Satan" (13, 14).

The ritual involving the priest's binding and sacrifice of the lamb, however, is the most stunningly prophetic element of this feast as it provides a remarkable foreshadowing of Christ's actual crucifixion: On the day of His death, Nisan 14, Jesus was bound and nailed to the cross at the third hour of the day, or 9:00 am (Mark 15:25), the exact date and time that the Jews had been binding the Passover

---

* The significance of setting the lamb aside for four days is rooted in the ancient belief that the Messiah would remain hidden from the world until four thousand years from the creation of Adam, thus alluding to God's "seven thousand year plan" (15).

Lamb to the altar for centuries on end. Jesus hung on the cross for the better part of the day and eventually died at the ninth hour, or 3:00 pm (Matthew 27:46, 50), the same time that the Passover Lamb, as instructed by God, had been sacrificed by the high priest for well over a millennia. Before He bowed His head and "gave up the ghost," Jesus uttered the same words that had long since been ritualistically uttered by the priest as he sacrificed the lamb: "It is finished" (John 19:30). Thus, in true rehearsal-like fashion, the Jews had sacrificed the Passover Lamb—representing Jesus Christ—on Nisan 14, for well over a thousand years before He had been born!

2) THE FEAST OF UNLEAVENED BREAD (HAG HAMATZAH)

HISTORICAL OBSERVANCE:

During the Feast of Unleavened Bread, which runs from Nisan 15 through Nisan 21, God forbade the Jews to have any leaven in their homes. Therefore, they would take care to remove all traces and eat only flat bread, or *matzah* (28).

A fascinating aspect of this feast centers on a traditional ceremonial dinner known as the Seder. This tradition, which remains a mystery to most Jews, is observed as follows: At a certain point during the dinner, the leader of the Seder picks up a linen bag from the table, which contains three pieces of matzah. He then removes the second, or middle, matzah and breaks it in half. Half is placed back into the bag and the other half is carefully wrapped in a linen napkin and hidden somewhere in the home. The piece that is hidden is known as the "afikomen" and reappears later in the service.

After the meal, the children are sent out to find the hidden afikomen; the child who finds it receives a reward. Rabbinic Law then requires that a small piece of the retrieved afikomen be eaten by everyone present at the service as a reminder of the Passover Lamb.[1]

SYMBOLOGY AND FULFILLMENT:

The removal of leaven (representing sin) from the home during this feast is symbolic of putting away the sin in one's life and, in turn, the corrupting influence that it has on the soul of the believer. Ancient Israel learned that keeping this feast meant a complete separation from Egypt's religion, as well as its worldly glory and splendor (32, 33).

The bread made without leaven, or matzah, also reminded the Jews of their ancestors, who hurriedly left Egypt for the Promised Land, not having time to wait for the dough to rise.

The symbology behind the ceremonial Seder dinner is perhaps the most remarkable though. For the Jews involved in this service, the question must be asked, why three matzahs? One rabbinic tradition holds that they represent the three groups of Jewish people: the priests, the Levites, and the Israelites. Another tradition holds that they represent the three patriarchs: Abraham, Isaac, and Jacob. However, there is no biblical basis for either of these explanations, and neither fit the symbolism behind the breaking of the bread ceremony. Basically, rabbinic tradition is at a loss to explain why the middle matzah must be broken.

The truth, though unrecognized by many of the Jews who routinely participate in this ritual, is that the trinity of the Godhead is being symbolized: three persons within the oneness of God, just as three matzahs are in the oneness of the linen bag. The second person of the Godhead, the Son, came to Earth as the Messiah. He was "broken" (on the cross), "wrapped in linen" (Christ's burial shroud was linen), and "hidden" away (buried in the tomb).[2] Thus is revealed the true spiritual meaning behind this feast: Jesus was buried and lay in the tomb on the Feast of Unleavened Bread. The matzah, which was traditionally pierced and striped, was seen as being symbolic of Christ, who was also "striped" (whipped by the Romans) and "pierced" (on the cross).

Interestingly, there is much debate among rabbis concerning the meaning of the word afikomen; this, perhaps, owing to the fact that the word afikomen does not even exist in the Hebrew language. Rabbinic consensus, nonetheless, usually maintains that it means "dessert," since it is eaten after the meal when a dessert would normally be eaten. Digging a little deeper, however, we find that afikomen is a Greek word—which makes a certain amount of sense considering that Greek was the common language of Jesus' day. Yet, oddly enough, it is the *only* Greek word in the Seder ceremony. Everything else is, again, in Hebrew. It is also the second aorist form (completion of an action, without reference to length of action) of the Greek verb *ikneomai*—a word with an electrifying translation: It simply means "*He came.*"[3]

Indeed, the death of Jesus—the man without sin—symbolizes the opportunity for the burden of sin to be removed from mankind forever. Perhaps the Prophet Isaiah put it best when he wrote, "with his stripes we are healed" (Isaiah 53:5).

3) THE FEAST OF FIRST FRUITS (BIKKURIM)

HISTORICAL OBSERVANCE:

As commanded by God, the people of Israel kept this feast on Nisan 18 as a *joyous* occasion. Chapter 23 of Leviticus details God's instructions:

> God said to Moses, 'When you enter the land which I am going to give to you and reap its harvest, then you shall bring in the sheaf of the first fruits of your harvest to the priest. He shall wave the sheaf before the Lord for you to be accepted; on the day after the Sabbath the priest shall wave it. Now on the day when you wave the sheaf, you shall offer a male lamb one year old without defect for a burnt offering to the Lord.
>
> —Leviticus 23:9-12

In Israel, barley would be the first grain to ripen, followed by fruit, olives, grapes, and finally, wheat. At the time of planting, the Jewish people would mark off certain barley in the field. Later, when the harvest season arrived, they would carry a sickle and basket and on command reap this specially designated grain. They would then march to the Tabernacle, bringing a sheaf of the "first fruits" of the harvest to the priest. The priest would then, as prescribed in Leviticus, wave the sheaf before the Lord, accompanied by burnt and meal offerings. This "first fruits" ceremony was a way of giving thanks to God for a good harvest by offering Him the very first of the larger harvest that yet lay in the field.[4]

Symbology and Fulfillment:

Representative of the "first fruits" of the "harvest of the redeemed," Jesus was resurrected from the grave during this feast. In 1 Corinthians, below, Paul confirms that Christ's immortal resurrected body, being the first, was the model, or prototype, of what believers have to look forward to when they are also given immortal bodies at the final harvest, or resurrection (36):

> But now Christ has been raised from the dead, the first fruits of those who are asleep. For since by a man came death, by a man also came the resurrection of the dead. For as in Adam all die, so also in Christ all shall be made alive. But each in his own order: Christ the firstfruits, after that those who are Christ's at His coming.
> —1 Corinthians 15:20-23

4) The Feast of Pentecost (Shavvot)

Historical Observance:

The fourth spring feast, known as "the Feast of Pentecost," occurs fifty days after the Feast of Passover. Pentecost was a one-day

Sabbath feast, a new meal offering to the Lord that was celebrated with two large loaves of leavened bread. Historically, this feast was a memorial of the giving of the Ten Commandments at Mount Sinai, which, according to the Bible, occurred exactly fifty days after the crossing of the Red Sea. It is said that at this time God recorded "the Law," or "the Torah," on two tablets of stone.

SYMBOLOGY AND FULFILLMENT:

After being crucified on *Passover* and then resurrected at *First Fruits*, Christ appeared to and spoke with the Apostles over a period of forty days. In His final words to them He said that He must return to the Father, but that He would send the "Holy Spirit" as a comforter. This came to pass just days later on the next Jewish feast, *Pentecost*, when He sent the Holy Spirit to dwell in the hearts of those who would receive Him (Acts 2:1-18). It is said that at this time God's Law was written not on "tablets of stone" but on the "hearts and minds" of all believers (41).

Thus, Pentecost was fulfilled by Christ's sending of the Holy Spirit, marking the beginning of the Church and the beginning of God's early "harvest" of mankind.

SUMMARY OF THE SPRING FEASTS

As we wrap up our look at the spring feasts, let us briefly review how each of them has been fulfilled by Jesus:

Jesus, who was our "Passover Lamb," was crucified on the day of Passover (Nisan 14). He, being the "bread of life" and the "man without sin," was lying in the tomb wrapped in a linen shroud on the Feast of Unleavened Bread.

Christ arose on the Feast of First Fruits as the first to rise from the dead and receive a resurrected body.

And finally, the Holy Spirit was poured out upon the first believers during the Feast of Pentecost, which marked the beginning of the Christian era.

Remarkably, these feasts, as recorded in Leviticus and observed by the Jews for over a millennia before Christ's appearance, were fulfilled to the very day and in at least one case—to the very hour—by Jesus when He came to carry out the most critical phase of God's redemptive plan.

At this point, before moving on to the fall feasts, we should take the opportunity to acknowledge yet another aspect of the feast cycle that is rooted in the underlying agricultural theme, which is the fact that there exists a significant span of time, or what some call a "gap," between the spring and fall feasts. Might this also hold some meaning?

THE SUMMER GAP

The season that lies between spring and fall is, of course, the summer season. In the context of the feast cycle, this "summer gap" symbolizes the span of two thousand years that began at Christ's resurrection from the dead and ends roughly at the present day. This time period is also known as the "summer harvest" and represents the growth of Christ's Church and the redeeming of those who have heard and responded to His call during this era.

This important element noted, let us move on to the fall feasts.

THE FALL FEASTS: TO BE FULFILLED BY CHRIST AT HIS SECOND COMING

The fall is arguably the most important time of year in Judaism and, though many Christians do not realize it, it should likewise be for them, as the fall feasts foreshadow the future return of Jesus Christ. For this reason, we are going to take a slightly more in-depth look at these holy rehearsals and what they portend—beginning with "the Feast of Trumpets."

5) THE FEAST OF TRUMPETS (ROSH HASHANAH)

HISTORICAL OBSERVANCE:

Tishrei 1 on the Hebrew calendar marks the Feast of Trumpets. Because it falls on the first day of the Jewish "civil" calendar, this feast represents a type of New Year's Day in Jewish culture. It is also viewed as a type of "birthday of the world," since, according to tradition, it is believed that Adam was created on this day (Mishnah, San Hedrin 38b).

The Feast of Trumpets was traditionally reserved as a time to consider the sins of the previous year and repent of them before the arrival of the next Jewish feast, the Day of Atonement.

SYMBOLOGY AND FULFILLMENT:

The ten days that fall between the Feast of Trumpets and the Day of Atonement are known as the "High Holy Days" or "the Days of Awe." Significantly, the Sabbath that falls within this ten-day period is called *Shabbat Shuvah*, or the "Sabbath of Return" (52, 53). Accordingly, several important themes related to the Messiah's return are associated with the Feast of Trumpets. Since each of these is fairly extensive, for the sake of clarity, we will list and discuss each separately over the course of the next several pages.

We begin with the most obvious theme:

Feast of Trumpets Theme (1): "The Sounding of the Shofar"

Considering the name of this feast—"the Feast of *Trumpets*"—it is no surprise that the sounding of the shofar, or trumpet, is the primary theme. Tellingly, the trumpet is often associated with the resurrection, or rapture, as we see in 1 Corinthians:

In a moment, in the twinkling of an eye, at the last trump: for *the trumpet shall sound*, and the dead shall be raised incorruptible, and we shall be changed.

—1 Corinthians 15:52

In the Torah, this feast is referred to as "The Day of the Sounding of the Shofar," or *Yom Teruah* (55). *Teruah* translates to *"an awakening blast."* In the Bible, the word *awake* is also often associated with the resurrection, as we note in Isaiah:

Your dead will live; their corpses will rise. You who lie in the dust, *awake* and shout for joy, for your dew is as the dew of the dawn, and the earth will give birth to the departed spirits.

—Isaiah 26:19

Teruah is also translated as "shout." In 1 Thessalonians we see the word shout used in connection with the resurrection:

For the Lord himself shall descend from heaven *with a shout*, with the voice of the archangel, and with the trump of God: and the dead in Christ shall rise first: Then we which are alive and remain shall be caught up together with them in the clouds, to meet the Lord in the air: and so shall we ever be with the Lord.

—1 Thessalonians 4:16, 17

Feast of Trumpets Theme (2): "Gates of Heaven Opened"

In accordance with the theme of the resurrection, it is also believed that the gates of heaven are opened on the Feast of Trumpets to allow the righteous to enter. We find this scene illustrated in the Book of Psalms (63, 64):

Open to me the gates of righteousness: I will go into them, and I will praise the LORD: This gate of the LORD, into which the righteous shall enter.

—Psalm 118:19-20

Feast of Trumpets Theme (3): "The Wedding of the Messiah"

The Hebrew sages considered marriage to be the ideal human state and the model for the relationship between God and Israel. Thus, the Jewish wedding ceremony was understood by early Christians to be a picture of the joining of Christ with His Church. Scripture confirms this in Ephesians, wherein the Apostle Paul draws this very analogy:

Husbands, love your wives, even as Christ also loved the church, and gave himself for it; That he might sanctify and cleanse it with the washing of water by the word, That he might present it to himself a glorious church, not having spot, or wrinkle, or any such thing; but that it should be holy and without blemish.

—Ephesians 5:25-27

Another example of the wedding analogy is, as we recall, found in "The Parable of the Ten Virgins" cited earlier in chapter 1. Here, again, Jesus is pictured as the bridegroom returning for His bride (the Church) at the end of the age:

And at midnight there was a cry made, Behold, the bridegroom cometh; go ye out to meet him...and they that were ready went in with him to the marriage...

—Matthew 25:6, 10

Many other scriptural references can be cited that link the return of Christ to the Jewish wedding tradition. For instance, in Jewish culture it was customary that after the bride had accepted the groom's proposal the bridegroom would depart, going back to his father's house to prepare the bridal chamber. It was understood to be the man's duty to go away to be with his father, build a house, and prepare for the eventual wedding. Before he departed, however, he would make the following statement to the bride: "I go to prepare a place for you; if I go, I will return again unto you." This, of course, echoes the well-known statement that Jesus made to the Disciples in John 14—just before leaving to return to His "Father's house" in Heaven:

> Let not your heart be troubled: ye believe in God, believe also in Me. In My Fathers' house are many mansions: if it were not so, I would have told you. *I go to prepare a place for you. And if I go and prepare a place for you, I will come again, and receive you unto Myself that where I am, there ye may be also.*
>
> —John 14:1-3

Here, we have a clear picture of the bridegroom (Jesus) returning to His Father's house (heaven) to prepare a place for His bride (the Church) (68).

Yet another reference to the wedding tradition was touched on, albeit briefly, in our first chapter. It is, again, the verse most often cited by those who insist that we cannot know the time of Christ's return:

> But of that day and hour knoweth no man, no, not the angels of Heaven, *but my Father only.*
>
> —Matthew 24:36

Focusing on the italicized portion of the verse, according to Jewish tradition, the timing of the wedding was contingent upon the father's approval of the groom's preparation of the wedding chamber.

So, when someone inquired as to *when* the wedding would be held, the groom would customarily answer, "Only my father knows." Needless to say, in comparing this customary turn of phrase to the above verse, the correlation becomes obvious! Therefore, the Jewish wedding, which, as we have established, is linked symbolically to the resurrection, is also linked by association to the Feast of Trumpets. All of this points to the fact that verse 36, above, which employs strong reference to the Jewish wedding tradition in speaking to the timing of Christ's return, is an obvious allusion to the fact that this return will take place at the Feast of Trumpets!

Continuing on, after the wedding it was customary for the bride and groom to remain in the wedding chamber for a week before emerging to take part in the "wedding supper" (44). As we recall, the Hebrew word for week is *shabua*. This, again, can refer to a period of seven days or seven years. In light of this, many believe that this week symbolizes a seven-year period immediately following the resurrection in which the saints will be in heaven, while, on earth, God's wrath is being poured out on an unrepentant world.*

At the conclusion of this week, the bride (or Church) and the groom (Jesus) will return to earth to take part in the "wedding supper of the Lamb." It is said that only the invited guests of the "father of

---

* As J.C. Alexander points out in *Kingdom of the Beast*, when reading the Book of Revelation it is crucial to understand that the "Tribulation" and the "Wrath of God" are two entirely different sets of circumstances that unfold during entirely different time periods (215). The resurrection, or rapture, which occurs at the opening of the "sixth seal," is the event that separates these two distinct periods. In Revelation 8, with the opening of the "seventh seal" we see the horrific events of God's wrath begin to unfold. The overall sequence of events, then, is as follows: 1) Tribulation (three and one half years in duration), 2) Resurrection-Rapture (both occur on the same day), 3) God's wrath (most likely seven years in duration) and, finally, Christ's return to earth with the resurrected saints. For those thinking seven years seems like a long time for the saints to be in heaven before returning to earth, we must keep in mind that the heavenly estate exists outside the confines of "time and space" as we know it. In other words, it is an *eternal* state where it is believed one is always "in the moment"—where the passing of time literally does not exist.

the bridegroom" (God the Father) will be present at this banquet meal (Revelation 19:9) (70).

Feast of Trumpets Theme (4): "The Hidden Day"

The Feast of Trumpets is also known as *Yom HaKeseh*, or "the Hidden Day." The term *keseh*, or *keceh*, is derived from the Hebrew root *kacah*, which means to "*conceal, cover, or hide.*" Every day during the month of Elul, a trumpet is blown to warn the people to turn back to God, except for the thirtieth, or last, day of the month—the day preceding the Feast of Trumpets. On this day the trumpet is not blown, but all is silent. This is done to underscore the fact that much about the Feast of Trumpets is concealed, or shrouded in mystery (72). This somewhat mystical aspect is alluded to in the Book of Psalms: "Sound the shofar on the new moon, in concealment of the day of our festival" (Psalm 81:3).

Part of the reason the Feast of Trumpets is considered mysterious, or hidden, owes to the fact that there was a fair amount of uncertainty with regard to observing this feast on the correct calendar day. As with all of the feasts, the uncertainty stemmed from a calendar that depended on the promulgation of the new moon, which marked the beginning of each new month as designated by the rabbinical court in Jerusalem. The problem with the Feast of Trumpets was further compounded by the fact that it falls on *Rosh Chodesh*, or the new moon, itself. Because the commencement of this feast hinged on the sighting of a tiny sliver of the Moon, even in Jerusalem it would have been difficult to let everyone know in time that the New Year had begun. To solve this problem, a *two-day* Feast of Trumpets was practiced, even in Israel. In the rabbinic view, these two days are regarded as a *yoma arikhta*, or one long day (54). For this reason, when speaking of the timing of the Feast of Trumpets the Jews would typically say, "Of that day and hour no one knows." Thus, in this theme we have yet another clear reference to Jesus' words in Matthew 24:36 ("of that day and hour knoweth no man") regarding the timing of

His return for the Church. This reference, in combination with the aforementioned Jewish wedding reference, "Only my father knows," leaves no doubt that Jesus' statement in verse 36, which has long been cited by those who argue that the time of the resurrection is unknowable, is actually a confirmation that this event will indeed take place on the Feast of Trumpets!

Feast of Trumpets Theme (5): "The Day of Judgment"

Yet another name for the Feast of Trumpets is *Yom HaDin*, or "the Day of Judgment." According to Jewish tradition, it was seen that on this day God would sit in court while all men would pass before Him to be judged. We see this fantastic scene described in the Book of Daniel:

> I kept looking until thrones were set up, and the Ancient of Days took His seat; His vesture was like white snow, and the hair of His head like pure wool. His throne was ablaze with flames, its wheels were a burning fire. A river of fire was flowing and coming out from before Him; thousands upon thousands were attending Him, and myriads upon myriads were standing before Him; the court sat, and the books were opened.
>
> —Daniel 7:9, 10

Since this judgment is taking place immediately following the resurrection, it is obviously a judgment of the *redeemed*. In other words, those being judged are believers only. Therefore, it is not a judgment of one's salvation, as that has already been determined, but a judgment of one's works, upon which rewards will be established. According to the Talmud, this is also known as the *Bema* judgment (61).

Now, keeping in mind the amazing revelation that the much anticipated resurrection or rapture of the Church will take place in some future year during the course of the two-day Feasts of Trumpets, let us move on to the second of the fall feasts, which happens to foreshadow an even more momentous event.

6) The Day of Atonement (Yom Kippur)

Historical Observance:

Leviticus chapter 16 specifies that ten days after the Feast of Trumpets, on the tenth of Tishrei, the high priest shall conduct a special ceremony to purge the shrine and the people of any defilement. To this end, he is to bring a bull and two goats as a special offering. First, the bull is sacrificed to purge the shrine and to make "atonement" for any misdeeds of the priest or his household (Leviticus 16:6). Secondly, one of the goats is chosen by the casting of lots to be sacrificed as a sin offering (Leviticus 16:7-9). The other goat, known as the "scapegoat," is not sacrificed but is sent away into the wilderness as a means to symbolically remove the sin from the people (74).

Symbology and Fulfillment:

The Day of Atonement is the most solemn and important of the Jewish holidays; its central themes are atonement and repentance. Jews traditionally observe this holy day with a full day of fasting and intensive prayer.

As with the Feast of Trumpets, there are also multiple themes associated with this feast so, once again, we will list and discuss them individually.

Day of Atonement Theme (1): "The Day of Face to Face"

The Day of Atonement is also known as a day of "face to face" with God. Referring again to the above-mentioned special ceremony involving the bull and two goats, it was during this offering, held only once a year on the Day of Atonement, that the high priest was allowed to go behind the veil of the Temple into the "Holy of Holies" to be in the presence of God (Hebrews 9:6, 7). Thus, the high priest was "face to face" with the mercy seat of the Lord (78-80). At that moment, the nation held its breath as their fate depended on God's acceptance of the sacrifice.

The term "face to face" also refers to the future physical return of Christ. We see both this theme and the historical, or priestly, reference alluded to in Joel, chapter 2:

> Gather the people, sanctify the congregation, assemble the elders, gather the children, and those that suck the breasts: *let the bridegroom go forth of his chamber, and the bride out of her closet. Let the priests, the ministers of the LORD, weep between the porch and the altar, and let them say, Spare thy people, O LORD, and give not thine heritage to reproach*, that the heathen should rule over them: wherefore should they say among the people, Where is their God?
>
> —Joel 2:16, 17

The "bridegroom" and the "bride" in this verse represent Christ and His Church returning to earth after the "wedding of the Messiah" that has taken place in heaven. The reference to the "priests" or "ministers of the Lord" that "weep between the porch and the altar" is a picture of the high priest ministering in the "Holy of Holies" on the Day of Atonement.

And so is revealed the future and ultimate fulfillment of the Day of Atonement. It represents the return of Christ to reign as King. This, of course, is not to be confused with the resurrection, or rapture, which has already taken place at the Feast of Trumpets. Here, Jesus has been joined with His bride, having presumably spent "seven days" in the wedding chamber, as they return to earth together.

At this time, according to Scripture, the Holy City is about to come under siege by the Antichrist and his forces.* This siege is interrupted, however, as the Lord returns to "destroy all the nations that come against Jerusalem" (Zechariah 12:9). This, perhaps, explains why the Day of Atonement is also known as the time when "a sentence in meted out." On this day, it is said that Jesus will stand upon the Mount of Olives in Jerusalem, but only after those who had rejected Him as Messiah are brought to mourning, "as one that is in bitterness for his firstborn," at the realization that He is indeed the Son of God (Zechariah 12:10, 14:4).

Day of Atonement Theme (2): "The Great Day"

As noted in chapter 3, it is believed that Jesus will proclaim a Jubilee when He returns. We also recall that a Jubilee can only be proclaimed on the Day of Atonement. Therefore, the ultimate fulfillment of both the Day of Atonement and the Jubilee will take place at the Second Coming of Christ on none other than the Day of Atonement! At this time the earth will at last be freed from the consequences of sin and come into full and complete rest from the curse brought upon it at Eden. It is no wonder then that this feast is also called "the Great day" (81, 82).

Day of Atonement Theme (3): "The Closing of the Gates"

Just as the Feast of Trumpets is known as the time when the gates of heaven are opened, the Day of Atonement is known as the time when the gates are *closed* (74). Accordingly, the last ceremony to take place on the Day of Atonement is called *neilah*, or the "closing of the gates." At this point, it is said that it is too late to make a decision to accept the Messiah into your life, as all opportunity has passed (85).

---

* This siege is described in Ezekiel 38 and is also infamously known as "Armageddon."

Again, just as we found the Feast of Trumpets to be a foreshadowing of the resurrection, the multiple themes associated with the Day of Atonement make it very clear that this feast represents the literal and bodily return of Christ and His resurrected saints to earth. Furthermore, as noted previously, if God's past faithfulness in fulfilling these "appointed times" is any indicator of what is to come, we can be certain that this glorious event will take place on this very calendar day at some point in the future.

And with that, we move on to the seventh and final feast.

7) FEAST OF TABERNACLES (SUKKOT)

HISTORICAL OBSERVANCE:

The Feast of Tabernacles, which occurs for seven days, from Tishrei 15 to Tishrei 21, is the last of the fall feasts and completes the sacred festivals of the seventh month. In contrast to the somber tone of the Feast of Trumpets and the Day of Atonement, this feast was to be a time of joy (91). Hence, there is a quick transition from a mood of remorse and judgment to one of rejoicing and celebration. At last, Israel has passed through the season of repentance and redemption and will know the joy of walking with, and knowing, God (87, 92).

During this observance, people were commanded to build a "tabernacle" and make it their home. The Hebrew word for tabernacle is *sukkah*, which means "*a booth, a hut, a covering, a pavilion or tent.*" The Greek word for tabernacle is *sk'en'e*, which also means "*a tent, hut, or habitation*" (89).

Historically, the Torah identifies this booth, or hut, with the temporary dwellings that the Israelites lived in after leaving Egypt while en route to the Promised Land (86).

SYMBOLOGY AND FULFILLMENT:

In a spiritual sense, the temporary dwelling represented by the hut, or tabernacle, is a picture of mankind, a spiritually eternal being who inhabits a temporary "covering," or body, as he dwells in the wilderness of this present world on his way to the *heavenly* promised land (87, 88).

The *ultimate* symbolic meaning of the tabernacle is grounded in the notion that Christ will eventually dwell, or tabernacle, with man here on earth—which leads us to the themes commonly associated with this feast.

Feast of Tabernacles Theme (1): "The Beginning of the Millennial Kingdom"

The fullness of the Feast of Tabernacles will be experienced at the return of Christ when He will begin to reign over the world during the Millennium. This will be a time of great joy for all believers and, according to Jewish tradition, the age of Israel's glory (103).

Feast of Tabernacles Theme (2): "The Feast of Nations"

This feast is also known as "the Feast of Ingathering," or "the Feast of Nations," as Jesus will literally dwell among *all* of the nations as He has promised (87). Moreover, the Feast of Tabernacles will continue to be celebrated throughout the millennial reign, not only by "Israel" as in days of old, but by *every* nation:

> And it shall come to pass, that every one that is left of all the nations which came against Jerusalem shall even go up from year to year to worship the King, the LORD of hosts, and to keep the feast of tabernacles.
>
> —Zechariah 14:16

During this time, the earth will be inhabited both by a remnant of mortal human beings who have survived the time of God's wrath as well as the resurrected saints, going all the way back to the biblical patriarchs, such as Abraham, Isaac, Jacob, Moses, and Daniel; a fantastic scene to imagine, to be sure, but nonetheless one that will soon enough come to pass!

SUMMARY OF THE FALL FEASTS

Now, having completed our look at the fall feasts, let us briefly summarize what each reveals about the future:

The first of the three feasts, the Feast of Trumpets, foreshadows the event that is next in line on the prophetic calendar, which is the resurrection, or rapture, of the Church. Christ will descend with a shout as He dispatches His angels to gather the elect. The dead will rise first and those who are alive will immediately follow, all being caught up into heaven together to take part in the "wedding of the Messiah," or the joining of Christ to His faithful followers.

The second feast, known as the Day of Atonement, marks the return of Christ and His saints to earth, at which time Jesus will destroy the forces gathered against Israel at what is commonly referred to as "Armageddon." On this day, the Lord will set foot upon the Mount of Olives and begin to rule over all the kingdoms of this world.

The last of the fall feasts, the Feast of Tabernacles, gives us a picture of the first thousand years of this reign, as Christ dwells or "tabernacles" with mankind, fulfilling the ultimate Sabbath and bringing to completion the "seven thousand year plan" of God.

FINAL SUMMARY AND CONCLUSION

As we conclude our look at the seven Feasts of The Lord, it should be noted that in studying these rehearsals we have only begun to plumb what is a seemingly inexhaustible well of insight into God's prophetic plans—both past and future. Nevertheless, we have touched on the most critical aspects and thus come away with a general understanding that each feast has a rich historical significance, as well as an important prophetic meaning.

Again, knowing that the spring feasts have already been fulfilled to the very day by Jesus, we can be certain that He will likewise honor the fall observances. Therefore, it could be said that we might indeed know the "day" (or "days" in the case of the Feast of Trumpets) on which certain prophetic events will transpire. The year, on the other hand, remains a matter of less certainty.

Be that as it may, considering our earlier revelations concerning the jubilee cycle and Daniel's "seven sevens," it seems we have identified in the year 2015, if nothing else, a target worth tracking.

Now, keeping in mind *all* of the compelling data that we have reviewed thus far, including God's seven thousand year plan, the Jubilee, Newton's interpretation of Daniel, and the feast days, it is time to move on to the next chapter, wherein we will examine yet another piece of the puzzle—a piece that seems to tie all of this together.

Multitudes, multitudes in the valley of decision: for the day of the LORD is near in the valley of decision. The sun and the moon shall be darkened, and the stars shall withdraw their shining.

—Joel 3:14, 15

Signs in the Heavens

―――――•―――――

It begins with the appearance of a tiny nick on the western side of the Sun. At first, the eye detects no difference in the amount of sunlight, but, as the minutes tick by, you begin to sense a difference in the quality of the atmosphere. Before long, the brilliant orb is more than half covered. The sky is still bright at this point, but the blue is a little duller, and the landscape takes on a steely gray metallic cast.

Soon, the crescent sun appears a blazing white sliver—like a welder's torch. The darkening sky continues to close in around what remains of the light, now swiftly engulfing it.

And then, all at once, where the Sun once stood, hangs an ominous black disk in the sky, outlined by the soft pearly white glow of the corona. The land is dark, but it is not the dark of night. As you gaze across the landscape at the horizon—beyond the shadow thrown by the eclipse—you discern an eerie twilight of orange and yellow. From this light beyond the darkness comes an inexorable sense of foreboding—and a feeling that time is limited.

―――――•―――――

SINCE DAYS OF OLD

Since ancient times, man has wondered at the inspiring phenomenon known as the solar eclipse. In many cultures, it was believed that a solar eclipse was caused by a dragon, or demons, who were attacking and devouring the Sun. The Chinese also believed that lunar eclipses were caused by the same monsters.

Often these ancient cultures would devise rituals designed to frighten the great dragon away. These usually involved making lots of noise by banging pots, chanting, or shouting into the air![1]

Obviously, modern man has a much better grasp of the actual mechanics behind the solar and lunar eclipse than most of his ancestors. Yet, in spite of this, or perhaps *because* of this, most take for granted the fact that these phenomena are in many ways as improbable as would be the actual devouring of the Sun by monsters! Indeed, the idea that a total solar eclipse is even possible seems to defy coincidence, or the notion of a random universe, as the combination of factors that conspire to bring about this wonder could not be more unlikely. These factors are, of course, grounded in the relative sizes and distances between the Sun, the Earth, and the Moon. During a total solar eclipse, the Moon, which appears from our perspective to be the same diameter as the Sun, effectively blots out this massive orb—no more, no less. They are a seemingly perfect match from our earthly vantage point. This is only possible because the Sun's distance from the Earth is roughly 400 times that of the Moon's distance from the Earth, and the Sun's diameter is about 400 times that of the Moon's diameter.[2]

Is this ratio of size and distance an accident of nature, or was it designed this way? And if so—for what purpose?

THE HEAVENLY BODIES: MORE THAN JUST A LIGHT SOURCE

As any astronomer would attest, the solar eclipse has afforded mankind the otherwise impossible opportunity to study the corona of the Sun and thus its mysterious properties. But more than this, the eclipse has enabled mankind to search the very secrets of the cosmos. For instance, Albert Einstein famously utilized this phenomenon as a means to prove his most important theory: On May 29, 1919, during a total solar eclipse, A.S. Eddington conducted the first empirical test of Einstein's theory of general relativity, which entailed the measurement of light by the Sun's gravitational field. Owing to the eclipse, Eddington was able to photograph the stars in the region surrounding the Sun. As per Einstein's theory, these stars should appear to have slightly shifted their position as their light is "curved" by the Sun's gravitational field. Eddington's experiment, needless to say, validated the theory, thereby radically altering our understanding of the Universe.[3]

Indeed, it appears that God, being all too aware of man's inquisitive nature, has gone out of His way to create circumstances that allow for him to satisfy this curiosity. But aside from man's scientific endeavors, it seems the Lord also had other purposes in mind when He designed the Sun and the Moon: As we noted in chapter 2, the luminaries were meant to "divide the day from the night" and to be for "signs and for seasons, and for days, and years" (Genesis 1:14).

Now, it goes without saying that dividing the day from the night is critical, as is our ability to mark the turning seasons and years. But what of God's allusion to using the heavenly bodies as "signs?" Could it be that from the very beginning He has planned to tell us something via the Sun and the Moon?

SIGNS IN THE HEAVENS: GOD'S PURPOSE FOR THE SUN, MOON, AND STARS

In this chapter, we are going to explore the fascinating notion that God has, in the past, and is now, at present, using "signs" in the heavens to draw our attention to certain prophetically significant dates and events. Before we dive into this topic, however, we need to first address a concern that many Christians harbor with respect to the concept of "signs in the heavens." This general unease is no doubt largely due to the fact that most of us have been taught that celestial signs are somehow akin to astrology, or "Godless paganism." What needs to be made clear, though, is that the type of signs we will be discussing here are in no way related to these occult practices. To the contrary, such signs are repeatedly mentioned in the Bible, particularly in regard to the end times. In fact, in Luke 21 Jesus tells us that in the last days, "there shall be signs in the Sun, and in the Moon, and in the stars." The Scriptures even speak of the Moon being "turned to blood" and the Sun being "darkened" or turned "black as sackcloth" as signals that the Day of the Lord is at hand (Joel 2:31, Revelation 6:12).

Moreover, the idea of God using heavenly signs to alert man to Christ's impending arrival is certainly not without parallel, as He previously employed a particularly well-known celestial sign to signal the magi of Christ's entrance into the world over two thousand years ago!*

There are also other Scriptural indicators that reinforce the notion of signs in the heavens. These we find rooted in the very Hebrew words translated as "signs" and "seasons" in the Book of Genesis. For instance, the Hebrew word for "sign" is *oate. Oate* means "*to come*" and denotes a meaning related to something or *someone* who will come.[4] The Hebrew word translated as "season" is *mo'ed,* also translated as "feast," which, as we recall, denotes an "*appointed time,*"

---

* The DVD feature entitled "The Star of Bethlehem" presented by Law Professor Rick Larson is a fascinating study of the actual celestial phenomena that resulted in the sighting of an unusual "star" above Bethlehem two thousand years ago. Using software designed for astronomers, he recreates the cosmic scenario at play during the time of Christ's birth. The "star" was actually the result of a very rare conjunction of two planets (Venus and Jupiter) resulting in a visual effect that appeared to the naked eye as the brightest star ever seen.

thereby pointing to the Feasts of the Lord, which are also, of course, "appointed" times.[5]

Therefore, even from the very beginning, when God spoke of the heavenly bodies as being "for signs and for seasons," it seems He was letting us in on His plan, which apparently involves using the Sun and the Moon to signal the "appointed time" of one (Christ) who is "to come!"

A SNAPSHOT OF THE HEAVENS IN THE LAST DAYS

So how does the Bible describe these solar and lunar signs of the last days? To get a feel for this coming period of darkness, let us take a look at some verses that speak of dramatic celestial phenomena occurring just prior to the Second Coming.

Our first example describes the opening of the "sixth seal" and a "great earthquake" that occurs in conjunction with the resurrection of the saints:

> And I beheld when he had opened the sixth seal, and, lo, there was a great earthquake; *and the sun became black as sackcloth of hair, and the moon became as blood.*
> —Revelation 6:12

Here, the Sun being turned "black as sackcloth" seems an obvious allusion to a total solar eclipse. Likewise, the Moon being turned to blood is an apt description of a total lunar eclipse, or "blood moon," a phenomenon wherein the Moon takes on a deep reddish tone as it passes behind the Earth, escaping the direct light of the Sun.

This next verse speaks of the same timeframe—that of the resurrection, or rapture. In this powerful depiction, we note that the Sun and the Moon are "darkened," seemingly referring to either a full or partial eclipse, just before Jesus appears in the heavens and sends His angels out to gather the elect:

> Immediately after the tribulation of those days shall the *sun be darkened, and the moon shall not give her light,* and the stars shall fall from heaven, and the powers of the heavens shall be shaken: "And then shall appear the sign of the Son of man in heaven: and then shall all the tribes of the earth mourn, and they shall see the Son of man coming in the clouds of heaven with power and great glory. And he shall send his angels with a great sound of a trumpet, and they shall gather together his elect from the four winds, from one end of heaven to the other.
>
> —Matthew 24:29-31

The Old Testament Book of Joel, similar to Revelation, also speaks of the Moon being turned to blood:

> *The sun shall be turned into darkness, and the moon into blood,* before the great and terrible day of the LORD come.
>
> —Joel 2:31

This next verse from Isaiah speaks of the outpouring of God's wrath, which, as noted previously, begins immediately after the resurrection, or rapture, of believers.

> Behold, the day of the LORD cometh, cruel both with wrath and fierce anger...*the sun shall be darkened in his going forth, and the moon shall not cause her light to shine.*
>
> —Isaiah 13:9-10

Later, in chapter 24, Isaiah puts a slightly different spin on his description of the same event:

Then the moon shall be confounded, and the sun ashamed, when the LORD of hosts shall reign in mount Zion, and in Jerusalem, and before his ancients gloriously.

—Isaiah 24:23

The above sampling represents just a fraction of the biblical references to various solar and lunar phenomena in the last days. Other examples are found in Mark 13:24, Luke 21:25-27, Acts 2:20, 21 and Joel 3:14, 15.

Considering the frequency of these references, it is obvious that God wishes to emphasize the fact that the Sun being darkened and the Moon being turned to blood are among the key signs that will precede the return of Jesus Christ. This, then, brings up an interesting question: Since a "sign" is by definition something perceived in *advance* to warn of something that is coming, presumably for the purpose of allowing one to prepare, how will believers be able to pre-identify the specific eclipses that the Bible speaks of as heralding Christ's return? In other words, assuming that the end-times eclipses mentioned in Matthew, Joel, Revelation, and Isaiah are intended as forewarnings to the Church and are thus also part of the naturally occurring eclipse cycle (and therefore predictable), how might one distinguish the end-times eclipses from the multitude of "regular" eclipses that take place on a relatively frequent basis?

The possible answer to this question—and I do stress *possible*—may lie in a recent finding.

AN INTRIGUING DISCOVERY

Our story begins with a remarkable discovery made in 2008. Intrigued by the numerous biblical references to solar and lunar phenomena in the last days, a pastor named Mark Biltz, who promotes and teaches the Hebraic roots of Christianity, decided to log on to a U.S. Government (NASA) website that provides precise tracking of past and future eclipse events. Biltz, curious as to whether he would find any significant eclipse activity over the next several years, was not disappointed. The first thing he noticed was four total lunar eclipses, or "blood moons," scheduled to occur, interestingly enough, during the Gregorian (Western) calendar years of 2014-15. The reason these particular eclipses caught Biltz's attention was the dates on which they happen to fall.[6] Note the Gregorian and Hebrew calendar equivalents below:

April 15, 2014, or Nisan 14 (Passover)
October 8, 2014, or Tishrei 15 (Feast of Tabernacles)
April 4, 2015, or Nisan 14 (Passover)
September 28, 2015, or Tishrei 15 (Feast of Tabernacles)

Interestingly, the Gregorian dates of these particular eclipses seem unremarkable, as April 15, October 8, April 4, and September 28 hold no apparent significance, prophetic or otherwise. In observing the Hebrew calendar dates of these eclipses, however, something immediately stands out: They all fall on feast days, namely Passover and Tabernacles, in two successive years. Therefore, hidden to the casual observer, it is only by viewing these eclipse dates within the context of the Lord's feast days or "appointed times," as Biltz did, that we see this pattern emerge: Passover and Tabernacles in 2014, and then Passover and Tabernacles in 2015.[7]

Also worth noting, as we consider this (Passover-Tabernacles) pattern, is the seemingly significant fact that these are not just any feast days but the very *first* and the very *last* of the seven feasts. Thus, this series of blood moons essentially "bookends," or forms a parenthesis around, the remaining feasts in both 2014 and 2015.[8]

AN UNCOMMON EVENT

The phenomenon of four consecutive total lunar eclipses, or blood moons, also known as a "lunar tetrad," is very rare. There will only be seven such occurrences this century. What is more, instances of tetrads occurring *in conjunction with consecutive Passover-Tabernacles feast days*, as the ones Biltz discovered, are *extremely* rare. In fact, according to the NASA website, which tracks this data as far as a thousand years out, the Passover-Tabernacles tetrad in 2014-15 is the only one that will be taking place in the foreseeable future.[9]

Further highlighting the rarity of what we will call "feast tetrads," a look back in history reveals that this phenomenon has occurred only three times over the last millennia or so: twice in the twentieth century and once in the late fifteenth century. Absolutely no tetrads occurred in the 1800s, the 1700s, or the 1600s. In the 1500s there were six, but none fell on consecutive Passover and Tabernacles feast observances.[10]

Nonetheless, the fact that this (feast tetrad) phenomenon *did* occur twice just last century would seem, at least on the face of it, to undermine the uniqueness of such an event and therefore any significance that one might attach to the upcoming tetrad in 2014-15—until, that is, one takes a closer look at these past occurrences and notes something very curious.

A COMMON THEME EMERGES

In taking a closer look at the past occurrences of feast tetrads, we at once notice something very peculiar indeed, which is the fact that they seem to be linked by what could be characterized as a common *theme*. More specifically, they have all occurred, strangely enough, in conjunction with what are arguably the defining moments in the history of Modern-day Israel. For instance, the most recent Passover-Tabernacles tetrad occurred in 1967-68—right after Israel fought the landmark Six Day War and recaptured Jerusalem. As we recall from chapter 4, the prophetic significance of this date is immense in that, according to Newton's interpretation, it may very well have marked the predicted latter-days restoration of Jerusalem that would set the prophetic clock ticking off the final forty-nine years to Christ's return!

The second most recent feast tetrad occurred in 1949-50 at the close of Israel's War of Independence, a battle that was fought to defend her triumphant rebirth as a state after nearly two thousand years of Jewish exile.[11] The significance of this event, needless to say, speaks for itself, as it is believed to be the fulfillment of the end-times regathering of Israel that was prophesied millennia ago in Deuteronomy (30:3-5) and Isaiah (66:8).*

The only other Passover-Tabernacles tetrad to have occurred over the course of the last 1,100 years or so happened in 1493-94, right after Columbus "sailed the ocean blue" in 1492 and Spain expelled the Jews, resulting in a massive Jewish dispersion. This was indeed a pivotal moment in Jewish history, as Spain had been a second Jewish homeland for well over a thousand years. In fact, so deeply woven into the fabric of Spain are the Jews, it is acknowledged that the history of either cannot be fully studied without considering the influence of the other. (Please see endnote for comments on a possible connection to Columbus's voyage).[12, 13]

COINCIDENCE—OR SOMETHING ELSE?

Having noted the rarity of tetrads, the *extreme* rarity of Passover-Tabernacles tetrads, and also the way in which each noted occurrence appears to be linked to pivotal events surrounding Israel's struggle for rebirth, survival, and ultimate restoration, it would seem the likelihood of all of this coming together as a result of sheer coincidence is near zero. And so we pose the obvious question: What might all of this mean? Or, more to the point, in light of the notion of God using

---

* At the close of the War of Independence in 1949, East Jerusalem fell to the Jordanians and was subsequently divided between the two countries via the Israel-TransJordan Armistice Agreement. Jerusalem would remain divided until the Jews recaptured the Eastern half of the city in the 1967 Six Day War.

the heavenly bodies as signs, what, if anything, could He be telling the Jews—and by extension the world—via the upcoming pattern of total lunar eclipses in 2014-15? Is it possible that these may have something to do with the lunar signs (Moon being turned to blood) that He has promised in the end times?

THE PARABLE OF THE FIG TREE

In speculating as to what the upcoming tetrad may portend, it is interesting to consider a passage familiar to most anyone who has studied end-times prophecy:

> Now learn a parable of the fig tree; When her branch is yet tender, and putteth forth leaves, ye know that summer is near: So ye in like manner, when ye shall see these things come to pass, know that it is nigh, even at the doors. Verily I say unto you, that this generation shall not pass, till all these things be done.
>
> —Mark 13:28-30

The popular interpretation of this passage, also known as "the Parable of the Fig Tree" holds that this current generation, the same one who witnessed the branch putting "forth leaves" (commonly interpreted as Israel's end-times regathering) is the one that will be on earth to witness the return of Christ.* Indeed, Jesus does not mince words in verse 30 when He says "this generation shall not pass, till *all these things* be done."

Now, assuming that the popular interpretation of this verse is correct, which I believe it to be, and also that God is using these feast

---

* This interpretation is based on the notion that Israel is repeatedly associated with the fig tree in Scripture. Read all of mark 13 to see the full list of signs that Jesus says will be witnessed by the final generation.

tetrads to mark certain prophetic events, as He seems to be, the simple yet profoundly important question arises: If the Lord were to employ the *last* such foreseeable feast tetrad to highlight any prophetic event for the final generation, what would it be if not the Second Coming or some event closely related?*

This, no doubt, is a question worth pondering at length, but let us set this 2014-15 lunar tetrad aside for the moment, as there is even more to consider.

NOTABLE SOLAR ECLIPSES: SUN TURNED INTO DARKNESS

As intriguing as the blood moons in 2014-15 are, there is yet another dimension to Biltz's discovery. As we recall from the verses cited earlier, in addition to the Moon being turned to blood, the Scriptures repeatedly describe what would seem to be *solar* eclipses as heralding the return of Christ.

Interestingly enough, while exploring the NASA website, Biltz also spotted some noteworthy solar phenomena. These solar events likewise occur in the 2014-15 timeframe and, similar to the lunar eclipses, they each happen to fall on some very significant Hebrew calendar dates:

(Total solar eclipse) March 20, 2015, or Nisan 1
(Jewish New Year)
(Partial solar eclipse) September 13, 2015, or Tishrei 1
(Feast of Trumpets)

These two dates are noteworthy indeed. Nisan 1, also called the *biblical* "New Year," or *Rosh Chodashim*, marks the very beginning of the seven-month religious (feast) cycle. Historically, it was on Nisan 1

---

* Biltz, in his many interviews on the topic, has made it very clear that while he believes something prophetically significant is coming in the 2014-15 timeframe he absolutely does not "set dates" for the Second Coming.

at the first anniversary of the Exodus that Moses raised up the tabernacle (the precursor to the Temple in Jerusalem) for the first time and the "glory of the Lord" descended[14] (Exodus 40:17, 34).

The second solar eclipse, which occurs on Tishrei 1, marks the Feast of Trumpets. The Feast of Trumpets marks the beginning of the *civil* New Year. But more importantly, as we recall, this feast also foreshadows the resurrection, or rapture, and is thus believed to be the very feast at which Jesus will return in some future year to gather the saints!

Again, these two eclipses are notable, not only because of the significant Hebrew Calendar days on which they fall, but because they fall within the seemingly parenthetical "brackets" formed by the lunar tetrads in 2014-15. In other words, while it is not unheard of for a solar eclipse to take place on a particular holy day, it is perhaps unheard of for it to occur in conjunction with a lunar tetrad on consecutive Passover-Tabernacles observances.

Might these solar eclipses also be signs? As we ponder this, let us consider some additional observations made by Biltz.

OTHER ECLIPSES

So far we have seen that several factors, including the jubilee cycles, Newton's interpretation of Daniel's "seventy weeks," and certain rare eclipse phenomena all seem to be pointing us toward a very narrow timeframe, more specifically, the year 2015. In fact, whether coincidental or not, we even have a solar eclipse on the Feast of Trumpets, or "resurrection day" in 2015!

Certainly, the combination of the above is enough to send the minds of prophecy enthusiasts reeling, but it seems these revelations are not the "end" of it as it were. Having identified the 2015 timeframe as one of possible if not likely prophetic significance, it is interesting to note something that we touched on briefly in chapter 4: Based on popular interpretations of Daniel, many prophecy scholars feel that the last "week" (or seven years) of the age will play out over the span of a sabbatical cycle. In light of this, it is interesting to note that seven years prior to 2015 a new sabbatical cycle happens to begin. It commences on Sept 29, 2008 and runs through September 22, 2015.[15]

Is it possible that this very sabbatical cycle could be the final "week" that so many are anticipating? Perhaps following this same line of reasoning, Biltz, further consulting the NASA website, found another obvious pattern of solar phenomena: During the years 2008, 2009, and 2010 there will be three separate total solar eclipses, each occurring on the *same* noteworthy Hebrew Calendar date. The Gregorian and Hebrew equivalents are as follows:[16]

August 1, 2008, or Av 1

July 22, 2009, or Av 1

July 11, 2010, or Av 1

Notably, Av 1 on the Hebrew calendar is an important day of mourning in Jewish culture. It is part of a larger three-week period of sorrow and lament that runs from Tammuz 17 (the day Jerusalem's walls were breached by the Romans in 69 AD) and concludes on Av 9 (the date both Jewish Temples were destroyed). According to tradition, beginning on Av 1 the mourning intensifies and remains at a heightened state until the conclusion of what is called "the three weeks" on Av 9. During this period, Jews purposely deprive themselves of any and all comforts, instead choosing to reflect on the past tragedies that have befallen their ancestors.[17]

Interestingly enough, the reason that Av 1 through Av 9 is reserved as a time of intensified mourning stems not just from the above-mentioned past tragedies associated with these dates but from the fact that the Jews believe Av 9 to be a day cursed by God. This curse is purportedly a consequence of something that took place much earlier than either of the destructions of Jerusalem: According to tradition, it was on the 9th of Av, over three thousand years ago, that the Hebrew spies who searched out the Promised Land (then known as Canaan) brought back an "evil report," relating that the land God had promised them was already inhabited by "men of a great stature" who in their sight were much stronger than they (Numbers 13:32). Thus, the Israelites demonstrated their lack of faith in God's promise and would therefore continue to roam the wilderness for forty years before inheriting the Land.

Incidentally, for those who are skeptical of the idea of a "curse," let us briefly note some of the events that have transpired on the 9th of Av since this infamous rejection of the Land:[18]

- Nebuchadnezzar destroyed the first Jewish Temple on the 9th of Av.
- Exactly six hundred years later, the Romans destroyed the second Jewish Temple on the 9th of Av.
- All Jews were forced out of England in 1290 on the 9th of Av.
- All Jews were forced out of Spain in 1492 on the 9th of Av.
- World War I started on the 9th of Av. (This war, referred to as the "parent" war to World War II, gave rise to widespread anti-Semitism throughout Europe and helped to shape Hitler's attitude toward the Jews).
- Hitler's proclamation to kill the Jews came on the 9th of Av.
- The disastrous 2005 evacuation of the Gaza strip occurred at sundown on the 9th of Av.

Needless to say, coincidence does not seem sufficient to account for the calamitous events that have befallen the Jews on the 9th of Av. Having noted this, we should reiterate that the eclipses Biltz noted do not actually fall on the 9th of Av, but rather on Av 1, the day that marks the *beginning* of the intensified period of mourning that culminates in an all day fast and time of lament on Av 9.

Lastly, we note that, just as we found with the lunar eclipses, the Gregorian dates of these solar events are seemingly random, while the Hebrew dates reveal a clear pattern in that all three instances take place on a particular day, a day that, again, according to Jewish tradition, marks the beginning of a time of sorrow.

PUTTING IT ALL TOGETHER

Now, to help us put all of what has been described thus far into perspective, let us take a moment to study the chart below, in which all of the various solar and lunar phenomena have been laid out in order of sequence:

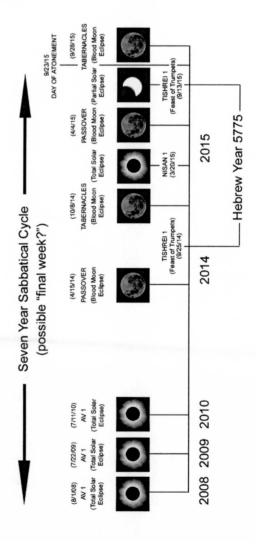

DECODING THE MEANINGS

In observing the full array of solar and lunar activity that is occurring over the course of the current sabbatical cycle, there is, again, no denying what seems to be an obvious, even seemingly *purposeful*, correlation between certain Jewish holy days and various eclipse phenomena. At this point, then, in our continuing efforts to make sense of these "signs," perhaps it will be further enlightening to consider a piece of the puzzle that has thus far gone unnoted, which is the belief that according to Jewish tradition solar and lunar eclipses hold different meanings. These meanings are detailed in the Talmud, as excerpted here:

> "Our Rabbis taught, when the sun is in eclipse, it is a bad omen for the whole world. This may be illustrated by a parable. To what can this be compared? To a human being who made a banquet for his servants and put up for them a lamp. When he became wroth with them he said to his servant, 'Take away the lamp from them, and let them sit in the dark'. It was taught: R. Meir said, whenever the luminaries [moon] are in eclipse, it is a bad omen for Israel since they are inured to blows. This may be compared to a school teacher who comes to school with a strap in his hand. Who becomes apprehensive? He who is accustomed to be daily punished. Our Rabbis taught, When the sun is in eclipse it is a bad omen for idolaters; when the moon is in eclipse, it is a bad omen for Israel, since Israel reckons by the moon and idolaters by the sun..."
>
> —Succah 29a

According to ancient rabbinical teachings, since the "idolater," or non-Jewish, world used a calendar based on the Sun (such as our Gregorian calendar), the *solar* eclipse was considered to be a bad omen for them. For Jews, however, whose calendar was based prim arily on the Moon, the *lunar* eclipse was considered an evil omen.

BLOOD MOON BODES BAD

In light of the Talmudic understanding of blood moons, namely their ominous portent, it is particularly interesting to take a second look at the three aforementioned blood moon tetrads that occurred in 1493-94, 1949-50, and 1967-68. In considering the events linked to these blood moons (Jewish expulsion from Spain and subsequent dispersion, Jewish War for Independence, and the Six Day War), we note that all three have been recorded in the annals of history as times of great peril, or, as the Talmud might put it, times at which "the strap" was brought to Israel. Thus, we see that just as the earlier proposed Jubilee occurrences of chapter 3 seem to fall in line with aptly themed events surrounding Israel (namely the two liberations of Jerusalem), so do the historical Passover-Tabernacles tetrads noted here seem to occur in tandem with times of great peril for the Jews. These correlations, then, seem to corroborate the traditional Talmudic understanding of the blood moon eclipse and what it means for Israel.

Of course, this Talmudic understanding of the blood moon also opens up the question of what exactly the 2014-15 lunar tetrads may be telling us about the nature of *forthcoming* events related to Israel. If these two series of blood moons, for instance, are indeed signaling the return of Christ or perhaps the accompanying periods of "tribulation" and/or "wrath," it goes without saying that the theme of "blood moon bodes bad" for Israel is still seemingly in effect, thereby further bolstering all that has been proposed here.

Now, setting aside the possible meaning of the upcoming blood moons for a moment, let us consider the Av 1 *solar* eclipses of 2008, 2009, and 2010. In light of the Talmudic understanding of what this type of sign portends for the world at large, can any similar type of correlation be drawn between these occurrences and world events?

THE FINANCIAL CRISIS OF 2008: JUST THE BEGINNING?

At the time of this writing, two of the three aforementioned Av 1 eclipses have already occurred. The first eclipse, which was seen from northeastern North America, most of Europe, and Asia took place on August 1, 2008. The current sabbatical cycle that runs from 2008 to 2015 commenced the following month, on September 29. With these dates in mind, and considering the traditionally ominous portent of the solar eclipse for "gentile" nations, it is remarkable to reflect on the now infamous events related to the global economy that began to unfold at precisely this time. For those whose memories—in addition to their 401Ks—have failed them, it all began with the bankruptcy of global financial services firm, Lehman Brothers, in early September of 2008. The crisis, which had apparently been building for months, almost immediately entered into an acute phase, marked by failures of prominent American and European banks. This same month, the Dow Jones Industrial average suffered one of its top ten most dramatic plunges since its inception in May of 1896, prompting world renowned billionaire investor William Buffet to describe the sudden turmoil in the financial markets as an "economic Pearl Harbor."[19, 20] As soon as early October, experts had acknowledged that "global recession" was imminent. They were, of course, correct.

Then, one year later, the second Av 1 eclipse (Gregorian date July 22, 2009), which was seen from East Asia, Indonesia, and the South Pacific was followed by an unprecedented string of natural disasters in Asia and the Pacific. An October 1 press release from the UN sponsored UNEASCAP (Economic and Social Commission for Asia and the Pacific) read, "It is almost unprecedented for any region to experience so many disasters over such a short period of time. Since last Saturday, 26 September, Typhoon Ketsana hit the Philippines, a tsunami struck Samoa, American Samoa, and Tonga, and two massive earthquakes hit the Indonesian island of Sumatra."[21]

Having noted the uncanniness of all of this, let me make clear that while it is interesting to consider how things have played out thus far, I would not go so far as to suggest that each of these eclipses is somehow signaling a separate round of disasters targeted at specific geographic regions. It is nonetheless indisputable that, whether coincidental or not, the first two of the three (2008-2010) solar eclipses have certainly lived up to their Talmudic reputation in regard to heralding trouble for the world at large, both in the specific and also in the broader sense.

Might these Av 1 eclipses, then, have been intended as a series of warning shots to the gentile or "idolater" nations that the world is entering into an unparalleled time of sorrow and judgment?

SUMMARY AND CONCLUSION

As we bring to a close this chapter, wherein we have noted some very intriguing solar and lunar phenomena, let us take a moment to summarize and reemphasize a few points that highlight the truly re-markable nature of these "signs" in the heavens.

Firstly, tetrads that occur in the pattern that Biltz found, falling on consecutive Passover and Tabernacles feasts, are extremely rare, so rare, in fact, that it has happened only three times during the course of the last millennia or so. Remarkably, in each of these three noted cases, the tetrads have occurred in tandem with events in which the Jews were faced with persecution or the sword, just as, according to the Talmud, blood moons would traditionally indicate.

This brings us to the upcoming lunar tetrad and the accompany-ing solar eclipses in 2014-15: What types of events, if any, might ac-company these occurrences? In considering this question, we should recall that God has gone to great lengths in Scripture to underscore the fact that the Sun being turned to darkness and the Moon being turned to blood will be among the chief signs that herald Christ's return. Could the upcoming eclipses, then, be *the* eclipses—the ones that the Bible says will occur just before the Second Coming? This, for now, is of course unknowable, but considering the days on which these particular eclipses fall, it is difficult to imagine a configuration of solar and lunar activity that could more aptly signal such an event.

Whatever the case may be, if the historical occurrences of feast tetrads are any indicator, it appears that something *major* (possibly a time of great peril) lies just over the horizon for Israel. For those who harbor doubts, I would encourage flipping back to the diagram on page 120 to reexamine the pattern of solar and lunar activity occurring during this sabbatical cycle. The fact is, beyond 2014-15, this configuration of celestial phenomena will not be seen again by this generation or any other for at least a thousand years. Thus, in the context of solar and lunar signs heralding the Day of the Lord, one could argue that it would make no sense that any generation other than the current one is destined to witness the Second Coming of Christ—and, by all indications, perhaps soon.

This leads to my final point, which is simply this: God has from the beginning chosen to reveal things to man, affording him an "expected end." From His promise in Genesis to use the Sun and the Moon for "signs" to mark His "appointed times," to His disclosing to Daniel the length of the Jewish captivity in Babylon, to warning Noah and his family to board the Ark seven days before the Flood began. It is my belief therefore that the Lord takes no pleasure in our uncertainty, nor does He wish to catch His Church unawares, or sleeping, at His return. In fact, according to the Bible, in that day He desires that all be found watching and in a state of knowingness.

And so we pose the ultimate question that arises from all that has been discussed in this chapter: Are these solar and lunar signs, discovered, curiously enough, just *seven* years prior to their culmination, a final wakeup call for those who will heed the sound of the alarm?

In closing, as we ponder the answer to this vital question, we are wise to take heed of Mark's most timely admonition:

What I say to you, I say to everyone: 'Watch!'

—Mark 13:37

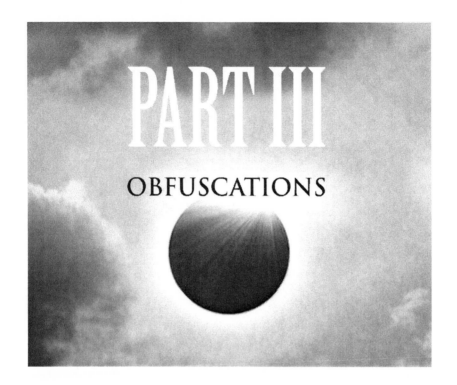

PART III

OBFUSCATIONS

SEVEN

...have nothing to do with the fruitless deeds of darkness, but rather expose them.

—Ephesians 5:11

2012

It is mid-summer in the heart of the Yucatan jungle, the year, 987 AD. The sweltering afternoon that had been punctuated only by the chatter of tropical birds is now alive with the sound of a steadily quickening drumbeat. Struggling to control the rising panic in his chest, a young native, daubed in blue paint from head to toe, is led up a column of steep narrow steps to the top of a massive pyramidal temple.

Reaching the top, he is abruptly laid down upon a stone altar and held in position by four Mayan priests. As the blinding Sun beats down on the victim's face, causing him to squint, a fifth priest, brandishing a ceremonial knife made of flint, begins to slice open the abdomen—continuing up though the diaphragm—until the lower chest cavity is opened. The priest swiftly thrusts in his hand, laying hold of the still beating heart—and tears it out. While still pulsating, the heart is placed in a bowl next to a statue of Quetzalcoatl, the god who is being honored, and the lifeless body is thrown down the temple stairs.

As this horrific scene plays out over and over again, the priests and audience gathered in the plaza below stab, pierce, and bleed themselves in a form of auto-sacrifice to the tune of hymns, whistles, and spectacular costumed dances.

Later, the arms and legs of the discarded body are cut off—in this case to be dined on by fellow tribesmen. The severed bleeding head is placed on a beam for display, and the remaining body parts and viscera fed to the animals in the zoo.[1]

A CURIOUSLY SADISTIC SOCIETY

It is reported that the above-described ritual was carried out as many as 20,000 times during a single ceremony for the re-consecration of the Great Pyramid of Tenochtitlan in 1487. Though, according to Ross Hassing, author of *Aztec Warfare*, the true number is not known and could have ranged anywhere "between 10,000 and 80,400 persons."

Today, researchers are only beginning to come to terms with the scale and depth of brutality that flourished in the Aztec and Mayan cultures. Unlike the sacrifices that God ordained for Israel, which included the humane slaying of a lamb or bull and ultimately the *self* sacrifice of His own Son for mankind's sake, the Mesoamerican version seems to have been focused on inflicting the maximum amount of pain and terror on as many human beings as possible: Victims were bound to posts and shot full of arrows, as well as being skinned, clawed, burned, or buried alive. The god Tlaloc preferred weeping boys in the first months. Teteoinnan, the "Earth Mother," required that female victims be flayed.[2]

Many had previously dismissed these graphic descriptions by the conquering Spaniards as exaggerated propaganda meant to showcase the sheer savagery of the natives. Yet the ever-mounting archeological and anthropological evidence seems to corroborate the Spanish accounts in substance, if not in number.[3]

Of course, all of this seems to beg a couple of questions: Firstly, why did the "gods" require human sacrifice on such a massive scale, and, further, why did they insist on such vile and grisly methods?

Going forward, the shocking answers to these questions will lend invaluable insight into what lies at the heart of the so-called "Mayan prophecies," as well as shed some much-needed light on a mysterious calendrical cycle that ends suddenly in 2012.

But first, in order to lay some important groundwork, we must pose a more fundamental question.

WHO WERE THE MAYA?

The ancient Maya, who for millennia on end occupied the same regions of Central America, are in many ways an enigmatic people.[*] Seemingly at odds with their famous warlike nature and penchant for human sacrifice, they are renowned for their architectural, artistic, mathematical, and scientific achievements. They left behind a series of super-human sized stone monuments and pyramids that boast precise calendrical computations. Moreover, they were extremely advanced in their study of celestial activity and possessed knowledge of the cosmos that far exceeded the information available to man before the invention of the modern telescope.

The Maya are probably most well known for the stunning accuracy of their complex series of calendars, which include a sacred 260-day calendar called the Tzol'kin, a 365-day calendar called the Haab, and a 52-Haab cycle called the calendar round, which synchronized the Tzol'kin and Haab cycles.[4, 5, 6]

The focus of our attention here, however, as per the mainstream today, is on yet another Mayan calendar known as the "Long Count." This calendar, unlike the Tzol'kin and Haab, deals in much larger cycles.

---

[*] Twelve hundred years ago, at the height of the Late Classic Period (AD 600-900), the total Maya population may have been as high as twenty million. They occupied the lowlands of Yucatan, Campeche, and Quintana Roo; Belize, parts of El Salvador and Honduras, and much of the States of Chiapas and Tabasco in Mexico.

THE MAYAN LONG COUNT CALENDAR AND THE YEAR 2012

Of origins still somewhat unclear, the Long Count calendar is based on the Mayan belief that there have been numerous "great cycles" in which the gods have created and subsequently destroyed the world, resulting in a cyclical pattern of creation-destruction events. These creation-destruction accounts are described in the *Popol Vuh*, which details the first four world cycles—the last of which purportedly ended in a great flood. Each of these cycles is said to be 5,125 years, or "thirteen *baktuns*," in length. According to Gregorian calendar conversions, the current (fifth) cycle, which began on August 11, 3114 BC, will end on December 21, 2012.[7]

While much attention has been given the notion that Mayan prophecy predicts the "end of the world" in 2012, the truth is that the Maya, who thought in terms of cycles, looked at this time as being as much about beginnings as it is about endings.* In fact, for them, the upcoming end of the current cycle was anticipated as a time of great transition and *spiritual advancement*, heralding the creation of a new world age.

Nonetheless, depending on the source, one can find all sorts of claims as to what one should expect during this time of transition: from cataclysm to enlightenment, from world war to world peace, massive earth changes and physical destruction, to a great spiritual awakening in which mankind will realize his inherent "oneness" with all things.

There is one thing, however, that virtually all sources can agree upon: Something very extraordinary is taking place in our galaxy at this time.

---

* Interestingly, this view of the current period as being one of immense spiritual activity is not new or even unique to the Maya but is shared by many ancient civilizations who lived on continents separated by vast oceans, including the Hopi, Egyptians, Essenes, Qero elders of Peru, Navajo, Cherokee, Apache, Iroquois confederacy, Dogon Tribe, and the Aborigines.[8, 9]

GALACTIC ALIGNMENT

In considering the mysterious 2012 end date of the current (5,125 year) great cycle, many believe that the Long Count calendar was designed specifically to point to an extremely rare Galactic alignment, which occurs only once every 25,800 years. During this alignment, the ecliptic (referring to the path travelled by the Sun, the Moon, and the planets through the sky) will cross over the Milky Way at a sixty degree angle near the constellation Sagittarius, thereby forming a type of "X." This cosmic cross, known to the Maya as the "Sacred Tree" or the "Crossroads" is exactly where the December solstice sun will be in 2012 AD.

Another feature of this alignment involves what is known as the "dark rift" at the center of the Milky Way galaxy. Referred to simply as the "Black Road" by the Maya, this dark rift, in scientific terms, could be described as a mass of dark cloud formations caused by interstellar dust, which, against the backdrop of the bright band of stars that is the Milky way, appears as a dark road. Remarkably, this "Black Road," believed by the Maya to be a portal into the underworld, or *Xibalba*, points directly at the above-noted cosmic crossing point (or the center of the Sacred Tree) which is, again, the precise location of our Sun in 2012 (see image below).[10]

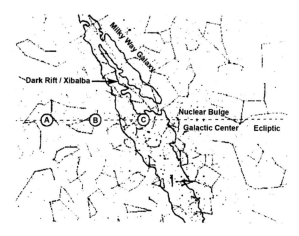

As seen from the Earth's perspective, position A is where the

December solstice sun was in relation to the Milky Way some 3,000 years ago. Position B depicts its location 1,500 years ago. Position C represents "era-2012," when the December solstice sun has converged as a result of the precession of the equinoxes with the center line of the Milky Way, or the "Galactic equator."*

It is believed that this galactic alignment held much significance for the Maya, representing not only a crossroads, or time of transition, but the opening of a doorway pointing to the "sacred source," or "cosmic womb," of the galaxy. Interestingly, the imagery of a cosmic womb, whether coincidentally or not, seems to infer knowledge of what modern astronomers have only recently discovered to be a massive black hole at the center of the galaxy, thus begging the question: How could the Maya have known?

A PORTENT OF DISASTER?

While both theories and conspiracies abound, no one knows exactly what physical effects, if any, the galactic alignment may have on the Earth. Though, as evidenced by the current number of books, films, videos, and seminars that broach the topic, there is no shortage of opinion as to what *could* transpire. Perhaps taking a queue from the Mayan theme of destruction and rebirth, many propose apocalyptic scenarios. Some of these, such as predictions of a massive asteroid impact, seem to be grounded more in the realm of

---

* It should be noted that because of the Sun's diameter and the fact that the precession of the equinoxes is such a slow phenomenon, the alignment actually takes place over a period of thirty-five or thirty-six years. Thus it could be said that the portal into *Xibalba*, or the Mayan underworld, opened in 1980 when the alignment began and will close in 2015-16 as the Sun passes through. It is therefore frequently noted by 2012 "purists" that the galactic alignment is not about a "date" but about a "window" of time.

imagination than that of reality. Some others, however, actually find a basis in scientific possibility. These center primarily on experts' predictions of a period of massive solar activity as we enter the peak of an eleven-year cycle called the "solar maxum" in 2012. Adding fuel to the fire, the Earth's magnetic field is currently known to be weakening, thus signaling an impending reversal (or trading places) of the north and south magnetic poles. Some surmise that such a reversal would dramatically affect the planet's ability to protect itself from the cosmic radiation and increased solar flare activity that will by all accounts accompany 2012's solar maxum.[*]

Somewhat reassuringly, most authorities agree that a solar flare event would by no means affect a "planetary catastrophe." Nonetheless, a recent study funded by NASA reports that a "super solar flare" followed by a severe geomagnetic storm could indeed result in widespread (possibly continent wide) power outages, as well as radio/satellite blackouts. This type of network failure would essentially disable GPS navigation, banking, finance, telecommunications, and all modes of transportation.[†] The end result, as detailed in the NASA study, is that vital necessities such as water distribution would be affected within just a few hours, while perishable foods and many medications would be lost within 12-24 hours, with no immediate capability to replenish. Other consequences would of course include the loss of all heating and air conditioning capabilities, sewage disposal, phone service, fuel re-supply, etc. On the upside, the report predicts that radio and GPS transmissions could come back online fairly quickly. On the downside, however, damaged electrical transformers, which are especially vulnerable to geomagnetic storms, can

---

[*] Scientists note that magnetic reversal is a naturally occurring phenomenon that takes place as often as every 10,000 years or so.

[†] In 1989 Quebec was hit by a large solar burst, causing a blackout that affected millions of customers. Several years earlier a solar storm caused Air Force One to lose all radio communications for several hours while en route to China. President Reagan was onboard.

take weeks or even months to repair. The bottom line, then, is that while a month-long continent-wide blackout would, again, not be a planet-changing event, it does have the potential to wreak even more havoc, at least on a human scale, than the most devastating of natural disasters.[11]

Of course, as recently as only fifty years ago solar flares did not pose nearly the threat that they do now, as our utter dependence on satellites and the modern interconnected power grid are both relatively recent developments in human history.

Another widely entertained "2012-apocalypse" theory speculates that as the Earth passes through the so-called "galactic equator" it could experience an actual polar shift.[12] During a true polar shift—rather that just the north and south magnetic poles trading places, it is said that the entire mantle of the Earth could shift in a matter of days, perhaps hours, actually tilting the globe and changing the latitudinal positions of the current north and south poles. It is hypothesized that such a shift would cause massive earthquakes, tidal waves, and volcanic activity the likes of which modern man has never witnessed.[13]

While most mainstream scientists insist that there is no reason to expect such an event circa 2012, many will nonetheless acknowledge that polar shift has indeed occurred in the past. In fact, results from a Princeton University study reveal that the area we now know as the North Pole once rested in the middle of the Pacific Ocean, placing Alaska at the equator![14] Many scholars who hold a biblical viewpoint believe that this very polar shift took place during Noah's flood. This theory, much to the chagrin of evolutionists, is bolstered by much physical evidence, not to mention the existence of completely intact ancient mammoth carcasses found buried under arctic ice with undigested grass, blubells, wild beans, and buttercups—foods typically available in equatorial climates—still undigested in their stomachs!

One account of discovered mammoth remains details that the "mouth was filled with grass, which had been cropped, but not chewed and swallowed." Apparently the grass froze so rapidly that it retained the imprint of the animal's molars (Brown, 165). Scientists conclude that such circumstances could only result from an unimaginably catastrophic event that unfolded in extremely short order. In fact, the animals would have had to have been buried and *deep frozen within a matter of hours*.

Walt Brown PhD, in his book entitled, *In the Beginning: Compelling Evidence for Creation and the Flood*, poses a theory that explains the current state of these found mammoth carcasses by attributing them to the biblical flood. Brown believes that the processes involved in the flooding of the entire globe included the opening of a great rupture in the Earth's crust, which he hypothesizes sat atop massive subterranean chambers of water.

Here, he sketches an outline of the event and poses his explanation for the preserved mammoth remains that we find today:

"The rupture of the earth's crust passed between Alaska and Siberia in minutes. Jetting water from the "fountains of the great deep" first fell as rain. During the next few hours, subterranean water that went above the atmosphere, where the effective temperature is several hundred degrees below zero Fahrenheit, fell as hail. Some animals were suddenly buried, suffocated, frozen, and compressed by tons of cold, muddy ice crystals from the gigantic "hail storm." The mud in this ice prevented it from floating as the flood waters submerged these regions after days and weeks. A thick blanket of ice preserved many animals during the flood phase. After the mountains were suddenly pushed up [due to the rupturing and shifting of the planet's crust], the earth's balance shifted, the earth "rolled," so what is now Alaska and Siberia moved from a temperate latitude to their present position. As the flood waters drained off of the continents, the icy graves in the warmer climates melted, and the flesh of those animals decayed. However, many animals, buried in what are now permafrost regions, were preserved (169).

Thus, according to Brown's theory, the Flood was a much more violent and complex event than most would imagine and included, due to some incredibly powerful streams of jetting water, the displacement of huge areas of land mass, creating massive mountain ranges which, in turn, shifted the balance of the whole planet. But perhaps the most significant thing to note about his explanation is that it makes sense of physical evidence that still baffles many evolutionary scientists.

For those interested in a scholarly yet easy to read treatise on the above topics, I highly recommend Brown's book, wherein he proposes a model for the Flood that accounts for virtually all of the strange features of the earth, including the existence of vast coal and oil deposits; layered strata and fossils; the massive trenches and hundreds of volcanoes that we find on the ocean floor; the major mountain chains, and also land canyons, particularly the Grand Canyon.*

Getting back to 2012, however, having noted that a polar shift is in fact a proven physical possibility, we should perhaps temper this speculation by also noting that in view of the timeframes and scenarios posed in this book, a calamity of this magnitude in 2012 seems unlikely, as the Bible speaks of a time of great "tribulation" before Christ's return to gather the saints, not an all-out planetary catastrophe. Nevertheless, it is interesting to consider the possibility of a polar shift taking place *after* the Tribulation and subsequent resurrection or rapture of the Church, during the time of God's "wrath"—especially in light of several prophetic warnings from Isaiah that seem to describe just such an event:

---

* Brown has extended a standing offer to debate any qualified evolutionist as to the overwhelming evidence for a young Earth and a catastrophic flood. This challenge has, for nearly two decades, gone unanswered (169).

Behold, the LORD maketh the earth empty, and maketh it waste, *and turneth it upside down*, and scattereth abroad the inhabitants thereof.

—Isaiah 24:1

The earth is utterly broken down, the earth is clean dissolved, *the earth is moved exceedingly. The earth shall reel to and fro like a drunkard, and shall be removed like a cottage*; and the transgression thereof shall be heavy on it; and *it shall fall, and not rise again.*

—Isaiah 24:19, 20

Therefore I will shake the heavens, and *the earth shall remove out of her place, in the wrath of the LORD of hosts*, and in the day of his fierce anger.

—Isaiah 13:13

Do these verses describe a polar shift in which the Earth will assume its original (pre-flood) position? Given Isaiah's utterly clear descriptions, it would be difficult to interpret otherwise.

Nonetheless, before getting too bogged down in matters of future planetary calamity, let us get back to the Maya and their legendary understanding of things thought beyond the grasp of "primitive" man. Thus, our next question.

WHO TAUGHT THE MAYA?

It is a question that has baffled scholars for years: From where did these seemingly primitive men attain such knowledge and expertise? How could they have known things about the cosmos that have only recently been "discovered?" Adding to this mystery is the fact that the "advanced knowledge" phenomenon is not limited to the Maya but is consistent throughout virtually all ancient civilizations going back approximately five thousand years to the beginning of recorded history.

In his highly acclaimed book, *The Omega Conspiracy*, Dr I.D.E. Thomas makes note of this phenomenon and poses some similarly pertinent questions:

"Unlike primitive savages roaming wild and naked in the bush, they [the ancients] planned the pyramids, built Babylon, engineered Stonehenge, and structured the Mayan Caracol.

A thousand years before Darwin formed his theory of evolution, ancient Mayans and Toltecs carved their own version of evolution in stone; their calendar was more precise than ours today, they even knew and used penicillin; and like the ancient Egyptians they designed great cities and mammoth pyramids. But from where, or whom, did they get their information and expertise?

Where did the ancient Dogon of the West African Republic of Mali receive their knowledge of Sirius's *invisible* satellite? Sirius, a star of the first magnitude in the constellation Canis Major, is 8.5 light years away, yet they knew the satellite's position, gravitation, and orbit. The star's white satellite was not discovered until 1844, and was not seen by telescope until 1862. But the Dogons knew of it long before the telescope.

Why did the Assyrians who lived more that 2,000 BC encircle the planet Saturn with a ring of serpents? How could they know of Saturn's rings? They depicted no other planet this way...They also recorded the different phases of the moon with an accuracy not seen again until the seventeenth century AD. But they did it [3,000 years earlier] in 1440 BC!

How did those Greeks know that there were seven stars in Pleiades? They could only see six! Did a higher intelligence inform them?

From whom did builders of the awesome structures of Tiahuanaco gain their knowledge thirty centuries ago? To erect such massive monoliths, the Lansburgs assert, would require "a colossal power crane or some secret of levitation unknown to us." Not only that, but those titanic blocks, some weighing fifty tons or more, were so precisely cut and interlocked that no mortar was needed to bind them. Even today one cannot pound a chisel between them. All this was accomplished without power crane or hydraulic lifts, elephant or oxen. How on Earth, then could they have done it? The only plausible answer is, "With nothing we know of on Earth" (Thomas 9, 10). (See Appendix for photos and details on Tiahuanaco and other ancient sites).

In answer to his own questions, Thomas concludes that these baffling anomalies are the result of "nothing we know of on Earth," thereby alluding to some type of "higher intelligence" that wielded powers beyond the understanding of modern man. But the question remains, from where did this higher intelligence originate?

THEY CAME FROM—THE STARS?

As outlandish as it sounds, according to virtually all ancient cultures, including the Inca, the Sumerians, and here, specifically, the Maya, this knowledge originated from powerful deities whose home was the stars. (See Appendix G for other cultural references to gods). In fact, like the Incas and Sumerians, the Maya believed that their gods came from the star system known as the Pleiades.[15]

Needless to say, these beliefs are so at odds with modern sensibilities that most dismiss them as shared mythology. But is it possible we have been too quick to judge? Might there be something more than mere imagination to these ancient and widespread beliefs?

In order to begin to unravel this mystery, perhaps the best course of action is to ascertain who exactly the ancients believed these gods—whether mythical or not—to be. And, to do so, what better way than to meet one?

THE FEATHERED SERPENT

Among ancient myths, including those of Egypt, Sumer, India, and even the fabled "Atlantis" among others, there is an entity who plays a key role as creator: In Mesoamerica and Peru he is known principally as "Quetzalcoatl" or the "the Feathered Serpent."*

The origins of this title stem from two associations: firstly, from the *quetzal* bird which, due to its beautiful green tail feathers, was regarded as the "most beautiful" or "most precious" of the winged creatures, and, secondly, from the dragon, or serpent, which translates as *coatl*; hence, the name "Quetzalcoatl," "Feathered Serpent," or even "Precious Feather Snake."† Other monikers include "the God of Wind," "the Creator God," "the Road Sweeper," and "Lord of the Morning Star."[16]

QUETZALCOATL'S FAMILY TREE

Quetzalcoatl originated as a water god and was said to be born in *Michatlauhco* or the "Fish Deeps" to his parents, Mixcoatl and Chimalma. Tradition holds that his mother, Chimalma, who was said to be a virgin, became pregnant with Quetzalcoatl by swallowing an emerald. Quetzalcoatl's father, Mixcoatl, was worshipped as the "Red"

---

* Author Constance Cumbey notes that it is probable that Atlantis existed, but as the world prior to the Noachian flood—a world that God judged and condemned (Cumbey, 250).

† The worship of "serpent deities" is endemic to virtually all ancient cultures.

aspect of the god Tezcatlipoca, or the "Smoking Mirror," who was the god of sorcerers, rulers, and warriors. He is also said to have brought fire to humanity and is thus known as a god of fire, as well as a god of war, and the hunt.[17, 18]

A GOD OF GREAT INFLUENCE

Quetzalcoatl was ascribed such import and power that nearly no aspect of daily life went uninfluenced by him. In fact, worship of this god was so ubiquitous among the Aztecs that the "great pyramid of Cholula"—the largest monument ever constructed anywhere on earth—was dedicated to him.[19]

But why was this god held in such high regard, and on what basis did he derive such widespread influence? Perhaps the answers lie in some important associations:

Knowledge:

Known as the Lord of Healing and magical herbs; known as a symbol of thought and learning, of the arts, poetry, knowledge, and all things good and beautiful, it is said that Quetzalcoatl taught men science, the calendar, and devised ceremonies.[20]

Sacrifice:

Quetzalcoatl is often depicted holding a thorn used to let blood (thought to be an act to honor his father, Mixcoatl). He is therefore credited with being the creator of auto-sacrifice, a forerunner to human sacrifice, which, as noted earlier, became rampant in Mesoamerican society. While some sources downplay Quetzalcoatl's association with this practice, archeological evidence, including the discovered remains of some two hundred victims of dedicatory sacrifice under the Temple of the Feathered Serpent, seems to argue otherwise.[21]

War:

Iconographers note that many artistic expressions of Quetzalcoatl are strongly linked to militarism and that by roughly 200 AD the symbolism of the Feathered Serpent came to denote power, sacrifice, and war.

Even in later years, many of the "plumed serpent" motifs were combined with images of soldiers and implements of war. For instance, panels found at Chichen Itza depict feathered serpents with warriors coming out of their mouths.[22]

The Planet Venus:

Quetzalcoatl is inextricably linked with the planet Venus. According to legend, he had been found to commit incestuous acts with his sister. And so, to escape guilt and shame, he determined to throw himself onto a funeral pyre in self-sacrifice. Legend holds that when he did, his ashes turned into birds and his heart was transformed into the planet Venus—which then ascended to heaven.[23]

Perhaps this association explains the Mayan obsession with Venus, as evidenced in the fact that there are six pages in the Dresden Codex (one of the few surviving Mayan hieroglyphic texts) devoted entirely to the accurate calculation of this planet's heliacal rising.[*]

Interestingly, Mayan rulers actually planned for wars to begin when Venus rose, lending credence to the notion that it was absolutely the most important astronomical object to the Maya, some claim even more so than the Sun!

Lightning:

Lastly, we note that lightning, as it contains a *serpentine* shape, was also associated with this god in the name "Xoneculli."

---

[*] Most Mayan books were destroyed by the conquering Spaniards as they were viewed as pagan or demonic.

Having noted some key associations, there are also a multitude of legends surrounding Quetzalcoatl. Here we have a brief summary of one of the more interesting.

LEGEND HAS IT

According to the ancients, Quetzalcoatl once described a journey in which he traveled to the Underworld to retrieve human bones after a great flood destroyed his world and his people. As the story goes, an old goddess ground up the bones of these ancestors as one would grind maze. She then placed the flourlike meal into a container. It is said that Quetzalcoatl then performed a bloodletting ritual in which he dripped the sacrificial blood onto the ground bones, giving them the potential for life. According to tradition, then, the present race of human beings is believed to be descended from those who, thanks to Quetzalcoatl, were reborn from their deceased state. Thus, Quetzalcoatl is credited with saving humankind![24, 25]

Now, having met the all-important god Quetzalcoatl, let us take a look at another major figure in Mayan lore who was apparently a mortal man but nonetheless deified and worshipped as a god following his death—after which, interestingly enough—he is said to have carried on communication with his descendants.

LORD PACAL

Known as a legendary ruler of the Empire of *Nah Chan Palenque*, Lord Votan Pacal was revered as a magician and seer who had been sent from the stars to teach about the mysteries of the current world, as well as the world to come.

Pacal has the distinction of being entombed in the only Mesoamerican pyramid built specifically as a funerary monument. Known as "the Temple of Inscriptions," it houses many outstanding examples of Mayan art, including, most famously, Pacal's own stone sarcophagus lid. This massive twelve-foot-long slab, which sits atop a monolithic sarcophagus measuring roughly six feet high, seven feet wide, and ten feet in length, has attracted a great deal of attention because of its fascinating depiction: A man, apparently Lord Pacal, is pictured in what appears to be a semi-reclined position in the midst of an intricately carved scene.[26] Around the edges, are glyphs representing the Sun, the Moon, Venus, and various constellations, locating this event in the nighttime sky. Above him is the "Celestial Bird" perched atop the "Sacred Tree" (represented by a cross) which, in turn, holds a serpent in its branches. At the foot of the tree is the Mayan water god, who guards the underworld.

Beneath Pacal are the unfolded jaws of a dragon, or serpent, into whose mouth he descends. Thus, the image is believed to portray Pacal between the heavens and the lower realms as he descends into *Xibalba*, or the Mayan underworld.[27]

IT'S ALL RELATIVE

Also found in the Temple of Inscriptions are six large verticals piers, or panels, that feature artistic sculptural reliefs made from plaster stucco. Several images depict human forms holding an infant-like figure described as having one human leg and one serpent leg. The human leg ends in a six-toed foot, which is cradled by the larger figure. This unusual infant is thought to be Pacal's son, Chan Bahlum II, who is often depicted in portraits as having six fingers on each hand and six toes on each foot.

According to *A Forest of Kings*, written by Maya researchers Linda Schele and David Freidel, it is also recorded in the tomb that Pacal's son was born after the likeness of the "first mother"—the first mother's line going all the way back into the historical darkness of a great catastrophe that struck the earth and from which her descendants escaped. Apparently, this line claimed some "special notice" and predominance above other lines.[28]

LEGENDS SURROUNDING PACAL

An interesting story involving Pacal is related in Irene Nicholson's book, *Mexican and Central American Mythology*:

"From some unknown origin he [Pacal] was ordered by the gods to go to America to found a culture. So he departed from his home, called Valum Chivim...by the way of the 'dwelling of the thirteen snakes' he arrived at Valum Votan...From there he travelled up the Usumacinta river and founded Palenque. Afterward he made several visits to his native home, on one of which he came upon a tower which was originally planned to reach the heavens but which was destroyed because of a 'confusion of tongues' among its architects. Votan [Pacal] was, however allowed to use a subterranean passage in order to reach 'the rock of heaven.'"[29]

Another noteworthy narrative involving Pacal relates how he taught the people about a civilization that had lived once upon a time in a land that was now buried deep beneath the waters. It seems that, like Quetzalcoatl, Pacal had ties to ancestors that had perished by way of a catastrophic flood.

THE KEY TO ALL UNDERSTANDING

Now, having been introduced to the Maya, their Long Count calendar, a prominent god, and a highly revered ruler-god, some may be wondering how all of this might be linked to the biblical end times or the return of Jesus Christ. In answer to this, we conveniently defer once more to Isaac Newton who, as we recall, believed that the Bible, at least in a general sense, held the solution to virtually every puzzle. Might this also hold true in the case of the mysterious Maya and perhaps, to some extent, *all* ancient civilizations?

Let us see if we can answer this question and thus validate Newton's assertion by dusting off the Bible and turning to Genesis chapter 6. It is here that we get a glimpse at what commentators say occurred roughly five hundred years after the creation of the world:

> And it came to pass, when men began to multiply on the face of the earth, and daughters were born unto them, That the sons of God saw the daughters of men that they were fair; and they took them wives of all which they chose. There were giants in the earth in those days; and also after that, when the sons of God came in unto the daughters of men, and they bare children to them, the same became mighty men which were of old, men of renown.
> —Genesis 6:1-2, 4

It is difficult to know where to begin with this passage, quite honestly, because it records such a bizarre turn of events. So bizarre, in fact, that many prefer to avoid it altogether and some who do not tend to want to misinterpret it. Nonetheless, what has occurred in the span of these few verses is that some individuals called "the sons of God" have become enamored with the "daughters of men" and taken them as wives. Immediately after, we learn that there were "giants" walking the earth. Apparently, the offspring of these unions grew to be men of abnormally large stature—"mighty men" and "men of renown." On the face of it, a fairly clear-cut, albeit strange, turn of events; but as we further consider the situation, certain questions come to mind, particularly regarding the cause of the apparent gigantism that has resulted from these unions.

Needless to say, as in most cases where an apparent abnormality occurs in a child, the closest link in that child's genealogy immediately becomes suspect. And so, in search of an explanation for what has happened here, we look first to the mothers in this scenario: Here we are told that they are simply "daughters of men," which seems an obvious allusion to regular (presumably normal) women. Thus, it seems we have no reason to expect anything unusual from this side of

150

the family tree. As we look to the other half of the parental partnership, however, the fathers, who are called "the sons of God," they, if for no other reason than their odd designation, seem to warrant further investigation. Who exactly would Scripture lead us to believe these sons of God to be?

WHO ARE THE SONS OF GOD?

While the answer to the question of who the "sons of God" are has been a matter of some controversy over the years, this author maintains (as many other commentators do) that if one simply follows the golden rule of biblical interpretation, which is to let Scripture interpret Scripture, the matter is actually settled quite easily: The Book of Job tells us in several places (1:6, 2:1, 38:7) that the term "sons of God" refers to angels.

Nonetheless, many reputable Bible commentators have rejected this seemingly clear-cut association on psycho-physiological grounds. How can one believe, they ask, that angels from heaven could engage in sexual relations with women on Earth? These same commentators commonly assert that the "sons of God" must refer instead to an exceptionally "godly" line of men from the line of Seth, the third son of Adam. Accordingly, they argue, the designation "daughters of men" refers not to women in general but specifically to those daughters born of Cain. Thus, this "unholy" union is supposed to have produced these "giant" offspring. This interpretation, however, while perhaps more palatable to those who wish to downplay some of the Bible's more fantastic claims, does not hold up to any level of scrutiny. The simple fact is, a plain reading of Scripture reveals that the term "sons of God" is used only to describe creatures that are created *directly* by the hand of God; this includes Adam (the first man) and also the angels.[30] The only exception to this rule is found in the New Testament where those who have accepted the Holy Spirit through Christ are called "sons of God." This, though, refers to a purely *spiri-*

tual state of being, whereas in the Old Testament (before the time of Christ), which is our area of focus, the term "sons of God" is, again (aside from Adam), used exclusively to refer to angels.[31]

A MATCH MADE IN HEAVEN?

Having settled the matter of who the sons of God are, let us get back to our story: Apparently these angels, also referred to as "the Watchers," became captivated by the beautiful daughters of men. They thus conspired to abandon their heavenly estate and marry the earthly women they found so irresistible. Later, the *hybrid* children born of these angelic-human unions grew to be mighty "giants," or in the Hebrew, "Nephilim," which comes from the root *naphal* meaning "fallen ones" (Thomas, 68).

Bizarre happenings, to be sure! It is no wonder that some are tempted to creatively misinterpret this passage. But there is another problem for those who do: Genesis is not the only source that records this strange turn of events; in fact, a well-known ancient text known as the Book of Enoch cuts through any lingering ambiguity.

ENOCH

Often referred to as "the lost Book of the Bible," the Book of Enoch, while not found in today's Scriptures, was nonetheless considered to be "Scripture" by many early Christians. It is noted, in fact, that the earliest literature of the so-called "Church Fathers," including the early second century "Epistle of Barnabus," is filled with references to this mysterious book.[32] Even Jesus, in the course of His teachings, mentioned many things that agree with what we find in Enoch, things that cannot be found elsewhere in the Old Testament Books available to Him at the time.

Further linking Enoch to the Bible, the New Testament Book of Jude contains a quote referencing the end of the age found in his writings:

And Enoch also, the seventh from Adam, prophesied of these, saying, Behold, the Lord cometh with ten thousands of his saints, To execute judgment upon all, and to convince all that are ungodly among them of all their ungodly deeds which they have ungodly committed, and of all their hard speeches which ungodly sinners have spoken against him.

—Jude 1:14, 15

So what did Enoch have to say about the events of Genesis 6? Here, the author essentially describes the same turn of events, agreeing with and expounding on what is stated in the Bible:

And it came to pass, when the children of men had multiplied, that in those days were born unto them beautiful and comely daughters. And the angels, the children of the heaven, saw and lusted after them, and said to one another: 'Come, let us choose us wives from among the children of men and beget us children.

—Enoch 6: 1, 2

A little later, in verse 10, Enoch alludes to the fact that the angels began to cohabitate with these women, introducing them to various occult practices:

...[they] took unto themselves wives, and each chose for himself one, and they began to go in unto them and to defile themselves with them, and they taught them charms and enchantments and the cutting of roots, and made them acquainted with plants.

—Enoch 7:1

Later still, in chapter 8, Enoch actually reveals the names of some of the angels who participated in these activities. He then details how they were involved in much more than just taking wives and teaching them sorcery. In fact, it appears these angels were inclined to share a whole variety of things—things perhaps best kept from fallen man:

> And Azazel taught men to make swords, and knives, and shields, and breastplates, and made known to them the metals (of the earth) and the art of working them, and bracelets, and ornaments, and the use of antimony, and the beautifying of the eyelids, and all kinds of costly stones, and all coloring tinctures. And there arose much godlessness, and they committed fornication, and they were led astray, and became corrupt in all their ways. Semjaza taught enchantments, and root-cuttings, 'Armaros the resolving of enchantments, Baraqijal (taught) astrology, Kokabel the constellations, Ezeqeel the knowledge of the clouds, Araqiel the signs of the earth, Shamsiel the signs of the sun, and Sariel the course of the moon. And as men perished, they cried, and their cry went up to heaven...
>
> —1 Enoch 8:1-4

Evidently, the angels were all too eager to pass on advanced knowledge to man, including the art of weapon making—an interesting development, indeed. The most remarkable thing about Enoch's narrative from our perspective, however, is the fact that it precisely corroborates the known archeological record. Today, modern archeologists and anthropologists acknowledge that technology, metallurgy, and weapon making all began about five thousand years ago, the precise timeframe, as asserted by Bible chronologists, that Enoch was referring to!

Here, noted anthropologist, Arthur Custance, comments on what the historical record reveals, then poses the obvious question:

> "...An unbelievably long time with almost no growth; *a sudden spurt leading within a very few centuries to a remarkably high culture*; a gradual slowing up and decay, followed

only much later by recovery of lost arts and by development of new ones leading ultimately to the creation of our modern world. *What was the agency which operated for that short period of time to so greatly accelerate the process of cultural development and produce such remarkable results?"* (Thomas, 114).

Is it possible that chapter 8 of Enoch holds the answer to Custance's question? Could it be that this "sudden spurt" of growth leading to a "remarkably high culture" was the result of advanced knowledge passed on to humans by fallen angels? However difficult to imagine it may be, the theory certainly seems to match the physical evidence.*

Nevertheless, in refocusing on Chapter 8 of Enoch, we see the upshot of this sudden explosion of knowledge: a sharp decline in morality and a sharp increase in behavior that the Bible condemns. Apparently, adultery and fornication were fueled by the use of jewelry, ornamentation, and makeup; murder and thievery were facilitated by the making of weapons; and idolatry was encouraged in the teaching of astrology and the attributes of the heavens. The bottom line: This sudden acquisition of knowledge had led humanity to become fascinated with the created rather than the Creator.

But this would not be the worst of it. Eventually, as the Nephilim or giant offspring of these human-angelic unions grew in numbers, they began to consume more than mortal men could produce, and, according to Enoch, rather than go hungry they turned to devouring mankind:

... [the giants] consumed all the acquisitions of men. And

---

* Conversely, it is interesting to note, though rarely pointed out, that the popular evolutionary notion of advanced culture *gradually* evolving over the course of tens of thousands of years does *not* seem to match the physical evidence.

when men could no longer sustain them, the giants turned against them to devour mankind.

—Enoch 7:3-4*

Thus, not so long after the time of creation we have a horrifying scene playing out on the face of the earth: due to the influence of these hybrid beings, or giants, mankind has become increasingly corrupted and even more disturbing has become a preferred food source!

SKEPTICAL?

Now, for many of us, the image of giants dining on human beings is a shocking one. And, for others, the notion of giants even having *existed* may be a little hard to swallow. For those who doubt, however, there is, again, much historical and physical evidence to support Enoch's claims. To begin with, the Bible, which has time and time again proven itself to be historically accurate, actually provides some fairly graphic descriptions of these giant beings:

For only Og king of Bashan remained of the remnant of the giants: behold, his bedstead was a bedstead of iron; is it not in Rabbath of the children of Ammon? Nine cubits was the length thereof, and four cubits the breadth of it, after the cubit of a man.

—Deuteronomy 3:11

---

* Interestingly, verse 5 reads, "And they began to sin against birds, and beasts, and reptiles, and fish, and to devour one another's flesh, and drink the blood." This has given rise to much speculation regarding the legends of strange hybrid beasts that once roamed the ancient world. It also illustrates how the giants were clearly intent on breaking all of God's rules, including His prohibition on consuming blood: "Only ye shall not eat the blood; ye shall pour it upon the earth as water" (Deuteronomy 12:16).

This description of Og's "bedstead" lends new meaning to the term "king-sized" bed. In modern measurements it was eighteen feet, six inches long, and eight feet, four inches wide!

Some giants carried spears that weighed from ten to twenty-five pounds. One carried a spear whose staff was "like a weaver's beam" (2 Samuel 21:19).

Goliath wore a coat of armor that weighed 196 pounds. He was said to be about nine feet tall (111).

Interestingly, some of these giants were said to have had six fingers on each hand and six toes on each foot (2 Samuel 21:20).

OTHER ACCOUNTS

In addition to the biblical accounts, we have other highly reliable historical references to giants. For example, Flavius Josephus, the noted first century historian to the Roman Empire, described these giants as having "bodies so large and countenances so entirely different from other men that they were surprising to the sight and terrible to the hearing." He also notes that in his day the bones of the giants were still on display (110).

But evidence of giants is not confined solely to the Middle East. Many cultures retain stories and historical records of exceedingly large beings, their height ranging from seven to twelve feet tall. In Australia, aboriginal people not only have tales of giants but also fossil evidence of extremely large tools.[33] Tools have also been found elsewhere: In a 3500-year-old copper mine, located near the coastal town of Llandudno in North Wales, archeologists have found a sledge hammer weighing in at sixty-four pounds that would have had a nine-foot-long handle. The largest typical sledge hammer available today is twenty pounds with a three-foot handle.[34]

Other physical evidences include actual footprints. Thomas notes in *The Omega Conspiracy* that massive fossilized specimens have been found in numerous locations: "Two dozen footprints of abnormal size have been found in the Paluxi riverbed in Texas, some of them measuring eighteen inches long. Other giant markings have been discovered in such diverse places as Colorado, New Mexico, Arizona and California" (111).

Giant *skeletons* have also been discovered in modern times. In 1936 Larson Kohl, the German paleontologist and anthropologist, found bones of gigantic men on the shore of Lake Elyasi in Central Africa. Other skeletons were later found in Hava, the Transvaal, and China (111). In the 1950s, during road construction in Southeast Turkey, it is reported that many tombs containing the remains of human giants were uncovered. At two sites, the femurs (thigh bones) were measured to be 47.24 inches. Joe Taylor, director of the Mt. Blanco Fossil Museum in Crosbyton, Texas was later commissioned to sculpt an anatomically correct and to scale human femur to represent these findings. (See Appendix D for photo). Estimates say that a being with a femur this size would have stood fourteen to sixteen feet tall with twenty-two inch feet.[35]*

The evidence for giants is, in fact, absolutely overwhelming. And while some fakes can be found on the internet, a careful search will yield the references alluded to here, as well as others.

Now, having established that giants actually existed and also the fact that, according to Enoch, they were up to no good, one begins to wonder how all of this was finally resolved. Of course, those familiar with the story are already aware that drastic measures were required.

JUDGMENT BY FLOOD

God made man in His own image, the highest of all earthly creations. While God said that everything He made was good, He con-

---

* The idea that giants actually existed obviously undermines the theory of evolution, which asserts that man's ancestors were, without exception, much smaller than we. Perhaps this explains why so much of this information is ignored by the mainstream.

sidered man to be *very* good. Indeed, man had been made for fellowship with God Himself, but as Genesis and Enoch reveal, he soon turned his back on his maker. Before many generations, the human race was being polluted by an abominable union with fallen angels. It was specifically because of this ultimate sin that God brought about a deluge of such magnitude that all life was drowned from the face of the earth (72). All life that is, except for one man and his family—which raises an interesting question.

WHY NOAH?

Most of us have been taught that because Noah was a godly man, he and his family were the only ones worthy of being saved from the Flood. While Noah was most definitely a "just man" and stood out as an example of righteousness and godliness in a perverse age, Genesis 6:9 reveals that there was more to it than just that. Here, we find that Noah was also "perfect in his generation"—an intriguing designation and one that immediately begs the question: What exactly does it mean to be "perfect" in one's generation? Obviously, this was not to imply that Noah—godly as he was—had attained a state of moral or spiritual perfection. In fact, Genesis 9:20-23 destroys any such illusion.

Here, Thomas describes the more likely reality:

> "The Hebrew word [for perfect] is Tamiym and comes from the root word Taman. This means "without blemish"...Just as the sacrificial lamb had to be without any physical blemish, so was Noah's perfection. In other words, this state of "perfection" refers not to any moral or spiritual quality but to *physical* purity. Noah was uncontaminated by the alien [angelic] invaders. He alone had preserved their pedigree and kept it pure, in spite of prevailing corruption brought about by the fallen angels" (73).

So we see that, while *relatively* godly, Noah and his family were preserved not because they were morally perfect but, in large part, because they were the only ones left untainted. And thus is revealed the motivation behind this angelic invasion: Satan wished to corrupt the flesh of all humanity! After all, doing so would not only mean the utter perversion of God's highest earthly creation but, conceivably, the thwarting of His plan of redemption, which centered on having His Son born from the seed of a woman. Satan, of course, realized that if the bloodline of every last woman could be defiled by these human-angelic unions, this would no longer be possible.

And so, to keep the Wicked One from accomplishing his goals, God moved to purge the earth.

THE FATE OF THE FALLEN AND THE ORIGIN OF DEMONS

While the Flood would succeed in destroying the giants, or Nephilim, the Bible tells us that God also dealt forcefully with the angels who had initiated all of this havoc. As punishment, He would imprison them in a place of darkness called "Tartarus" (translated as "hell" in most English Bibles), where they remain to this day, awaiting judgment at the end of the age:

> For God did not spare the angels who sinned, but cast them down to Tartarus and delivered them into chains of darkness, to be reserved for judgment;
>
> —2 Peter 2:4

So, the giants are drowned and the angels have been imprisoned. All is well that ends well as they say. Though, in the case of the Nephilim, perhaps we have spoken too soon. While the *bodies* of these giants were destroyed, it seems their disembodied *spirits* survived. This simple fact, which often gets glossed over, is actually crucial to understanding the origin of the malevolent spiritual forces that mankind contends with even today. These are the very entities who have come to be known as "evil spirits," or "demons."

In chapter 15, speaking of their respective fates following the Flood, Enoch highlights the differences between these "demons" and the fallen angels who sired them:

> And now the giants, who are produced from the spirits and flesh, shall be called evil spirits upon the earth, and on the earth shall be their dwelling. Evil spirits have proceeded from their bodies; because they are born from men, and from the holy Watchers [angels] is their beginning and primal origin; they shall be evil spirits on earth; evil spirits shall they be called. As for the spirits of heaven, in heaven shall be their dwelling, but as for the spirits of the earth which were born upon the earth, on the earth shall be their dwelling. And the spirits of the giants afflict, oppress, destroy, attack, do battle, and work destruction on the earth, and cause trouble: they take no food, but nevertheless hunger and thirst and cause offences. And these spirits shall rise up against the children of men and against the women, because they have proceeded from them.
>
> —Enoch 15:8-12

According to Enoch, the angels, who are "spirit" beings, remain in a non-earthly realm, while the disembodied spirits of the giants who were born on Earth as "men of renown" will roam the planet as demons, afflicting and tormenting men at every opportunity. These are the same demons mentioned frequently in the New Testament; the same demons that Jesus, on numerous occasions, cast out of people. They, of course, no longer have a physical form of their own but nevertheless continue to hunger and thirst and so desire to inhabit the bodies of other living humans and even animals.

But the story does not end there. Apparently, the demons were not content to merely make trouble for humanity. In chapter 19, speaking of the judgment of the fallen angels whose actions brought about the Flood, Enoch reveals something critical to our understanding of the relationship between their demonic offspring and man.

> …Here shall stand the angels who have connected themselves with women, and their spirits assuming many different forms, are defiling mankind, and shall *lead them astray into sacrificing to demons as gods*; (here shall they stand) till the day of the great judgment in which they shall be judged until they are made an end of.
>
> —Enoch 19:1

The key words to note here: "sacrificing to demons as gods."

And "We" Shall be as Gods

It is said that power corrupts, and absolute power corrupts absolutely. So, apparently, does knowledge. With their superior intellect, these evil spirits had succumbed to the sin that became the downfall of Lucifer: pride (1 Timothy 3:6). But more than mere pride, such knowledge wedded to an already arrogant nature had led to self-deification, thus fulfilling the demons' desire to receive religious worship and to rule over men. And from such men, these demons, or "gods," would demand an unending flow of blood and sacrifice.

Here, then, is where our story picks up with the Maya.

Connecting the Dots

Having spent the last dozen or so pages discussing giants, the Flood, and the resultant demons who roam the earth today, we are finally prepared to explore what all of this means with regard to the

Maya, their gods, and the year 2012. What is revealed via this exploration, I believe, not only corroborates and thus further reinforces what the Bible and Enoch have to say on many topics, but also dispels many, if not all, of the earlier discussed mysteries surrounding the Maya.

Let us begin "connecting the dots," then, by simply pointing out some highly significant parallels between the biblical record and Mayan lore: First and most obviously among these is a narrative that speaks of a great flood, the Bible's version, of course, being Noah's flood, the Mayan version being the cataclysmic deluge that destroyed Quetzalcoatl's world. In drawing this parallel, the question immediately arises: Might the Mayan traditions, like so much of world mythology, contain kernels of truth and therefore be a reference to an actual devastating global flood in the past—perhaps the same one mentioned in the Bible?*

In posing this question, one begins to wonder how the historic timeline of the Maya aligns with what Bible chronologists have to say about the timing of the Flood.

TIMELINES: THE MAYA AND THE FLOOD

While the exact date of Noah's flood is not known, Josephus puts it at a little over 5,000 years ago, in 3146 BC. Ussher placed it some 4,357 years ago, which equates to approximately 1,656 years after biblical creation, or 2,348 BC (based on his 4004 BC creation

---

* Flood myths are common to at least two hundred cultures worldwide, including the Eskimos. According to Plato, the Flood also submerged "Atlantis." Bible skeptics often dismiss these as merely isolated references to what were actually *local* flood events, but this does not account for how or why all of these civilizations, who were separated by vast oceans and different languages, would share such similar stories. The only logical answer: They are but locally and culturally modified remnants of one tale of an actual global catastrophic flood that has been handed down through the generations, originating from the time of Noah.

date).[36, 37] Thus, the generally accepted time range for the Flood is between 2000 and 3000 BC, though likely closer to 3000 BC.

The precise origins of the Maya are shrouded in the mists of time. According to some researchers, the first clearly "Maya" settlements were established circa 1800 BC in the Soconusco region of the Pacific Coast.[38] Though many experts assert that the Mayas' predecessors, the Olmecs, from whom many aspects of Mayan culture are derived, can be traced back to as early as 2000 to 3000 BC.

Interestingly, the origins of the famous Long Count calendar are even more ambiguous. While some speculate that it was devised circa 500 BC, the earliest Long Count inscriptions uncovered thus far date back to only 36 BC.[39]

What makes all of this yet more mysterious, however, is the fact that the Long Count calendar itself, which, again, according to Mayan lore, was supposedly given by the "gods," has a very definite "start date" which is, as we recall, 3114 BC. Why is this? No one seems to know.*

THE LONG COUNT START DATE AND THE FLOOD: A POSSIBLE CONNECTION?

In light of the seemingly inexplicable start date of the Mayan calendar, and, as we have just begun to hint at, a possible connection between the Mayan gods and the demons of the Bible, it is, if nothing else, fascinating to consider a couple of things: First, according to the Book of Jubilees, the fallen angels, or Watchers, initially descended to Earth on 461 Annus Mundi, a date that Ussher would interpret as 3543 BC. Considering the allowable margins for historical dating, it is interesting to note that this date of descent falls relatively close to the 3114 BC start date of the Long Count calendar. The second

---

* Many speculate that the Long Count calendar is indeed a product of a civilization that preceded the Maya.

point to consider is Josephus's estimated date for the Flood, which is, again, 3146 BC. This date also falls very close (only thirty-two years prior) to our Long Count 3114 BC start date.

Needless to say, the proximity of both of these events in relation to the start date of the Long Count calendar, seems to raise some interesting possibilities: For instance, is it possible that the original (possibly demonic) architects of the calendar, in choosing 3114 BC as a start date, were in fact referencing a date of great significance from their perspective, perhaps the first descent of the fallen angels, or even the first irruption of their (Nephilim-giant) offspring? Or, along these same lines, might it be possible that they were marking the date of the Flood that sealed their fate, or just after? To a certain extent, this scenario seems even more likely, given the "creation-destruction" theme associated with the beginning and end of the Long Count calendar cycles.

WHEN THE PIECES FIT

In view of the above possibilities, we are led to consider a further possible connection between the Long Count calendar and the Bible's chronology: Interestingly enough, based on Ussher's proposed creation date of 4004 BC, we can calculate that a span of roughly 890 years of earth history precedes the Long Count calendar's start date of 3114 BC. Now, by simply adding this 890 year span to the length of the Mayan great cycle, which is 5,125 years, we arrive at a total of 6,015 years of earth history. Why is this significant? This total, as you will notice, falls stunningly close to the all-important six thousand year mark from biblical creation, the year believed by many to pinpoint the time of Christ's return!

Significantly, the creation date estimates of other respected scholars yield even closer results. For instance, Petavius calculated creation to have occurred twenty one years later than Ussher's estimate, in 3983 BC. If we plug this number into the above equation we arrive at an earth history total of 5,994 years—only six years off the six thousand year mark!

Again, while ultimately speculative, the notion that the "great cycle" that runs from 3114 BC to 2012 AD ends at what is essentially the six thousand year mark from biblical creation gives one pause and also seems to bolster the notion that the Mayan Long Count calendar may indeed be a product of either the pre-flood patriarchs (Nephilim) or the post-flood demons—beings who would, for obvious reasons, be intensely aware of not only the Flood date but even more so the time remaining from that event until the six thousand year mark from creation—the time of Christ's return!*

If what we are proposing here is correct, perhaps the length of the Mayan "great cycle" is not such a mystery after all; in fact, perhaps the Long Count calendar is actually nothing more than a demonic countdown to the Millennium.

OTHER CORRELATIONS

Considering all that we have discussed thus far, it seems a growing number of indicators are pointing to the likelihood that the Mayan deities may have indeed been the same demons who, according to Enoch and the Bible, were later worshipped as gods. But there is even more evidence to consider: As you may or may not have noticed, interlaced throughout our introduction to the Maya were many uncanny references that seem to indicate a demonic association. In fact, there are so many of these that the only practical way to highlight them effectively is to list them. Thus, over the course of the next several pages we have done so, first by noting the Mayan (god) attribute

---

* Considering the Bible's description of signs not only in the Sun and the Moon, but in the "stars" in the last days, it is interesting to speculate as to whether the so-called "galactic alignment" that has been associated with the Mayan prediction of a new age is but yet another sign or indicator of what the Bible calls Christ's millennial age.

and then by countering it with the biblical (demonic) correlation. While some of these are fairly subtle, most are surprisingly not, leaving one to question: If we are truly dealing with demons here, why would they be so conspicuous? We will pick up this question on the other side. For now, let us simply take note of the many correlations:

MAYAN: The Mayan god Quetzalcoatl is referred to as a *serpent* (Feathered Serpent), and a *snake* (Precious Feather Snake).

BIBLICAL: Satan is repeatedly referred to as a serpent in the Bible, most infamously in the Garden of Eden: "And the woman said, the *serpent* beguiled me, and I did eat" (Genesis 3:13).

MAYAN: One Mayan legend tells of Quetzalcoatl's journey to the underworld to retrieve human bones after a great flood destroyed his world and his people.

BIBLICAL: According to the Bible, a worldwide flood destroyed the Nephilim, transforming them into disembodied spirits, or demons.

MAYAN: The Maya believed that their gods came from the stars.

BIBLICAL: In the Bible, angels are referred to as "stars." For instance, the Book of Revelation refers thusly to a "third part" of the angels who took part in Satan's rebellion: "*And his [the dragon's] tail drew the third part of the stars of heaven, and did cast them to the earth...*" (Revelation 12:4). In another example, Satan himself is pictured as a "star" falling from heaven: "And the third angel sounded, and there fell *a great star* from heaven..." (Revelation 8:10).

MAYAN: It is said that Lord Pacal taught about a people who lived in a land that is now buried deep beneath the sea.

BIBLICAL: Ancient cities boasting paved boulevards, temples, massive columns, and even pyramids continue to be found buried deep beneath the ocean in such places as off the coasts of Spain, Cuba, Japan, and the southern United States. Modern archeologists acknowledge that during the period these cities would have been above water there should not have existed a civilization old enough or advanced enough to have built them. Many Bible commentators and theorists believe that these cities were, in fact, built with the assistance of the Nephilim during the pre-flood era and were subsequently buried by the deluge (and the likely accompanying polar shift) sent to destroy them.[40, 41]

MAYAN: Prominent Mayan figures are linked to serpents and water, or the sea. For instance, the god Quetzalcoatl was originally a "water god" and was said to be born in Michatlauhco, or the *"Fish Deeps."* Also, on Pacal's famous sarcophagus lid is pictured the Mayan *water god* who guards the underworld as Pacal descends into the unfolded jaws of a dragon, or serpent.

BIBLICAL: In the Book of Isaiah, Satan is referred to as a serpent, or reptile, that is in the *sea*: "In that day the LORD with His severe sword, great and strong, Will punish Leviathan the fleeing serpent, Leviathan that twisted serpent; And He will slay the *reptile that is in the sea*" (Isaiah 27:1).

MAYAN: Legend holds that Quetzalcoatl's mother became pregnant by swallowing an *emerald*. It is also noted that the traditional ceremonial regalia for Quetzalcoatl included a headdress decorated with precious stones.[42]

BIBLICAL: According to the Bible, Satan was created with a covering of incredibly beautiful precious stones: "You were in Eden, the garden of God; *every precious stone was your covering*: the ruby, the topaz and the diamond; the beryl, the onyx and the jasper; the lapis lazuli, the turquoise and the *emerald...*" (Ezekiel 28:13).

MAYAN: Some legends attribute certain Christ-like attributes to Quetzalcoatl. For instance, Aztecs believed that Quetzalcoatl's mother, Chimalma, was a "*virgin.*" Also, as we recall, Quetzalcoatl is not only portrayed as a "creator," but is credited with shedding his own blood in an act of self-sacrifice to save the "ancestors."

BIBLICAL: In Isaiah 14, Satan declares his intention to be like God: "I will ascend above the tops of the clouds; *I will make myself like the Most High*" (Isaiah 14:14). Thus, the notion that the Devil or his minions would attempt to impersonate Christ to one degree or another seems highly plausible.[43]

MAYAN: Lord Pacal's son, Chan Bahlum II, is depicted in Mayan art as having six fingers and six toes. Moreover, legends, statues, and petroglyphs from around the globe, i.e., North America, Egypt, French Polynesia, Easter Island, and Peru depict figures or objects of worship as having six fingers and six toes.[44] (See Appendix C for photos).

BIBLICAL: The giants, or Nephilim, of the Bible were described as having six fingers and six toes: "And there was yet a battle in Gath, where was a man of great stature, that had on every hand six fingers, and on every foot six toes, four and twenty in number; and he also was born to the giant" (2 Samuel 21:20).

MAYAN: Quetzalcoatl is inextricably linked in Mayan lore with the planet Venus (also called the morning star) and is thus referred to as "Lord of the Morning Star" or "Lord of the Dawn."

BIBLICAL: In Isaiah, Satan is called the "morning star" and "son of the dawn": How you have fallen from heaven, *O morning star, son of the dawn*! You have been cast down to the earth, you who once laid low the nations! (Isaiah 14:12).*

MAYAN: Iconographers note that the ancient artistic expressions of Quetzalcoatl are strongly linked to militarism and war.[45]

BIBLICAL: In the Bible, the Antichrist (a man indwelt by Satan) is pictured as worshipping a "god of fortresses," or a god of *war.* "But instead he will honor *a god of fortresses...*" (Daniel 11:38).

MAYAN: Quetzalcoatl is called "the God of the Wind." Also, in an illustration in the Borgia Codex, this deity appears as the god of breath and *air.*[46]

BIBLICAL: In the Bible, Satan is called "prince of the power of the air" (Ephesians 2:2).

MAYAN: The Maya (perhaps under the advisement of their gods?) are known to have practiced cannibalism.

BIBLICAL: The giants, or Nephilim, are said to have turned to devouring mankind (Enoch 7:11-13).

MAYAN: Lightning, as it contains a serpentine shape, was associated with Quetzalcoatl in the name "Xoneculli."

BIBLICAL: At Satan's fall, he is described as "lightning": "And he

---

* Leading physicist, Dr Irwin Ginsburgh, draws an interesting parallel between the biblical description of hell and the planet Venus, which is described as having a searing atmosphere and a surface heat of 850 degrees Fahrenheit. The planet is also wreathed in dense sulphur clouds, with sulphuric acid droplets—liquid and solid, dripping from the clouds (Thomas, 141).

said unto them, I beheld Satan as *lightning* fall from heaven" (Luke 10:18).

MAYAN: Often depicted holding a thorn used to let blood. Quetzalcoatl introduced auto-sacrifice, a forerunner to human sacrifice, which became rampant in Mesoamerican culture. Also, further linking Quetzalcoatl to sacrifice, hundreds of sacrificial victims have been discovered under the Temple of the Feathered Serpent.

BIBLICAL: The writings of Enoch tell us that fallen angels caused men to sacrifice to false gods, or "demons." The Bible reports the same in Jeremiah 19, wherein the Phoenicians and Canaanite tribes offered human sacrifices to the "gods" who, as Scripture reveals, were actually demons.

MAYAN: The Mayan god Quetzalcoatl was associated with and thus adorned with the plumes of the quetzal (meaning *most beautiful*) bird.

BIBLICAL: In the Bible, Satan is spoken of in the following terms: "Thus saith the Lord GOD; Thou sealest up the sum, full of wisdom, and *perfect in beauty*" (Ezekiel 28:12).

MAYAN: Lord Pacal's son, Chan Bahlum II, is portrayed in ancient Mayan reliefs as having one serpent leg and one human-looking leg.

BIBLICAL: The Nephilim of the Bible were hybrid beings: half fallen angel (of the serpent) and half man.

MAYAN: Legends speak of Pacal's travels, relating how at one point he had come upon an unfinished tower that was originally planned to reach the heavens, but which had been destroyed due to a "confusion of tongues" among its architects.

BIBLICAL: Many theorists believe that, due to a later (post flood) incursion of fallen angels, the Nephilim, or giants, may have had a hand in building the infamous Tower of Babel, which took place relatively soon after the Flood.*

MAYAN: The Mayan god Quetzalcoatl, known as a symbol of thought and learning, is said to have imparted much wisdom, including science, the calendar, arts, and poetry.

BIBLICAL: In the *Satanic Bible*, Lucifer is acknowledged as the bringer of intellectualism and enlightenment. Ezekiel describes Satan as being "full of wisdom" (Ezekiel 28:12). Moreover, the Greek word *daemon*, from which the words daimon and demon are derived, denotes "genius and intelligence."

MAYAN: The current great cycle of the Mayan Long Count calendar, presumably given by the "gods," begins in 3114 BC (about the time of the Flood) and ends 5,125 years later in 2012 AD, supposedly marking the beginning of a "new world age."

BIBLICAL: While a margin of error exists, according to Bible chronologists, the Flood occurred circa 3000 BC (essentially the same time that the current Long Count calendar cycle begins). Also, the expected time for Christ's millennial reign to begin (the six thousandth year from biblical creation) is approximately 2012 AD, which happens to coincide with the end date of the Long Count cycle.

---

* Genesis states that some giants existed *after* the Flood: "There were giants in the earth in those days; *and also after that...*" (Genesis 6:4). Commentators agree that this was due to a second, albeit limited, incursion of Watchers, or fallen angels. This post-flood appearance of Nephilim is also the reason God ordered the Israelites to "*utterly destroy*" the people in Canaan before they took the Promised Land (Deuteronomy 20:17). They were descendants of the giants!

MAYAN: According to legend, Quetzalcoatl's heart was transformed into the planet Venus just before he ascended to the heavens.

BIBLICAL: Interestingly, modern astrologers identify the planet Venus as having been known by the name "Lucifer" in Roman astrology before being given its current name. Also, Lucifer (Satan) says in Isaiah, "I will *ascend* to heaven; I will raise my throne above the stars of God..." (Isaiah 14:3).

As we noted at the outset, most of the parallels drawn here seem shockingly obvious, which, again, begs the question, why would demons masquerading as gods not be more discreet? One can only speculate as to the answer. However, there is one possibility that seems highly plausible: Perhaps, like the serial killer or the thief who cannot resist leaving behind a tantalizing clue as to his identity, these beings are simply far too egotistical to conceal their true origins.

While some would suggest that many of the above-noted parallels are merely the result of Christian influence via the conquering Spaniards, it should be noted that a number of these references, including those alluding to the destruction of the world by flood, are rooted in the Dresden codex as well as the Popol Vuh, both of which denote origins that would seem to predate any possible Christian influence.[47, 48] But even if one ignores this fact, thereby assuming that a certain amount of Christian influence did later creep into Mayan lore, a fundamental question must be asked: Why would the Maya adopt virtually *every* nuanced attribute of Satan, the Bible's foremost villain, and ascribe them so deliberately to their most highly revered figures? This scenario makes absolutely no sense!

Therefore, it seems the most likely explanation for all of the correlations we have identified here is that the Mayan gods, the myths surrounding these gods, and even the mysterious Long Count calendar are simply a corollary of the Bible's demons, whose origins are chronicled in the Book of Genesis, as well as the writings of Enoch.

And so, it seems, we may finally have our answer to the question posed at the beginning of this chapter as to why human sacrifice and unabashed brutality became so endemic in Mesoamerican culture: The shamans, who were in continual contact with the "spirit world," even as they ruled as kings over the Mayan people, were essentially taking their marching orders from Satan's minions.

Now, as we begin to wrap things up, let us take a look at one last piece of the Mayan puzzle that seems to make all of this even more relevant as we approach 2012.

THE RETURN OF QUETZALCOATL

Among the most compelling legends surrounding Quetzalcoatl is one concerning a promise he purportedly made to the ancient Maya—a promise to one day return. While there is some confusion and debate as to the exact details of this myth, it is inarguable that the theme of "return" is central to the Mayan lore surrounding this god.[49]* It is even today echoed in the words of Mayan shamans, one of whom in a recent interview stated:

> "The ancestors are returning, my brothers and sisters, and we do not have long. Now is the time that the prophecies will be fulfilled."[50]

Needless to say, the return of Quetzalcoatl or, according to this shaman, the "ancestors," is not only much anticipated but believed to be imminent. In fact, many are convinced that the forthcoming end of the great cycle, along with the accompanying galactic alignment, and also two extremely rare Venus transits, one on June 8, 2004 and

---

* The narrative of "gods" who brought knowledge to Earth and then left, promising to one day "return," is found in many ancient cultures.

the other on June 6, 2012, may be the signs that herald this return.*

Significantly, within the ever-growing New Age community, which has become deeply involved in what is now commonly referred to as the "2012 phenomenon," some claim to have "channeled" information from "spirits" or "star beings" that agrees with the above message, adding that anyone who is able to connect to the "oneness of all" will become a "living incarnation" of Quetzalcoatl; also adding, interestingly enough, that "to become real, the energy of Quetzalcoatl must manifest in human beings."⁵¹

Might they be on to something?

BY WAY OF THE BLACK ROAD

In considering the "return of Quetzalcoatl," whether merely in a symbolic sense or somehow, as New Ageists suggest, in pure "energy" form, it is fascinating to overlay the imagery of this myth with the powerful symbolic significance of the so-called "galactic alignment" in 2012. Though perhaps nothing more than an exceedingly rare celestial event to modern astronomers, for many observers, the notion of the Sun and the Earth being in direct alignment with the entryway to the Mayan underworld evokes a certain sense of expectation: Might Quetzalcoatl be planning a return trip to Earth via the legendary Black Road?

Of course, while speculation on what amounts to myth should be given no more credence than it deserves, it is interesting, in light of this legend, to cite a certain passage from Revelation in which Satan and his angels find themselves cast down from heaven in the last days:

And there was war in heaven: Michael and his angels fought against the dragon; and the dragon fought and his angels,

---

* A "Venus transit" takes place when the planet Venus passes directly between the Sun and Earth, obscuring a small portion of the solar disk.

And prevailed not; neither was their place found any more in heaven. And the great dragon was cast out, that old serpent, called the Devil, and Satan, which deceiveth the whole world: *he was cast out into the earth, and his angels were cast out with him.*

—Revelation 12:7-9

Could the Mayan myth of Quetzalcoatl and the "ancestors" returning to Earth be some type of demonic allusion to Satan and his fallen angels being cast down from heaven in the last days? For now, it is impossible to know. In considering the prospect, however, it is interesting to speculate as to a possible scenario and to pose a final question: As most are aware, it is believed that the Antichrist (a man indwelt by Satan) will be revealed toward the very end of the age, at the beginning of what many believe will be a three and one-half year period known as the "Tribulation." Considering, as we have, 2015 as a possible timeframe for the Second Coming, one cannot help but note that the current Long Count cycle happens to end roughly three and one-half years prior, in 2012. Might this year, therefore, mark the beginning of this "indwelling" by Satan and thus the emergence of the Antichrist and the start of said Tribulation?

SUMMARY AND CONCLUSION

Here we have taken a look at the mysterious Maya from a somewhat different perspective than that usually offered by the mainstream, noting first that their history follows a storyline similar to that of many ancient cultures: Far back in the mists of time, the "ancestors" were purportedly visited by gods from the stars who brought with them great knowledge and wisdom. In the case of the Maya, this included science, the arts, poetry, and even the calendar. At some later point in time, the gods apparently had to leave abruptly but promised to one day return.

We also noted that, though revered by modern scholars for their remarkable mathematical, astronomical, and architectural achievements, the Maya were evidently not as progressive in other spheres. In fact, seemingly at odds with their state of intellectual development, they are known to have slaughtered tens of thousands of human beings in some of the most gruesome ways imaginable. Moreover, in what could be viewed as profound irony, this barbarism was presumably practiced to appease the very gods who had enabled their stunning advancements.

For this reason and others, the Mayan culture remains a topic of fascination to many, a dramatic example of civilization at its best and at its worst—yet ultimately an enigma—until, that is, one holds it up next to the Bible and shines a comparative light on it. Suddenly, the Mayan gods are unmasked as fallen angels and demons; the son of Lord Pacal (Chan Bahlum II) with his six fingers and six toes conjures images of the Nephilim; the traditions that speak of the last "great cycle" ending in a watery deluge is recognized as an allusion to Noah's flood; and finally, the current cycle of the Long Count calendar, which begins inexplicably in 3114 BC and ends in 2012 AD, is seen as perhaps marking the time of the Flood (or the destruction of the Nephilim), as well as pointing forward to the six thousand year mark from creation, the time at which many believe Christ will return to Earth.

Of course, this invaluable insight is lost on those who reject or are ignorant of the Bible's teachings. Today, due to widespread promulgation of the "Mayan prophecies" and an increasing appetite for alternatives to the Christian brand of spirituality, many are focused on 2012 and the seemingly incredible foresight of the Maya in predicting the transformational "earth changes" that we are now seeing. This, I believe, has facilitated a type of mass deception whereby a series of myths perpetrated by the "gods" have succeeded in muddying the waters and obscuring the singular truth of Bible prophecy.

Thus, the common question today: How could the Maya have

known? The answer, quite simply: they had some help. But these helpers did not then, nor do they now, have humanities' best interests at heart.

EIGHT

For we wrestle not against flesh and blood, but against princi-
palities, against powers, against the rulers of the darkness of this
world, against spiritual wickedness in high places.

—Ephesians 6:12

MESSAGES FROM THE DARK SIDE: UFOS, ALIEN VISITATIONS, AND THE NEW AGE

"Everywhere, Mother Earth is rapidly advancing the endgame of this reality, which is transforming it into something entirely different. These continuing changes are alarming many of your atmospheric and climate specialists. Your present reality is slipping away as the vast changes in climate formation and the increase in various types of seismic activity together produce something new and different. All this heightened activity points to one simple fact: Mother Earth cannot hold this reality together as it presently is for very much longer. What is now urgently called for is a big shift in your global society, and this includes public acknowledgement of the fact that a great consciousness shift is well underway. And yet this is a mere prelude to the reality that is coming. Your world needs to plan for this, and begin to comprehend the huge implications of this monumental process."[1]

—A message "channeled" from an extraterrestrial being belonging to the so-called "Galactic Federation," Dec. 9, 2008

WHAT WAS OLD IS NEW AGAIN

Rudyard Kipling once wrote that "East is East, and West is West, and never the twain shall meet." If this was ever true, perhaps it can no longer be said, as an Eastern "pantheistic" worldview has long since spread to the West and is now flourishing in both hemispheres. The primary vehicle of this supposed new transmission of ideas has been what is today called the "New Age" Movement.[2]

Emerging in its current distinct form in the late sixties and early seventies, then, later gaining momentum in the eighties, the New Age Movement, sometimes called "the Human Potential Movement," or "Humanism," is difficult to define because there is no formal hierarchy, dogma, doctrine, or membership card. In the simplest terms, though, it consists of a worldwide network of organizations and individuals who are bound by a distinct set of beliefs. These beliefs generally lead adherents to strive for what might be described as a higher, or "advanced," state of spirituality, yet ultimately to reject what they view as the "narrow minded" or "patriarchal religious doctrines" commonly associated with Christianity or Judaism.[3]

In a revealing article, National Director of Probe Ministries, author and radio host, Kerby Anderson, describes the major tenets of the New Age Movement:

> "First is the belief in monism. New Agers believe that "all is one." Everything and everyone is interrelated and interdependent. Ultimately there is no real difference between humans, animals, rocks, or even God. Any differences between these entities are merely apparent, not real.
>
> Second is the belief in pantheism. Since New Agers already believe that "all is one," the next logical assumption would be that "all is god." All of creation partakes of the divine essence. All of life (and even non-life) has a spark of divinity within.

The third major tenet of the New Age follows as a logical conclusion from the other two. If "all is one" and "all is god," then we should conclude that "we are gods." We are, according to New Agers, ignorant of our divinity. We are "gods in disguise." The goal, therefore, of the New Age Movement is to discover our own divinity.

Fourth, we discover our own divinity by experiencing a change in consciousness. The human race suffers from a collective form of metaphysical amnesia. We have forgotten that our true identity is divine and thus must undergo a change of consciousness to achieve our true human potential (hence the name, the Human Potential Movement).

A fifth tenet is reincarnation. Most New Agers believe in some form of reincarnation. In its classic form, the cycles of birth, death, and reincarnation are necessary to work off our bad "karma" and to reach perfection. The doctrine of karma says that one's present condition is determined by one's actions in a past life.

The Western version of reincarnation held by many New Agers places much less emphasis on bad karma and postulates an upward spiral towards perfection through reincarnation. This view has been espoused by such people as Shirley MacLaine, Sylvester Stallone, George Patton, and Henry Ford.*

---

* Perhaps one of the most effective modern-day proponents of the New Age is Oprah Winfrey, who regularly features and promotes New Age writers and gurus on her show via her "Book Club" list. Since the beginning of 2008, Oprah has offered daily classes on her XM radio station on the book *A Course in Miracles*. "A Course in Miracles" (or ACIM for short) was written by a major player in the New Age movement, Helen Schucman, who claims that the book was dictated to her by an "interior voice," which she identifies with Jesus Christ. In this course, the listener is taught that there is no sin, and to not make the "mistake" of "clinging to the old rugged cross;" also, that the name of "Jesus Christ, as such, is but a symbol."

A final major tenet is moral relativism. New Agers think in terms of gray, rather than black or white. Denying the law of non-contradiction, New Agers will often believe that two conflicting statements can both be true. They will therefore teach that "all religions are true" and "there are many paths to God."[4]

Anderson goes on to note that the so-called "New" Age Movement is, in all reality, not so new after all:

"The New Age is really old occultism in new linguistic garb. Many of these concepts can be found in basic form in Genesis 3. Notice these statements made [by the Serpent] to Eve in the Garden: "You will be like God" (pantheism), "You will not surely die" (reincarnation), "Your eyes will be opened" (change of consciousness), and "Did God really say" (moral relativism).[5]

Therefore, as Anderson points out, from a Judeo-Christian standpoint, the Serpent, or Satan, might be traced as the original progenitor of New Age thought. After the fall at Eden, these teachings flourished and became dominant in the pre-flood world. In fact, as highlighted by Constance Cumbey in her book *The Hidden Dangers of the Rainbow*, many of today's New Age "esoteric" historians proudly acknowledge that their traditions originated in the pre-flood, obviously ill-fated, utopia known as "Atlantis" (Cumbey, 250). As the story goes, the cataclysmic destruction of this once great city caused their "White Lodge" of "Ascended Masters" to withdraw from the Earth, leaving the planet temporarily in control of the "Black Lodge."[*]

---

[*] Cumbey notes that a clear reading of the New Ageist's literature reveals that they define "Black Lodge" as the source of Judeo-Christian tradition and "White Lodge" as the source of their occult (New Age) teachings.

According to New Ageists, these Atlantean teachings were pre-served in the ancient land of Babylon and surrounding Plains of Shinar and from there disseminated throughout the globe—providing a foundation for the Taoist doctrines of China, the Hindu/Buddhist teachings of Asia, the Great Spirit teachings of the American Indians, and, significantly, the Mayan-Aztec teachings of Central and South America (251).

THE MAYA AND THE NEW AGE

Considering that modern New Age teachings can be traced back to so many ancient cultures, including, most notably here, that of the Aztec and Maya, it is perhaps not surprising that, as noted in the previous chapter, today's New Age Movement is deeply involved in what we have termed the "2012 phenomenon." Playing off the Mayan themes of "change" and "transition," this ever-burgeoning community is actively involved in promoting the idea of a mass "shift in consciousness" as we near the end of a great cosmic cycle and the beginning of a new one.

On the topic of new beginnings, it is interesting to note that while Christians, for the most part, also believe we are entering into an era of great change, the view they hold of man's role in this transition differs greatly from that of the New Age. From the Christian standpoint, believers look for Christ to return and implement His righteous rule over the planet, thus guiding humanity into an era of true peace and harmony. In the New Age way of thinking, however, this transition is more dependent upon man's own will and *self*-determination.* The Christian's "problem," therefore, from a New Age

---

* New Age adherents generally do not openly repudiate Christianity. More subtle than that, they often clothe New Age concepts in Christian language, undermining Christianity while pretending to be its friend. A commonly used term is "Christ consciousness." The term Christ is thus not limited to any one individual, but relegated to a "spiritual experience" that can be attained by all. In other words, Christ is not a man, but an "office" (Cumbey, 146, 147).

perspective, is that in focusing on his "religious doctrines" and "antiquated teachings" about the respective roles of God and man, he is blinded to his *own* abilities. In other words, his inability to recognize his own divinity and power has stunted his spiritual growth and consequently his ability to advance to the "next level."

There is hope, however, New Ageists will tell you. This spiritual blindness can be overcome by the use of various techniques for unlocking the hidden (divine) potential within each of us. These include meditation, parapsychological experiences, such as telepathy, clairvoyance, and psychokinesis, and often the use of a wide range of psychedelics or hallucinogens.[6] The employment of psychedelics, like New Age thought itself, is not a new phenomenon, as shamans and mystics have since ancient times used consciousness-altering substances to open up pathways of communication to "spirits" or "ancestors" in other realms.

A LACK OF BIBLICAL PERSPECTIVE

As brought to light in the previous chapter, the vast majority who are exposed to the so-called Mayan prophecies are getting a severely limited reading of what is really a much larger story. In fact, most will never be introduced to the biblical perspective discussed here, as virtually all mainstream sources, including the various History Channel "Mayan-2012" documentaries, routinely ignore this aspect except for occasionally noting the supposed similarities (in the apocalyptic sense) between Mayan and biblical prophecy. We do, however, find from these same mainstream sources an abundance of speculation as to a possible "extraterrestrial," or "ET," connection. This notion, famously promoted by Erich von Däniken in his 1968 best seller, *Chariots of the Gods*, essentially rejects a literal interpretation of the Bible's account of fallen angels visiting the earth, instead proposing that the biblical record was simply man's best attempt at describing what was actually an ongoing incursion of

"aliens," or "astronauts," from other planets. Many in recent decades
have developed similar theories; one example being well-known
author Zecharia Sitchin, who postulates that these ancient astronauts
may have had a hand in genetically manipulating homo erectus
(man's supposed predecessor) into homo sapiens (modern man) using
their own extraterrestrial DNA.

THE PROPHETS OF A NEW AGE

Today, due to massive increase in UFO sightings, the resultant
broader public acceptance of the phenomenon, and the multiplying
influence of internet and radio shows like *Coast to Coast AM*, the
"ancient astronaut" theory is more popular than ever, especially
among those who reject the Bible, or who are predisposed to New
Age teachings.* Consequently, a cadre of mystics, teachers, and gurus
have garnered an ever-growing following to which they preach what
some have termed the alien, or "cosmic," gospel.

One of these so-called "prophets of the New Age" is author,
educator, and mystic, Jose Arguelles. Arguelles is credited with being
the first to introduce the date of December 21, 2012 to the
mainstream. Though he has been criticized as not being endorsed by
any authentic Mayan scholars, Arguelles has nonetheless been
instrumental in introducing Mayan lore to the modern-day New Age,
Metaphysical, and UFO movements. He has thus exposed untold
millions to the concept that current events reflect nothing less than
the fulfillment of Mayan prophecy, thereby downplaying the notion
that the fulfillment of Bible prophecy might be a factor.

Arguelles is currently the director of the *Noosphere II Project*,

---

* *Coast to Coast AM* is an extremely popular radio show that is broadcast nightly on
over five hundred United States affiliates, as well as numerous Canadian affiliates.
The show is also broadcast on XM Satellite Radio in the US.

established for the purpose of linking a network of organizations around the globe that will collectively promote a "positive shift of consciousness by 2012."[7]

Another 2012 guru of sorts is David Wilcock. In a 2009 interview with *Coast to Coast AM* radio host, George Noory, Wilcock cited a book by George Hunt Williamson entitled *Road in the Sky* (published 1958). Interestingly, the author of this book was said to be heavily involved in contacting "beings from outer space" via automatic writing, Ouija, and channeling. He believed that "space brothers" in the distant past had taught the human race the rudiments of civilization. He also apparently received Ouija-revelations to the effect that some ancient South, Central, and North American civilizations actually began as colonies of human-appearing extraterrestrials. Moreover, Williamson believed that spacemen had helped materially in the founding of the Jewish and Christian religions, impersonating "gods" and providing "miracles" when needed. The underlying theme to all of this being that aliens, or space brothers—not the God of the Bible—are the source of man's current existence and continuing evolution. Nonetheless, during this particular interview, Wilcock relates how *Road in the Sky* details several accounts of people receiving messages from extraterrestrials who warn of future interplanetary "climate change." Apparently, the ET's explained that this change would fulfill all of the ancient prophecies that speak of a coming golden age. Further commenting on the book, Wilcock says, "So they're [the extraterrestrials] not doom and gloom at all...I find it fascinating because if they tell you that the solar system is going to be doing this before it happens, and then you see the proof, then why would you be willing to discount what they say about what it's really going to do?" He then speculates that the "real" purpose of these extraterrestrials is to "promote our evolution and get us to the next level."

Wilcock's statements epitomize what many would describe as the current New Age co-opting of Bible prophecy, whereby "extraterrestrials" and their earthly spokesmen, like himself, in lieu of Scripture, provide the answers to what is *really* happening to the planet.[8, 9]

Yet another member of the New Age community who is heavily involved in promoting a shift of consciousness as we approach 2012 is popular author and speaker, Daniel Pinchbeck. Also featured in a recent *Coast to Coast AM* interview, Pinchbeck, a seemingly lucid and articulate proponent of using psychedelics to attain higher states of consciousness, spoke of what seems to have been an unsettling personal experience: Apparently, in 2004, while participating in a ceremony of the *Santo Daime*, a Brazilian religion that uses the psychedelic brew *ayahuasca* as its sacrament, he began to hear a "powerful voice" in his head that identified itself as "Quetzalcoatl." Over the course of a week, he purportedly continued to receive what he calls a kind of "prophetic transmission."* Though, interestingly, Pinchbeck relates that this was not an affirming or "self-aggrandizing" experience as one seeking the enrichment of one's spiritual beliefs might expect. He relates instead that it was as if this voice was merely "using him as a vessel of transmission to get [a] message out to the people." At one point during the interview, Noory, questioning Pinchbeck about the experience, asks, "Was this message difficult to translate...was it easy to understand?" Pinchbeck replies, "Well, it took some work, it was [more like] a ferocious experience. The voice was very powerful and brought up [some] karmic baggage in my own life, and what seemed to be memories of other past lives...In a way, it was almost somewhere between humbling and humiliating to suddenly find myself the vessel of some other form of consciousness."

It seems that "Quetzalcoatl," or whomever was actually behind the ferocious voice in Pinchbeck's head, was not the least concerned

---

* Mayan shamans used a number of methods to converse with the gods, including the use of various hallucinogens but also the occult practices of crystal, water, and mirror gazing. An integral aspect of communication with the gods was the "vision serpent." It is said that during Maya bloodletting rituals, participants would experience a vision in which they communicated with the "ancestors" or gods. These visions took the form of a giant serpent, which served as a gateway to the spirit realm.[12]

with the mental well-being of his vessel of transmission but focused squarely on getting "the message" out. Pinchbeck, apparently not willing to disappoint Quetzalcoatl, has proven an effective vessel indeed, via speaking engagements before large crowds as he promotes his 2007 book, entitled *2012: The Return of Quetzalcoatl*. The main theme of Pinchbeck's book is that humanity is in the final stages of a fundamental shift from a society based on materiality to one based on spirituality.[10, 11]

THE MESSAGE

So what is the ultimate aim of these prophets in their promotion of Mayan prophecy and a shift in consciousness as we near 2012? Obviously, as evidenced by the growing metaphysical section at the local Barnes & Noble, it is to educate, or, as Pinchbeck puts it, to simply "get a message out" to the people. This is being accomplished in large part by popular figures such as these, as well as other lesser-known proponents who claim, similar to the Mayan shamans, to be involved in ongoing contact with beings, or "extraterrestrials," from other realms.

The message of these beings: "Prepare for change. It is coming, on a grand scale—and soon."

UFOs AND THE NEW AGE: A PARTNERSHIP FORGED IN HELL?

As we are beginning to see, it is virtually impossible to discuss either the New Age Movement or the 2012 phenomenon in any depth without touching on the subject of so-called extraterrestrial contact, or "UFOs." So where is all of this leading, you may ask? Obviously, not to a comprehensive study of these topics, as this would take us too far afield from our main subject. Yet, in order to lay some important groundwork for what will later be discussed in this chapter, we do need to establish a couple of things: First, while many offhandedly dismiss or simply ignore the notion of UFOs or ETs, for those who have open-mindedly considered the ever-mounting evidence, it is not so much a question anymore as to whether or not they exist, but more or less a question of *who* they are and *where* they might be coming from. Significantly, this sentiment is not limited to "UFO enthusiasts" but has spread into the scientific community. In fact, in recent decades, many noted scientists and scholars have come to the conclusion that UFOs are indeed "real." Underscoring this, in *The Omega Conspiracy*, Thomas quotes a leading scientific specialist at the University of California as saying, "I know of no scientist who has become professionally involved with UFO investigation who doesn't believe in the extraterrestrial phenomena" (Thomas, 33). One of these scientists was the late Dr. J. Allen Hynek, former chairman of the Astronomy Department of North Western University and a previously avowed skeptic, who more than two decades ago stated, "There is sufficient evidence to suggest that we are not alone" (28).

The overwhelming majority of the American public—about seventy percent—agrees.* What is more, most believe that these strange craft, often sighted by witnesses with rock solid credentials, including Astronomers, Astronauts, Cosmonauts, Air traffic controllers, Government officials, Doctors, Police, Military personnel, and Radar operators, are most likely guided by "intelligent beings" from other worlds or dimensions.[13]

Many UFO sightings have been experienced by dozens, hundreds, or even thousands of people simultaneously; the descriptions of these sightings, given by various reliable independent sources, almost always agree on an overwhelmingly large percentage of facts and details. Recent examples include the widely covered 2008 Stephenville, Texas mass sighting and also the legendary Hudson Valley sightings wherein literally thousands of witnesses observed boomerang-shaped

---

* According to the United Nations, since 1947 approximately 150 million people have sighted UFOs throughout the world. This, in spite of the fact that, as well-known author on UFO topics, Jacques Vallee, notes, it is estimated that only one in ten witnesses come forward to report a sighting (Vallee, 18).

craft, or crafts, moving silently through the sky over New York and Connecticut between 1982 and 1995.

One of the most stunning mass sightings in recent years is known as the "Phoenix Lights" incident, which occurred in March of 1997 over the course of several hours and a span of about three hundred miles, from the Nevada line, through Phoenix, to the edge of Tucson. That evening, thousands of witnesses reported seeing an extremely low-flying "v-shaped" or "carpenter-square-like" craft that was by many accounts a mile or more wide, yet "completely silent" and travelling so slowly that it almost appeared to be hovering. Many witnesses noted that it was flanked with amber colored lights that strangely threw no glare but appeared to the eye as "canisters of swimming light." One witness was then Arizona Governor, pilot, and former Air Force Officer, Fife Symington who was quoted as saying, "I'm a pilot and I know just about every machine that flies. It was bigger than anything I've ever seen…It was enormous and inexplicable…And it couldn't have been flares because it was too symmetrical. It had a geometric outline, a constant shape." Later, in a CNN interview, he added, "It just felt otherwordly…In your gut you could tell it was otherworldly."[14]

Ian Mclennan puts it in perspective when he says "Hundreds of thousands of people cannot make independent observations of the same optical phenomenon over thousands of square miles under a fantastic dose of mass hysteria" (30). Indeed, while a percentage of UFO sightings might be dismissed as fakes, as naturally occurring phenomena, or as perhaps a secret government program, too many cannot. Thus, the growing consensus: Something very strange and unexplainable is going on in the skies over planet Earth and—as revealed in the historical record—has been for a very long time. From the earliest civilizations, such as the Sumerians, whose "gods" came from heaven to earth in "winged discs," to Alexander the Great's run in with "two great silver shields" that repeatedly dove at his army, panicking the men and animals in 329 BC, to the mysterious lights that appeared "in sudden and passing gleams" to Christopher Columbus and Pedro Gutierrez in 1492, just hours before discovering land. The accounts are simply too widespread, too similar, and too numerous to be discounted.

The second and more simple to make point in regard to UFOs is that modern man, it seems, is no closer to understanding this phenomenon than the Sumerians, Alexander's troops, or Columbus. In fact, perhaps even less so: While the ancients typically thought them to be gods, we in modern times assume them to be highly advanced visitors from other worlds. The problem with this theory, however, is that the possibility of a planet existing in proximity to allow for this type of travel, even at the speed of light, has all but been completely discredited as *physically impossible.*

For this reason and others, such as the often noted peculiar behavior of these craft and their presumably "alien" occupants, another theory has emerged in recent decades. This theory tends toward a belief that these craft and their pilots may actually hail from an unseen, perhaps parallel, dimension, or dimensions.*

Taking this "other-dimensional" concept a step further, some observers have developed a further hypothesis concerning the true origins of these visitors. And many, who have held suspicions all along, have had these suspicions confirmed.

DEMONIC VISITORS?

Today, the notion that the UFO phenomenon is perhaps more *supernatural* rather than an "extraterrestrial" in nature is becoming increasingly popular. Many Christian authors and scholars, such as Chuck Missler, the aforementioned I.D.E Thomas, L.A. Marzulli,

---

* An intriguing feature of a concept called "string theory" (a developing branch of theoretical physics that combines quantum mechanics and general relativity into a quantum theory of gravity), involves the prediction of *extra dimensions.* Interestingly, a scientific article entitled "The Universe's Unseen Dimensions," released in August, 2000, postulates that we may before long have scientific proof of other dimensions.[15]

and Thomas Horn, among others, have written and spoken elo-
quently and convincingly on the topic. But even more significant,
many highly respected agnostic or *secular* scholars have reached similar conclusions. For instance, scientist and astronomer Dr. Jacques
Vallee, here citing the extensive research of Bertrand Meheust notes
that "The UFO beings of today belong to the same class of manifesta-
tion as the [occult] entities that were described in centuries past."[16] In
other words, Vallee, who has immersed himself in the topic since the
mid-sixties, equates the modern UFO and ET phenomenon with the
ancient legends of fairies, dwarves, elves—and demons. Moreover,
lending support to the notion that the phenomenon is indeed likely
other-dimensional rather that otherworldly, Vallee notes in his writings that "The UFO phenomenon represents evidence for other dimensions beyond space-time." This increasingly popular hypothesis,
again, holds that UFOs do not, in fact *could not*, come from outer
space but probably originate from what might be described as a "parallel reality."[17]*

Dr. Pierre Guerin, senior researcher at the French National
Council for Scientific Research (CNRS), holds a view similar to that
of Vallee's, noting that "UFO behavior is more akin to magic than to
physics as we know it."[18] Here, Guerin alludes to the fact that these
craft do not seem subject to the laws of physics as we understand
them. For instance, they have been observed to suddenly appear and
then to vanish virtually into thin air, to pass through solid objects, to
merge with one another and change shape dynamically, and to perform aerial maneuvers that are physically impossible, such as turning
and accelerating so fast that any *metal* spaceship, even if it were a
solid iron ball, would disintegrate (Vallee, 144). Only adding to this
strangeness, these craft have also been observed emerging from and
descending into water, where they travel with the same ease.

Based on these observations, as well as the full body of his research in the field of UFOs, Guerin, like Vallee, comes to the ulti-

---

* Christians might refer to a dimension beyond space-time as the "spirit realm."

mate conclusion that "The modern UFOnauts and the demons of past days are probably identical."[19]

"IF IT WALKS LIKE A DUCK AND QUACKS LIKE A DUCK..."

So what, then, aside from the apparently physics-defying behavior of these alien craft, has caused these secular experts to equate the UFO phenomenon with the ancient legends of the supernatural, the spiritual, and ultimately the demonic? The justification for such a point of view is actually overwhelming, so much so that we cannot explore it to its fullness here. For the purpose of illustration, however, let us touch on the basics: To begin with, there are the countless testimonies of reliable witnesses who claim contact with the "pilots" of these UFOs. While a few report that the creatures behaved shyly or in some cases in a seemingly friendly manner, even waving or beckoning to them on certain occasions, many more report frightening, aggressive, taunting, or even "animalistic" behavior. One instance of this, which happens to be one of the most well-known and well-documented cases in the history of UFO incidents, unfolded in Hopkinsville, Kentucky in 1955. What began with the sighting of strange lights in the sky ended with two families being harassed and terrorized over the course of many hours by an unknown number of "gremlin like" beings who approached the farmhouse they were occupying. Though the creatures purportedly never attempted to enter the house, witnesses said they would pop up in the windows and at the doorway, working the children into a hysterical frenzy. This was interpreted by some at the time as persistence on the part of these beings in instigating fear and panic. Eventually, the families fled to the local police station and returned with twenty officers who also reported seeing and hearing strange lights and sounds. Later speculation among those involved as to the motives of the creatures ranged from field study, to curiosity, to outright malevolence.[20]

Still other seemingly sinister distinctives are brought to light as one thumbs through the voluminous files of recorded encounters with extraterrestrial beings. For instance, it seems the ETs "prefer darkness, and lonely, or isolated, places; they have, oddly enough, been known to advocate drug use (particularly LSD or hallucinogens), as well as pre-marital sex, violence, and even racism.* They have also been known to carry strange devices, or "weapons," which they use to "paralyze" or immobilize their victims. Moreover, they are often described by witnesses as being accompanied by an unpleasant odor that is said to be irritating, or nauseating, "like the inside of an old tennis shoe," or even "sulphur like" (143-145). In addition to these characteristics, which would seem to be at variance with a supposedly highly advanced or enlightened race of beings, we have the remarkably consistent *physical* descriptions of these entities, which uncannily parallel the traditional descriptions of demons: large heads, narrow, pointed chins, slit-like mouths, huge almond-shaped or slanted eyes and even claws or talon-like appendages!

Lastly, and perhaps most tellingly, UFO beings have been known to use biblical terms and references, and have purportedly shown a marked interest in what Christians refer to as the "end times." Some even bring up Jesus Christ, or God, in conversation (140-142). One incredible example of this is the testimony of long-time UFO contactee, Jim Sparks. In a recent *Exopolitics* interview, he explains how at one point he was so overcome with anger stemming from his ongoing *involuntary* contact with the ETs that he unleashed in an unrelenting barrage of obscenities until one of the beings walked up to him,

---

* In regard to promoting violence, in *Messengers of Deception*, Vallee notes how one alien contactee was instructed by a "voice from space" to kill a newsman who had written several books on UFOs (Vallee, 59). Concerning "racism," the author notes an extraterrestrial inspired version whereby the ETs promulgate the notion that "some" of us on Earth are of extraterrestrial descent and therefore constitute a "higher race." In light of this, it is interesting to note that one "race" of ETs are consistently described as tall "Aryan" types with blue eyes and long blonde hair (112).

looked him in the face, and said (telepathically), "Your behavior is
not pleasing to God." Sparks relates that this made him even madder,
and so responded, "No way are you guys connected to God!" The being, according to Sparks, replied in a decidedly unemotional manner
with two simple words: "We're demons." Sparks, apparently uncon-
vinced that demons would be caught flying around in "UFOs," went
on to relate to the radio host how he cynically rejected this response,
reasoning that it was some type of "copout" or an attempt at evasive-
ness on the part of the ETs.[21]*

In addition to all of the above, as if these indicators were not
enough to set off the internal alarms of any objective observer, some
of these "alien" beings appear to be involved in much more than just
performing miraculous maneuvers in their physics-defying craft, or
engaging unwitting earthlings in some playful scaring or harassment.
Sometimes they invite humans aboard these craft with what are described by many to be sinister intentions.

THE ABDUCTION PHENOMENON

Today, even those unfamiliar with the UFO phenomenon have
almost certainly heard the term "alien abduction." Alien abduction is
an expression coined to describe an experience in which an individual
is taken aboard an alien spaceship for a time and "examined," among
other things, presumably by beings from another planet.

Interestingly, in looking at the historical record, we find that, like
the UFO phenomenon itself, similar types of abductions have been
occurring since ancient times. In centuries past, as frequently noted
by Vallee and others, people believed they were taken by faeries,

---

* Logic would seem to dictate that one of two things is going on here: Either these
"ETs" who are largely described as being humorless and emotionless, were only
"kidding around" with Sparks, or perhaps (assuming them to be demons), faced
with a victim who they *knew* would reject the notion, they chose to be uncharacter-
istically forthcoming about their true identities.

dwarves, and elves. Faeries, in fact, were said to have abducted new-born children from pregnant women in order to raise them as their own. In the middle ages, a great number of people were being abducted by airships believed to be piloted by powerful magicians from the mythological "Magonia land, far away and beyond the horizon."[*] In modern times, however, it seems that space aliens have taken over the task of kidnapping humans.

The earliest widely publicized case of so-called alien abduction is that of Barney and Betty Hill, who in September of 1961 reported that they had been taken from their car while stopped on a dark road in New Hampshire. Since this time, alien abduction seems to have burgeoned from a relatively unheard of, or *unspoken of*, happening, to one that has become an integral part of our popular culture. Whether the abductions are actually increasing or if, due to increasing exposure, they are merely perceived to be, is unknown. Yet it seems that this generation more than any other has been targeted. In fact, a decade-old Roper Poll noted that nearly five million Americans have had certain "indicator" experiences of the abduction phenomenon. Thus, it is believed that at least three to four million in the U.S. alone may have been "taken" at some point (Jacobs, 123).

EVIDENCE OF ABDUCTION?

Though many remain skeptical of abductees' claims, investigators note that there is often both subtle and robust physical evidence that corroborates their stories, including bruising, redness, "surgical scars," and strange circular or triangular markings on the skin. Some *multiple*

---

[*] Vallee notes that "It is difficult to find a culture that does *not* have a tradition of little people that fly through the sky and abduct humans. Often they take their victims into spherical settings that are evenly illuminated and...subject them to various ordeals." He further adds that "sexual or genetic interaction is a common theme in this body of folklore" (144).

abduction cases have inexplicably turned up separate victims who have somehow received identical markings.

Perhaps the most compelling evidence for the reality of the phenomenon, though, is the utterly life-altering effect it has on the abductee. Susan A. Clancy, a skeptic at Harvard Medical School who studies abductees' psychology, has notably observed that "all of the subjects, without exception, said they felt 'changed' because of their experiences...Abductees have said, it 'enlarged my world view,' or 'expanded my reality.'" Being abducted by aliens, Clancy concludes, is inarguably a "transformative event."[22]

According to the vast majority of case studies, however, the type of transformation that manifests in the life of the abductee is not of a positive nature. In fact, many previously normal, productive, and often exceptional individuals have had their lives transformed for the worse, suffering from recurring nightmares, depression, a sense of humiliation and loss of control, obsessive thoughts, paranoia, posttraumatic stress and, consequently, the breakdowns of relationships and marriages.

A TYPICAL EXPERIENCE

It is significant that, although experienced by people from all walks of life who live at all points around the globe, the common elements of the abduction experience, as well as the descriptions of the aliens themselves, are extremely uniform. In a typical abduction, the victim usually reports a sense of anxiousness or foreboding that "something" is about to occur. Eventually, the experiencer will undergo an apparent "shift" into an altered state of consciousness in which they are rendered docile and thus incapable of resistance. They often liken this to having every part of their body "completely paralyzed," except for, in most cases, their eyes. Often a strange and powerful light, or lights, will appear. Most describe it as "bluish white" and "intense," emanating from a source outside of their window. Others claim that the lights are in the room with them and then transform into "alien" figures.[23]

These figures, often described as tiny grey beings with large heads and enormous black almond-shaped eyes, are said to communicate telepathically with each other and with the victim as they remove him or her from their earthly surrounds.*

The victim is then taken aboard a "craft" where their clothes are removed and they are made to lie on a table. Here, a series of frightful physical, mental, and reproductive procedures are performed in which the body is probed and examined. Most often, sperm is taken, or eggs harvested. The procedures are also frequently said to involve the taking of skin samples and sometimes the insertion of extremely long needles into the nasal passages or, in the case of women, the navel.[24, †]

Some victims even claim that "implants" are inserted under the skin.

Oddly enough, at no time are these "alien examiners" said to wear any type of protective gloves or mask as one might expect of a highly advanced race of beings involved in performing medical procedures. Moreover, it is noted that in most all cases the examiners lack any type of "bedside manner," routinely displaying a cold, callous disregard toward the examinee.[25]

In addition to all of this, the aliens are said to perform "staring procedures" which consist of gazing into the abductees' eyes at a dis-

---

* Significantly, experiencers of "NDEs" ("near death" or "out of body" experiences) relate that communication with other beings is "telepathic" in nature. Vallee actually compares the entire experience of abduction to that of the near-death experience, noting that "the UFO phenomenon is able to act upon the minds of human beings, to induce thoughts and images that are similar to those described by people who have had near-death or out-of-body experiences and even to medieval witnesses of demons and elves" (152).

† Betty Hill reported that during her abduction an extremely long needle was inserted into her navel. Interestingly, a fifteenth century French calendar, the Kalendrier desbergiers, shows tortures inflicted by demons on the people they have taken. The demons are depicted piercing their victims' abdomens with long needles.

tance of only an inch or two. This procedure, victims claim, is some type of neurological manipulation that enables the alien to "enter into" one's mind.[26]

After the above "table procedures" are completed, many abductees report that they are taken into another room; here, some are shown "visions," which are sometimes presented on a screen and at others said to be projected into one's mind. These visions commonly consist of scenes of nuclear war or environmental calamities that are understood to take place in the future.[27]

In some instances, abductees report that they are required to perform tasks, or that they are "tested" in some way, sometimes by strange machines, apparently designed for this purpose.

Additionally, many abductees say they are required to have skin-on-skin contact with "unusual looking" babies, further relating that these babies seem to be a cross between humans and aliens.[*] These strange beings are popularly termed as "hybrids." Abductees also report seeing hybrid toddlers, older youth, adolescents, and adults. Even more disturbing, some claim to have been coerced into having various forms of sexual intercourse with these hybrids.[28]

Victims often relate that at some point during the course of the experience the aliens will apologize for the cruel treatment given them during the initial kidnapping and "examination" phase.[†] They will sometimes even explain their motives to the captive, or reveal why

---

[*] David M. Jacobs, PhD, Associate Professor of History at Temple University believes that the "reproductive procedures" and subsequent appearance of "hybrids" lies at the heart of the "alien agenda." This is interesting in light of the fact that the original incursion of fallen angels essentially involved the same type of program— the creation of human-angelic hybrids.

[†] Vallee notes that "The 'medical examination' to which abductees are said to be subjected, often accompanied by sadistic sexual manipulation, is [also] reminiscent of the medieval tales of encounters with demons. It makes no sense in a sophisticated or technical framework: any intelligent being equipped with the scientific marvels that UFOs possess would be in a position to achieve any of these alleged scientific objectives in a shorter time and with fewer risks" (13).

they were "chosen." Still, it seems the beings are often reluctant to disclose certain details, especially regarding their origins. For instance, one abductee related that when he asked them (the aliens) where they were from they gave the decidedly enigmatic answer: "Nowhere and everywhere." Thus, some abductees feel that their captors are being, at the least, evasive, or, at the most, dishonest or deceptive.

Curiously, as was noted earlier, the aliens will now and again weigh in on spiritual matters, sometimes referencing prophesied calamitous events and even broaching such heady topics as the nature of God. In this arena, they seem to share a view startlingly similar to that espoused by proponents of the New Age, such as belief in an impersonal God; endless improvement in the hereafter (read reincarnation); men are not lost sinners in need of divine mercy (as the Bible teaches); and, further, that Christ was only divine in the sense that *all* men are divine (Thomas, 142).

Finally, at the conclusion of what is often characterized as an intermittently wondrous, albeit largely terrifying, experience, the abductee is apparently returned to their normal environment and within seconds forgets what has just happened—noting only that, upon checking a timepiece, they are "missing" a significant amount of time.[29]

In most cases, the memory of the abduction is later triggered by some particular event or circumstance. Some subsequently pursue a more complete recall of the encounter via hypnosis or regression therapy.

IS THE ABDUCTION PHENOMENON REAL?

While the alien abduction phenomenon has been dismissed by some mainstream psychologists as "sleep paralysis," virtually every doctor or scholar who has studied the phenomena in depth—many avowed skeptics—later became convinced otherwise. For instance, Pulitzer Prize Winning author and former head of Harvard's Psychi-

atric Division, the late Dr. John E. Mack delved into the alien abduction issue almost twenty years ago to prove it was the product of some
type of mental illness. After digging into the facts, however, and con-
ducting a comprehensive scientific investigation that lasted over a
decade and involved some two hundred test subjects, he completely
changed his view. Mack was later quoted by the BBC as saying, "I
would never say, yes, there are aliens taking people. [But] I would say
there is a compelling powerful phenomenon here that I can't account
for in any other way…I can't know what it is, but it seems to me that
it invites a deeper, further inquiry."[30]

Mack, who had spent many years exploring how one's perception
of the world affects one's relationships, subsequently developed a
keen interest in the spiritual or transformational aspects of the
abductees' encounters and suggested that the experience of alien
contact itself may, in fact, be more *spiritual* than physical in nature—
yet nonetheless "real." He also noted, similar to Vallee and others
who cite legends of dwarves and faeries, that there is a worldwide
history of this type of visionary or spiritual experience; one example
being the "vision quest" phenomenon common to some Native
American cultures. Only fairly recently in Western culture, noted
Mack, have such visionary events been interpreted as aberrations, or
as mental illness.[31, *]

Though Mack, to this author's knowledge, did not entertain the
possibility of a demonic aspect to abduction, it is interesting to note
that his characterization of the phenomenon being "more *spiritual*
[rather] than physical in nature" parallels the view of our previously
noted scholars as well as yet another significant researcher, Lynn E.
Catoe, who, after preparing a comprehensive compilation of UFO

---

* Because of his foray into "alien abduction," in 1994 Mack became the focus of an
investigation ordered by the Dean of Harvard Medical School. In view of this, it is
telling that a highly esteemed scholar such as Mack felt strongly enough about the
"reality" of the abduction experiences to put his career as a tenured professor on the
line in order to investigate a topic that is to this day considered taboo in academic
circles.

data for the Air Force Office of Scientific Research in 1969, concluded the following:

> "A large part of the available UFO literature is closely linked with mysticism and the metaphysical. It deals with subjects like mental telepathy, automatic writing and invisible entities as well as phenomena like poltergeist [ghost] manifestation and 'possession.' Many of the UFO reports now being published in the popular press recount alleged incidents that are *strikingly similar to demonic possession* and psychic phenomena."[32]

Thus, it seems Catoe, as well as others who are willing to go where the evidence leads, are more and more associating UFOs and ETs with supernatural or psychic phenomena—particularly and most interestingly—demonic possession.

...AND THIS RELATES TO THE SECOND COMING *HOW?*

Having spent the last dozen or so pages establishing the link between the UFO/alien abduction phenomenon and the demonic— even "demonic possession" as it were—a legitimate question might be *why* have we established this connection? In other words, what might this type of activity have to do with the timing of Christ's return?

A CHANCE DISCOVERY

During the course of researching this book many web searches were performed on the year "2015," which, of course, yielded a multitude of results; these included global financial forecasts, weather trends, and budget projections for various organizations, among others. Among these completely irrelevant results, however, surfaced two very well-documented and highly compelling cases of alien abduction. Notably, each of these cases fit the profile of the commonly related abductee narrative as discussed earlier in that, among other things, both abductees were shown "apocalyptic" visions of things to come. The element that stood out about these particular cases, though, and which led to a deeper investigation is the fact that, independent of one another, each of the noted abductees was given by his abductors a *timeframe* in which these visions were to become a reality. That timeframe—as you may have already surmised—is the year 2015.

Needless to say, I found this very intriguing, and in light of the timeframes we have discussed in this book, determined to include these testimonies. Having done so, however, I must make something absolutely clear at the outset: This information is included only with an *italicized* and "ALL CAPS" qualifier attached, which reads, *while all of this is fascinating to consider and MAY shed some additional light, this type of testimony is NOT to be regarded as necessarily reliable.* The obvious reason being that we are essentially relying on two non-biblical sources: the "alien" (likely demonic) abductor who presumably supplied the future "vision" and the abductee who has relayed the information. Thus, anything gleaned from these testimonies should be filed under "interesting possibilities" that seem to corroborate the overall thesis laid out in this book—but for now, perhaps nothing more than that.

RELIABLE WITNESSES?

Again, considering the "alien" source, skepticism is always appropriate. In the case of the individual abductees involved, however, while skepticism is also highly appropriate, I want to emphasize here that both come across as highly credible, having clearly gone to great lengths in documenting their respective experiences. Thus, both present themselves as exceedingly genuine in their conviction that they have indeed been "abducted" by aliens. This sincerity seems further bolstered by the simple fact that each claims to have been shown events in "2015" and beyond. The reason we find this significant is that 2015 has not heretofore been considered a year of note among the "apocalyptic" community, such as we find with the ever-hyped date of 2012. Of course, on the flip side, the fact that these abductees *have* identified 2015 of all possible years seems to raise the question (in light of Mark Biltz's recent discovery), might they have somehow become aware of the "blood moon" tetrads in 2014-15 and been influenced? This, however, seems unlikely, if not impossible, as their actual "abductions" and even their relatively recent postings describing them were recorded well before Biltz's discovery.

As for the topic of Bible prophecy in general, it is also noteworthy that neither abductee appears to have had any prior interest in the subject. In fact, one made his disdain for any "religious talk" clear in one of his postings. The other seems to take a somewhat "New Age" view in terms of the Bible, suggesting, after apparently being enlightened by the aliens concerning their earlier involvement in human affairs, that our "Genesis story of Adam and Eve is [merely] a metaphor" intended to explain how "knowledge that should have belonged to *all* men was kept secret."

As an interesting aside, some researchers who have sought to create a profile of the typical abductee note that virtually all victims, without exception, have had some prior connection to occult or metaphysical activity. This includes interest in Eastern religion, or a New Age world view, or involvement in psychic, meditation, or consciousness-altering practices, including channeling, Ouija, or the use of hallucinogens. Equally as interesting, some Christian researchers have noted that very few if any "born again Christians" appear to have been targeted for abduction by these aliens. Some even submit that attempted abductions have been thwarted by invoking the name of Jesus Christ. Thus, it seems those involved in direct contact with aliens or UFOs are not typically of a resolutely Christian mindset and have also most likely, either knowingly or unknowingly, previously opened doors to the dark side of the supernatural world.[33]

These things noted, let us take a look at these two fascinating accounts.

MEET THE ABDUCTEES

Our first abductee story comes from a thirty-one year old male who lives in Northern England. He has two children, a girlfriend, and is a staff trainer for a fairly large mail order company. He describes himself and his motives for posting his story thusly:

"I am a pretty down to earth fellow, I try to remain objective and take everything I hear with a pinch of salt...I am not trying to convince anyone of the reality of my own experiences...I have built this [web] site with other abductees in mind, to share my own methods of dealing with these experiences and to share and compare my experiences with other abductees."[34]

This individual, who chooses to remain anonymous, claims that his first alien encounter occurred when he was about four years old. At this time, he says, he was confronted with what is referred to as the classic "Grey" alien, described earlier as having a small spindly body, a large head, and massive black almond shaped eyes. He recalls the event:

"I remember waking up in the middle of the night and having weird conversations with myself, I think in hindsight that I was actually conversing with the creature that I was about to see...I got out of bed and walked to my window and opened my curtains. When I look out I saw a pair of feet directly in front of my face, I then followed them up with my eyes and was confronted with my first full image of a Grey. At the time I believed that the almond shaped eyes almost certainly denoted the creature as evil or angry, so I reacted with abject terror. I don't remember any more of that encounter, but I am sure that prior to my confrontation with the creature, that I was actually having a conversation with it, in which it was persuading me to come to the window to meet the spaceman, who had come to visit me."[35]

The abductee goes on to detail numerous other abduction experiences that he has been able to recall, with and without the aid of hypnotic regression. The most intriguing, however, with regard to the thesis set forth here, is the following experience wherein he is shown a vision of the future:

"This is a recent memory…I remember standing in a room after being laid on a medical bench, I was with two hooded beings and a stereotypical Grey.

I believe that the hooded Grey is female and the hooded brown fellow is male. I remember talking with them for a while after which they showed be an Apocalyptic image which seemed both three dimensional and yet cast upon the room's wall.

The illusion was so great that I really felt that I had been transported to an external location, I could feel the wind in my hair and smell the acrid smoke of the fires around me.

I don't remember very much about the encounter above, but I will go into as much detail as I can. Quite often my memories of my encounters with the visitors go from hazy to clear to complete black outs. I believe that the visitors are able to manipulate my recall to such a degree that they are able to allow me to remember specific conversations or images, but nothing else of these encounters…I remember that they had just done some kind of medical procedure on me, I don't remember what it was. I don't remember being taken from my room or being lifted up to the ship or wherever it was, the memory just starts with me sitting up on a bench. As is usually the case I was completely naked...I remember that the brown fellow was saying something to me, but for the life of me I cannot remember what it was. I saw a TV size image appear on or just above the surface of the wall in front of me. I remember that I was getting an explanation of what I was seeing from both the brown fellow and the grey lady. The image was an area of land near to my home. As I watched, the image grew larger and larger. If anyone remembers when Cinemas had curtains the experience was similar to the moment when the curtains open, while the projector is running; the growth of the image was about as quick and smooth as that. After a short while I noticed that the ground just in front of me seemed to be part of the image, complete with grass and dirt. I remember that I stepped onto the grass just to see whether my feet would go through the image, but to my surprise the illusion was completely solid. I don't know whether this was a holographic effect or whether my senses were being manipulated by the psychic presence of the entities around me. I suspect that it was 50/50 of both.

As I watched I remember being told that I was seeing a span of a small number of years unfold in front of me over the span of a couple of seconds. This wasn't like time lapse, it was more as if the image was morphing. I saw the low lands toward Manchester become completely flooded and the sky became almost completely black with thick clouds of smoke. I remember asking things like, has there been a nuclear war and is this as bad as it gets and how far is this? I remember that the beings did not think that there would be an exchange of nuclear arms in our future, which I found very relieving. I think that I was told that this was ten years into our future, which would put the year around 2015, but

I also remember that 2020 is also supposed to be an eventful year. I remember asking how bad will it be for humanity and what are the contributing factors to this scenario. I was told that the sea level will rise very suddenly sometime over the next decade. There will also be a huge tectonic shift, which will be more due to the changes in the way the ocean mass is distributed over the tectonic plates than the changing mass of the ice at the Earth's poles. The smoke is due to the huge amount of volcanic activity, but also the waters will become extremely polluted by the deep ocean volcanic eruptions. The flood waters will have radioactive contamination from the radioactive materials that will become submerged, that were held within the world's power stations, nuclear weapons sites, plutonium mines and factories. These sites will be very localized but the long term effects will be devastating.

I was told that our government, (I don't know whether this is the US, British or worldwide) has been given this exact information, but they have chosen to ignore it. They also said that it is never too late for them to act, but the later we leave it the more lives will be lost. I don't know whether they are talking about taking global warming seriously or whether they want our governments to request contact somehow. I do know that the future that they showed me is an incredibly dark one. The survivors will have to brave terrible air pollution, a huge loss of land mass and near starvation. I got the feeling that there is an alternative, but they never go as far to explain what it is. I don't remember how the encounter ended and as time has passed since this encounter more information has presented itself, but as I said before I believe that the visitors are extremely skilled at editing my memories of these events, so perhaps as the time comes closer I am being allowed to see deeper into the meaning of these messages."[36]

Obviously, the overriding theme of this abductee's account centers on what seems to be a major environmental calamity—but not just any calamity; he explicitly describes increased volcanic activity, a sudden rise in sea level, and a huge tectonic shift due to a redistribution of ocean mass. In considering his characterization of the calamity, it is interesting to note that while it seems to be in agreement with the overwhelmingly popular message voiced by climatologists, namely the belief that the planet is going to experience a drastic rise in sea level, it is in fact at odds with the popularly cited *cause* for this future calamity, which would be *the melting of ice at the poles.* The abductee instead offers a completely novel explanation, relating how he was shown that, more so than any melting of polar ice, tectonic shift is the primary culprit. This description, interestingly enough, corresponds precisely with what some experts predict in the event of an actual *polar shift.* We, of course, find the notion of polar shift interesting because, as alluded to in the previous chapter, many believe that Isaiah predicts just such an event during the time of God's wrath.

Speculating further, it is strange that even the timeframe he describes—2015-20—would seem to fit the roughly sketched scenario discussed earlier, which points to a possible resurrection or rapture around 2015, to be followed by the time of God's wrath over the course of subsequent (perhaps seven) years.

It is also interesting to consider the aliens' motives for showing this individual, along with so many others, these dark visions of the future. The abductee speculates that it may stem from their desire that man play a proactive role in saving the planet, perhaps even by requesting "contact" or assistance from the aliens. To this point, it is noteworthy that many who propose that aliens are, in fact, the same demons of the Bible suggest that their ability to intervene in earthly affairs is somehow contingent on man's overall state of consciousness. In other words, demons are ultimately subject to man's God-given freewill. The more accepting or *open* an individual or, in this case, *humanity* is toward the ETs, the more latitude they have to interact.

This might explain the overarching emphasis in New Age circles on the need for a "shift in consciousness."

Our second abductee story comes from a forty-one year old male who also prefers to remain anonymous. In one of his postings, he justifies his anonymity by likening himself to a victim of rape, which is actually a common sentiment among abductees.

This individual has been interviewed several times, mostly, it appears, on obscure UFO-themed radio shows. He has written a synopsis of his experience that is posted on his personal page at a popular social networking website and has also posted a series of very compelling videos on a heavily trafficked video-sharing site.

It is noteworthy that throughout all of the various tellings of his story (interviews, written accounts, and videos) he remains utterly consistent. There seems to be no element of hoax or contrivance in his presentation or demeanor. Moreover, this abductee seems not to be seeking any type of notoriety or financial gain. In fact, for the reasons noted above, he has gone so far as to disguise his voice and mask his appearance, when needed, to maintain his anonymity. Also, like our first abductee, this individual seems unconcerned with trying to convince anyone of the *reality* of his encounter. Thus, he seems more or less motivated by a need to share what he has been shown and to connect with others who may have had the same experience.

He describes his encounter, which took place over twenty years ago:

> "I will try to cut most [of the] details out and get to the main story. It was 1988. I usually would be asleep by 8:00 pm nightly. I had to be at work by 5:30 am every morning so I made sure to get my sleep. Anyway. One night I was awoken by a bunch of dogs barking loudly. I was very confused when I woke up because I wasn't in my bed when I woke up. I was actually in the middle of my street walking. I found out the dogs were barking at me.
>
> At this time I realized that I had no control of myself.

All I could move were my eyes. The next thing I remember was I was walking to this wooded bike trail area near my home. As I crossed a little bridge I knelt down on one knee. With two hands on my bent knee I peeked through some trees and bushes and saw a craft of some type. It was ball shaped, no lights, and landed under these huge power lines. I never saw the craft from the outside fly. As I looked at the craft an opening opened up and two [beings] smaller than me came out of the craft.

The next thing I remember was that I was boarding the craft. As I walked onto the craft the two beings followed me in the craft. The craft was kind of cramped and dark. It was dark but you could see like a neon kind of darkness. I then bent down and asked the being where we are going. They answered me and said they are taking me behind the moon. I then asked why? They said they couldn't be detected on earth's radar from there. I said okay, then we took off. I looked out of some kind of window type thing and saw us leaving the earth. We passed the moon then made a u-turn type of turn back. This took less than 10 seconds. For some reason I wasn't scared at all. I actually acted like I knew them. The next thing I recall was the only time I was really scared. I woke up again, this time naked in a funnel-shaped pool filled with a greenish black gel type liquid. The pool had to be 20 yards wide all around. And pretty deep. The pool was made of some kind of shiny metal. With the gel it made the surface very slippery and you would slip under the gel if you tried to get out. I then realized something very odd at that time. I wasn't alone. There were at least 15 other humans with me. All of them screaming and panicking. This is what scared me. I didn't know what they were screaming about. I thought they knew something I didn't, so I got scared. Some were under the gel moving around I could see. Most were trying to escape. One man kept climbing half way out. The closer he got to the top he would get hit by some sort of beam then he'd slide back into the pool. I thought this guy was insane, if he did get out where would he go?

I didn't see who was telling me but they where telling me not to be scared. They told me I would be fine and that I could breathe the gel. They said I could eat it and digest it. I couldn't drown in it. We could live in the gel. It also recycled human waste back into the gel.

I believed some of the humans were in the pool for years by the way they were acting. I figured a way to be under the gel and still breathe air. That way they wouldn't hit me with the beam and make me slide under. I blacked out after that. The next things I remember are some pretty vivid memories. I must let you know that I am deathly frightened of frogs. I know it sounds crazy but it's my one phobia. It's their skin.[*]

Back to the story: I was rudely awakened by a being, armpit high [to me], holding my hand, taking me somewhere. I remember the touch of their hands it's [what] woke me up from whatever I was under. I tugged away and started to threaten them. I clenched my fist like I was going to fight. I said, get away from me, and if they touched me again I was going to hit them. He told me if I would do that I would change the world as we know it. I knew if I hit them in the head my fist would go right through them. I didn't like the feel of their skin and I thought I sure wouldn't want its brains all over me. So I was kind of stuck

---

[*] In reference to these aliens reminding him of "frogs," it is interesting to note the following verse from Revelation: "Then I saw three evil spirits that looked like frogs; they came out of the mouth of the dragon, out of the mouth of the beast and out of the mouth of the false prophet. They are spirits of demons performing miraculous signs, and they go out to the kings of the whole world, to gather them for the battle on the great day of God Almighty" (Revelation 16:13, 14).

in defending myself or making a huge nasty mess all over
me. That's when I realized that I was communicating to
them without my mouth. I knew what they were thinking
and they knew what I was thinking. It made things difficult
for me at first. That's when the smaller beings brought over
this taller being, a little taller than me. As the taller being
approached me, he told the smaller being that this is a
'prophet.'*

I looked at his face for maybe half a second. His face
grossed me out so I never looked at him again. If I looked at
him again then he'd know how I felt about his appearance. I
didn't want to offend him because I liked this one, he made
me feel comfortable.

He explained that they wanted to do some medical ex-
aminations on me and if I would cooperate. I made a deal
with him if they didn't touch me, hurt me, or scare me then
I would do it. He promised, then I allowed them to do what
they wanted. He also said he would answer all my questions
that [I] asked. He walked me around as we talked. I looked
at the ground the entire time so [as] not to look at him. The
next thing I remember was the medical examination:

First thing that I remember was coming out of a blackout lying on a table. I was not scared whatsoever. I trusted
them. And by being able to read their minds I know they
weren't lying to me. As I remember, they took some skin
from my right arm. It was like the thinnest layer possible.
Invisible to my eyes, but all they needed. Next they took
semen from me. I didn't understand this. Again I won't go
into too much detail simply because this story would be
about nine hundred pages long. I asked about this procedure later. The last thing they did to me was the strangest of
all. They took my right eye out of my head. I actually saw

---

* It is interesting that these purportedly highly advanced space beings use the biblical term, "prophet" for this abductee.

the back of my eyeball and a cord or veins connected to it. I instantly asked about this. Next they put a baby like metal ball in my eye socket. About the size of a broken piece of rice. I asked, "What's that for?" They said so they can monitor me from space. I thought it was so they could see everything that I can see, like a video camera or something. Then they put my eye back in, then that was that. My next memories were the taller being [and I] talking...This was the best part because he answered my questions and showed me things in my head.

I don't know the exact order of my questions but I did ask away. I must inform you that they communicated to me like an adult would talk to a five-year-old child. With simple words. Stuff like that. I thought it was funny. Anyway, the first question was about my semen. Why? He told me so they can make baby humans in space. I simply said, "ooh." But then, as I asked him questions, he put visions in my head and showed me in an instant how they do it. As we were walking and talking about the humans in space he walked into this doorway that you can't even see until you look in it. Just as we were talking about humans in space these two kids, about thirteen to fifteen years old, one male, one female, turned to look at us. Both human. Full blooded perfect human beings. They were both sitting down facing away from us. They turned around [and] looked in my eyes. He sort of introduced us I guess. Then they turned around and continued to do what they were doing. Believe it or not they were either controlling, driving or operating the craft or building [we] were in. They were in control of [or] operating something. I was tripping on this because they knew what they were doing and [they were] just little kids. They totally trusted them. Crazy stuff. And being that you can read minds in this situation I knew the kids weren't scared or uncomfortable. They were programmed to master their

job. There is much more to this topic also but that will
scratch the surface of it. As we left, I noticed he was taking
me somewhere else. This was kind of confusing to me also.
This time it's like the room just appeared. We were just instantly in it. I think it's their doorways. They are unexplainable.

Next thing I see is a dead cow hanging, I believe, head
up, butt down. Nothing, to my eyes, was holding it up. I
was baffled. I know cows can weigh tons but it was just
hanging. Next thing they did was dip it into some kind of
gel in a box-shaped pool just big enough for the cow to fit
in. Strangely enough, the gel didn't overflow when they put
the cow in. The pool was filled up. Next they lifted the cow
out and it was cut, dead, and I was starting to get scared.*

I thought I was next. But then he showed me why they
do this. It's all related to the humans in space. He said, what
do humans eat as a child or infant? I said, milk. He said, exactly. What do adult humans eat? I said hamburgers, steaks,
and food. Again, he said, exactly. Then he put a vision again
in my head and explained it all. They can't just take earth
cows in space. They do just like they told me; he said, we
make our own cows in space. Germ free, no fleas, no ill-
nesses, pure cows. Just like the space humans, perfect
specimens. Like I said, I have much more information on
that topic also. Then I asked about monitoring me behind
my eye. They said humans do it all the time. He explained
like this: How does a tiger explain to itself when it hears a

---

* This is an interesting visual in light of the innumerable well-documented cases of
"cattle mutilation" commonly associated with UFO sightings. A noted hallmark of
these incidents is the surgical nature of the mutilation; also, the characteristically
precise wounds tend to be cauterized by an intense heat with no bleeding evident.
It is consistently found in these cases that the flesh has been removed down to the
bone in an exacting manner, i.e., removal of flesh from around the jaw exposing the
mandible.

helicopter coming out of the skies in the jungle? A big metal...scary object. Then all of a sudden they feel a pain in their hip and lose all control of everything except their eyes. Then creatures come out of the object and start doing things to it. Like tagging its ear. Like even taking teeth. They even take semen to preserve the species from extinction sometimes. Basically scaring the crap out of the tiger, for its own good, in a way. He said, so why is it cruel for them to do it, but not for humans? Again I said "ooh."

I'm not positive but I believe the implant is still there behind my eye, or I believe it actually dissolved. If I'm correct, I believe that's what they told me. Then he started showing me things I didn't ask about. He even showed me things that you can't explain in human words. I saw human history in a way. I saw how humans got here, I seen why we are here.

They showed me the day modern-humans make contact here on earth. I actually know what happens the day they "ARRIVE!!" To me this is going to be an incredible time in the history of "ALL" life. Not just human life. The skies will be filled with huge enormous crafts just hovering, silently. This will be a shock for all human eyes and human minds. Many will not survive (not a great mass but a mass of life will be lost) not by the hands of the visitors, but by their own hand of fear. They didn't show me how but they showed me that we are getting ready for the next human extinction. They didn't say when or even if we will be extinct, they just showed me they are prepared to keep the human race alive (again). They showed me the process and how they do it. I was part of that process..."[37, *]

---

* Abductees are often told that they have a special purpose, role, or task. Some theorize that this is a subtle form of seduction wherein these beings appeal to the human ego to garner their participation in carrying out the larger "alien agenda."

In viewing this abduction experience through the lens of the
"aliens equals demons" hypothesis, perhaps one of the most telling
aspects is how the element of fear is employed by the abductors. Interestingly, the abductee notes more than once that he felt fairly
"comfortable" and that he actually "trusted" his captors. Then, at certain points during the encounter, the beings seem to (purposely?)
place him in situations that evoke outright terror or panic. The question that arises is why was this done? It is obviously not due to a lack
of understanding of "fear" as a human emotion, as the beings at one
point tell him "not to be scared" and then later promise not to further frighten him if he will allow a "medical examination."

Might, then, the beings be using fear as a means of control? This
also seems unlikely considering their demonstrated ability to immobilize the captive at will. Moreover, one would assume, having abducted tens of thousands or perhaps millions of subjects, that such
advanced beings would be adept at avoiding situations that elicit un-
necessary panic, if for no other reason than to make their own task as
abductor easier. It seems, therefore, that only a couple of plausible
possibilities remain: Either the beings simply lack empathy or do not
care about the emotional state of their abductee, or, to put a more
sinister spin on it, perhaps, as in the case of the earlier cited Kelly-
Hopkinsville encounter, some sense of gratification is derived by in-
citing fear or panic in human beings.

Continuing to look at this experience in the context of the *spiritual* or possibly *demonic*, we also note that there seems to be an element of what Vallee has described as the "staged" or theatrical" at
play here (176): Certain frightening visuals, including the removal of
an eyeball and the insertion of an implant during the medical examination evoke an "advanced technology" feel that helps to convince
the abductee that he is indeed in the presence of a race of highly advanced beings. Other visuals push the very bounds of imagination:
The abductee admits to being baffled by doorways and rooms that
seem to appear out of nowhere and a cow, of all things, that hangs

suspended by nothing that can be discerned.* In search of an explanation for all of this, it is tempting to assume that this may be a simple "nightmare," or fantasy. Yet either possibility seems unlikely for a couple of reasons: Firstly, because this account, while highly bizarre and unique, *does* fit well within the bounds of the typical abduction scenario as discussed earlier and as reported by countless experiencers around the globe. Nightmares or psychotic fantasies, however, as John Mack noted in an interview, are highly *individual* and thus not prone to fitting any sort of template. Secondly, and most significantly, there is the commonly noted life-altering effect this experience has had on the individual. He, for lack of a better term, seems to have found "religion," albeit not in the Christian sense. For instance, in one video posting he speaks of his alien-given insight into the cyclical and eternal nature of life (read reincarnation), further noting that a hundred years is but a day in the life of your soul.† The beings also showed him a vision of the "dying experience" which he described as "falling up" through a tunnel.

Interestingly, though perhaps not surprisingly considering our thesis, they further informed him that "heaven and hell are merely man-made inventions" and that "it makes no difference whether you kill ten people or adopt ten kids and raise them" because we all "go home" regardless of what we have done in this life.[40, 41]

Once more, the notion that these revelations might stem from a

---

* Vallee speculates that, "Actual beings are staging simulated operations very much in the manner of a theatrical play or movie, in order to release into out culture certain images that will influence us toward a goal that we are incapable of perceiving" (176).

† At one point the abductee notes that the beings actually disclosed exactly when and how he would die. He says this realization "scared him half to death"; so he sat bolt upright and screamed at them to "fix" whatever was wrong and spare him from the certain death they had foreseen. He goes on to relate that the two beings who had informed him of the nature of his future demise looked at each other and then at him with what he read as an "amused" expression, telling him simply "not to worry about it."[38, 39]

mere dream seems highly implausible. The fact of the matter is, few among us are likely to recall, much less be affected by, a dream experienced two weeks ago, let alone one experienced more than two decades ago.

Lastly, we note a reference that is, again, highly typical among abductees to what seems to be a possible breeding program wherein aliens are creating their own "humans in space." Obviously, as footnoted earlier, this bears striking parallels, for those coming at this from a biblical perspective, to the Bible's account of the "Watchers" siring hybrid beings. It also calls to mind the earlier cited reference to "faeries" kidnapping human infants and raising them as their own. Indeed, it seems the theme of non-human beings becoming involved in human sexuality and reproduction reaches back millennia and spans all cultures.

Nonetheless, whether one believes that all of this actually took place in the physical realm, merely in this individual's imagination, or was perhaps somehow "projected" into his mind to simulate a "real" experience, he is utterly convinced of its reality.

Moving on, the most relevant aspect of this story is what the abductee later has to say about the day they (the aliens) appear to the masses. The following is transcribed from a video posting in which he details what he calls "the arrival."

"It seems like everybody, well not *everybody*—a lot of people—are interested in 2015. What everybody's talking about, 2012, and what's going on with that…I don't know. I honestly do not know what's happening with 2012. I really don't think it's the end of the world or anything like that because 2015 is what I know about. So, if the world ends in 2012, how could what I say be true? So [again] I don't know about 2012 at all. I'm not really into it because I don't know about it. Whatever happens, I'm gonna make it. That's all that matters to me.

But anyway, 2015. I like to call it "the arrival." It's—let

me start with how I know it starts or whatever…I don't know what country, but humans—I don't know if it's America, China, Japan, or whatever…we find evidence of alien life; we visually see it…it's unquestionably going to be there. We first discover…these structures…man made. I don't know how you want to say it but just basically 'alien' structures. We find them on the moon.* I don't know if in 2012, that's when we go to the moon—but somebody's going to the moon, and somebody's going to find some important things up there: important artifacts, structures, buildings, crafts—just positive proof—evidence that humans did not do this. So anyway, that's how we find it. That's how we discover alien life. And it's going to—a lot of people still won't believe it. We don't actually find beings or anything up there, but we just see it…I don't know what year this is, when we discover that, but that [happening] opens up to [the events of] 2015.

I don't know if it's because we don't believe they're there, or whatever, but in 2015—I don't know when—I call it "the arrival." They're going to come here. They're going to fill up the skies and show proof positive that they exist. I don't know *why*, but I think it's just so people know that they simply exist. As far as I know, they don't…actually physically land and show themselves, but they show their crafts…They're [only] going to be here for a short time. I don't know if that's when I have to do what I have to do— what they were telling me. When my time comes, I'll know, they say…But, as far as I know, they'll leave as fast as they came. Basically, it's [just] for us to realize that they exist—

---

* Interestingly, an AP article dated August 24, 2007 reports that China and Japan are both currently planning lunar missions. Of course, it is impossible to tell whether the information given the abductee is an allusion to possible future events or simply more "staging" for dramatic effect.

no question about it.

But there will be some problems. One thing I was shown was mass suicides. A lot of people will question God.* A lot of people will think it's the end of the world. There's going to be mass suicides at an incredible level. But I think it would be stupid [to kill yourself]...[Regardless] It's going to happen...I don't know if I'll still be around to witness [all of] this, but it's documented [here] so, basically, that's 2015. I haven't really studied it or [really] gotten into my head. It's kind of like a meditation thing that I have to get into, but I don't do [it] that often. So basically that's it. I don't know what you want to call it—a (unintelligible) prediction or whatever. I'm just basically here to tell you what's going to happen. Believe it or not, I really don't give a damn...I'm just answering a few of my friends...Hopefully this will help them out. I can't tell you what I don't know. Ya know, I can't tell you everything...[like] *why* and all that stuff...but I'll tell you what I [do] know. So that's basically it—2015. Like I said, I don't (unintelligible) 2012, but if I was you, I wouldn't kill yourself when you see them. They're not here to kill us. If they were here to kill us, we'd be...dead a long time ago. Don't worry about it. It's going to happen anyway. Deal with it. Be prepared (unintelligible)."[42]

Again, one of the most remarkable things about this individual's testimony is that unlike the innumerable observers, skeptics, and believers alike who have expressed profound interest his story, he seems completely unconcerned with and in fact oblivious to the hype surrounding 2012. He is instead focused squarely on what he has been shown to happen in 2015. It is also significant that he admits to not knowing "everything" about the motives of the aliens or about other

---

* Perhaps this is a primary goal of these beings.

details, such as the nature of the special task that they appear to have in mind for him. It is often noted that when someone has fabricated a story they usually *do* know everything; or if, perchance, they do not, they are usually more than happy to make something up.

Of course, the most noteworthy aspect of this part of the story is the abductee's description of what essentially amounts to a massive UFO sighting in 2015. Apparently these "craft" will suddenly appear to the masses, perhaps, he speculates, simply to show that they "exist," but they will not "physically land" or attempt to make contact. Even so, this, he says, will leave humanity in a state of shock—to the degree that many will take their own lives.

Needless to say, all of this might be viewed as highly significant by certain Christian UFO researchers who have for years theorized that as part of the end-times deception Satan plans to counterfeit the resurrection, or "rapture," event. The thinking goes like this: The Bible tells us that the coming of Christ will take place very suddenly, "just as the lightning comes from the east and flashes even to the west..." (Matthew 24:27). At this time, the Lord will send His angels to "gather together his elect from the four winds, from one end of heaven to the other" (Matthew 24:31). This, as some imagine it, may appear to earthly observers as a host of illuminated bodies, or beings of light, suddenly filling the skies, only to vanish almost as quickly as they had appeared.

Now, with this image in mind, as well as the one evoked by the abductees' description of "the arrival," let us read carefully the following passage from the book *Project World Evacuation*, written in 1993 (Inner Light Publications). It was allegedly channeled from an extraterrestrial named Ashtar, "Leader of the Ashtar Command," who is by all accounts a very powerful being and a prominent name in UFO circles:

"The Great Evacuation will come upon the world very suddenly. The flash of emergency events will be as lightning that flashes in the sky. So sudden and so quick in its

happening that it is over almost before you are aware of its
presence...Our rescue ships will be able to come in close
enough in the twinkling of an eye to set the lifting beams in
operation in a moment. And all over the globe where events
warrant it, this will be the method of evacuation. Mankind
will be lifted, levitated shall we say, by the beams from our
smaller ships. These smaller craft will in turn taxi the persons to the larger ships overhead, higher in the atmosphere,
where there is ample space and quarters and supplies for
millions of people."[43]*

Interestingly enough, Ashtar's description of the supposed
"evacuation" of Earth sounds eerily similar to the Bible's characterization of the resurrection-rapture event.

In another message channeled in September of 2008 from a
completely different source, an ET speaks of a similar mass "appearance" and the aftermath. This message is aimed at those who will *not*
be leaving the planet and thus seems designed to allay any fear of a
"hostile" alien invasion, as well as prepare those left behind for the
ensuing period of chaos and dislocation:

"I, and others like me, are now present aboard starcraft in
orbit about your planet...We will make our appearance
shortly...I cannot tell you the date or time. It is like the
massive invasion of Normandy that took place during your
WWII. There was a date set, but many factors came into

---

* In *Omega Conspiracy* Thomas notes that *many* contactees and mediums claim to
have received messages from "Mr. Ashtar." Interestingly enough, Ashtar, or Ash-
taroth, was a female goddess worshipped by the Canaanites in biblical times. Worship of this goddess purportedly involved orgies and other wicked practices, all of
which helped to bring the land of Canaan to an all-time low in moral degradation.
This, combined with the fact, as noted in the previous chapter, that many of the
Canaanites were descendants of the Nephilim (giants), again, explains why God ordered their complete extermination at the hands of the Jewish tribes (Thomas 143,
144).

play, many ships [were] needed, many individuals needed to be coordinated. Having said that, I hasten to assure you that your brothers and sisters from other star systems are not invaders. Rather, having been invited, we are coming by invitation to assist, and only assist.

First there will be the unmistakable appearance of ships from other planets and dimensions. This will be followed by events leading to the bifurcation. Those who choose will remain on earth...Those that remain will be charged with returning Earth to her pristine condition and creating a new civilization. Many on your planet are choosing to participate in this grand transition.

Those who fear to be a part of the lighter density of earth will awaken on another planet believing they have always lived there. They will continue their lives in physical density, but one that is not controlled by the dark energy. As things now stand, the majority of her people will leave earth.

Some families will be torn asunder because some will decide to stay while others leave. Some houses will be occupied, some will not. There will be dislocations in the first days. That is why we have advised you to store water and food, and to secure shelter. We are taking steps to minimize the predicted earth changes. Be willing to accept some momentary dislocations; the greater good of all will emerge from this transition.

Those who understand will greet these changes with a positive attitude. They will show others that there is nothing to fear, that we come in peace and are here to assist. They will greet the ships that land.

This is coming more suddenly than many had anticipated. Preparations are speeding up because we wish to thwart any reaction by those who serve the dark. Everything is now in place for the mass appearance..."[44]

According to this and many similar channeled messages, the reason for evacuating certain people from the planet is to save them
from the "earth changes" and the resultant "lighter density" that they
are not prepared for. These earth changes, the ETs insist, are being
brought about by the presence of pollution within the body of
Mother Earth. Consequently, like a living organism with an infection, Mother Earth needs to cleanse herself of this pollution as well as
those who "fear" and who "serve the dark."

Of course, the "dark energy" spoken of by this ET is a reference
to the same "Black Lodge" mentioned earlier, and should be interpreted as Christians, a group whose thought patterns are of the past
and who are thus holding back the earth and keeping the more
enlightened among its inhabitants from evolving to a higher state of
consciousness.

It is also interesting to note the reference to those left behind
who will "understand" and who will apparently be tasked with showing others that "there is nothing to fear" from those who have only
"come to assist." Might this be the special task that the abductees are
being groomed for—to essentially serve as crowd control and to
calmly direct the panicked masses whose reality has suddenly been
turned upside down by an "alien" invasion?

ARE WE BEING CONDITIONED?

What is the ultimate purpose, then, of this massive and decades-
long campaign on the part of the ETs to prepare mankind for an
alien arrival? Again, looking at this through the lens of the "aliens
equals demons" hypothesis, there seems to be only one plausible explanation: For those who will presumably be left on earth following
the resurrection, or rapture, there will already be in place, via a multitude of alien contactees who have been "programmed" with messages
like the ones we have just read, a seemingly plausible and non-biblical
explanation for what has happened, which is, of course, the very

227

event that was foretold by God's Prophets millennia ago, namely Christ's end-times gathering of the saints.

Indeed, any way one slices it, it appears that the groundwork is being laid for mass deception.

A FINAL NOTE OF DISCLAIMER

Lastly, as we marvel at the way in which these "channeled messages" and "abduction visions," presumably from the same (demonic) sources, seem to mesh eerily not only with what the Bible predicts but with the timelines discussed throughout this book, it is very important to factor into the overall equation something noted earlier, which is the fact that demons are deceivers! They will lie and also mix elements of what seems to be the truth with lies—the latter perhaps being the most effective method of deception.

Moreover, many so-called prophetic visions given by "extraterrestrials" have proven to be completely false. One well-known example is a UFO contactee who in the sixties was told that New York City would be submerged under the ocean on July 2, 1967. This date was accepted as genuine by the UFO community and also by a large part of the New York hippie community. But New York, at last check, is still above sea level (142).

On the other side of the coin, one could speculate that if these aliens are indeed demons they may very well know something (perhaps more than most of us) about the timing of the end and are therefore, as just alluded to, merely laying the groundwork that must be laid in order to counterfeit what will undoubtedly be, up until that point, the most dramatic event in all of human history. Whichever the case may be, you, the reader, are now prepared for either eventuality.

CONCLUSION

In this chapter, we began by identifying a distinctive belief sys-

tem that is embraced and actively promulgated by the so-called New
Age Movement. The core tenets of this belief system are shared by
many ancient religions, such as that of the Maya, as well as found interlaced throughout the "alien" gospel espoused by the supposed extraterrestrial occupants of UFOs. This same belief system, in all its
various forms, can be traced directly back to the Serpent who
tempted Eve in the Garden. The message of the Serpent, which runs
contrary to what the Bible teaches about the nature of God, man, and
the Universe, has throughout time been taught by shamans, seers,
and mystics who claim to have acquired their knowledge from gods
whose home is the stars.

Whether deliberately channeled via human vessel, delivered in a
vision aboard an "alien craft," spoken in one's mind in a powerful
voice that identifies itself as "Quetzalcoatl," or in a subtle one that
claims to be "Ashtar, Leader of the Ashtar Command," the message
of these beings is consistent. It centers on warning man of coming
planetary calamities and urging him to request help from his "space
brothers." Most secular scholars who study the alien contact phenomenon agree that the ETs have a definite agenda or end goal in
mind and that humanity is seemingly being prepared for "something," yet they are at a loss to explain what it might be.*

Are these ET messages real? Whether one believes they are or not,
there is no question that the effects on those who have received them
is real. For this reason and others, Harvard's top psychiatrist was so
convinced of their reality that he put his reputation on the line by in-
vestigating a phenomenon considered not worthy of study by most
serious minded academics. In the end, Mack found the evidence for
abduction so compelling that it caused him to broaden his investigation into considering the merits of an "expanded notion of reality."[46]

Thus, as far as alien abduction is concerned, it seems the ultimate

---

* Jacobs, on the alien agenda: "All I hear is how everything is going to
be...wonderful in the future when they are here with us, but I don't hear that it's
going to be 'wonderful' for *us* necessarily...They [the aliens] tend to talk almost exclusively from their perspective and their perspective is very different than ours."[45]

question is not *if* this type of contact is happening, but *why* is it happening? And furthermore, the earlier posed and still unresolved question (at least among secularists): From *where* do they come? Mack, in the earlier cited interview, did not seem preoccupied with the answer to the latter question but did suggest, as Vallee and others have, that we move away from the literal thinking of this star system or that, adding that "They may come from another dimension."

Who are these entities that have been contacting man since the dawn of civilization? Are they the mythical faeries, elves or magicians our ancestors described? Are they "alien astronauts" who have somehow subverted the laws of physics and discovered a way to travel to Earth from another star system? Or, are they the same demons who have tormented man since the time of Noah and who are now busily putting the final touches on the ultimate end-times snare for humanity?

Considering the havoc they have wrought in the lives of those whom they have visited, perhaps Matthew provides the best instruction in determining their true origins:

"You shall know them by their fruits…" (Matthew 7:16).

CONCLUSION

"All truth goes through three stages. First, it is ridiculed. Then, it is violently opposed. Finally, it is accepted as self-evident."

—Arthur Schopenhauer

CONCLUSION

REVIEW OF KEY POINTS

B ecause such a diversity of topics, some rather involved, have been discussed in this book, for the sake of the "big picture" we have prepared a review of some highlights from each chapter. We will afterward close with some final thoughts.

Chapter 1, *Can We Know?*

Here we learned that God has, on numerous occasions, revealed the timing of future events. Examples include the timing of the Flood (Genesis 7:1, 4), the timing of the Jewish return from captivity in Babylon (Jeremiah 25:11), and the timing of Jesus' birth, death, and resurrection (Daniel 9:24-27). Yet based on Christ's statements, "Ye know neither the day nor the hour wherein the Son of man cometh" (Matthew 25:13), and "I will come on thee as a thief, and thou shalt not know what hour I will come upon thee" (Revelation 3:3), most believe that the timing of the Second Coming is unknowable. A closer look at the context of these statements and others, however, reveals that they are aimed specifically at those who are *not* watching, i.e., the "foolish" virgins and the *sleeping* church.

As for the sober, or *watching*, church, the Apostle Paul tells us that they, being the "children of light," will not be caught unawares by the thief in the night (Christ at His return), as they know full well the "times and the seasons" of the "day of the Lord" (1 Thessalonians 5:1-6).

Chapter 2, *God's Sevens*

Here, we discovered how God's use of the mystical number seven in His weeks and sabbatical cycles foreshadows His overall seven thousand year plan for the earth. We also learned that, though the precise year is not known, Bible chronologists have determined that we currently stand at the threshold of the six thousand year mark from biblical creation, the time at which many early Christians, including Irenaeus, Barnabas, and others believed Christ would return to begin His millennial reign.

Chapter 3, *The Jubilee*

Here, we learned that every fiftieth year on the Day of Atonement a special Sabbath, or "Jubilee" was proclaimed, thus granting liberation to the people and their land. The Jubilee foreshadows Christ's *ultimate* granting of liberty (from the bondage of sin) that will take place at the end of the age. Therefore, it is believed that the Second Coming will occur during a jubilee year.

While the original jubilee cycle is thought to be lost, we cited several sources that point to 1917-18, 1966-67, and 2015-16 as being jubilee years. This proposed cycle is bolstered by the fact that events surrounding Israel (specifically Jerusalem) during the two most recent presumed Jubilees (1917-18 and 1966-67) exemplify the theme of "liberation" for God's Holy City. This lends plausibility to the notion that God may, in fact, be using prophetically significant events that have occurred at a forty-nine year interval to call attention to the jubilee cycle, thereby pointing forward to 2015-16.

Chapter 4, *Daniel's Seventy Weeks*

Here, we discovered how in Daniel 9:24-27, also known as "the prophecy of seventy weeks," God laid out a series of timespans based on multiples of weeks that would be benchmarked by events related to Jerusalem's restoration, thus revealing the timing, to the year, of key events related to the Messiah. Preeminent genius and Bible scholar, Isaac Newton, proposed that virtually all of these events had been fulfilled before his (Newton's) own lifetime, except for one—the period of "seven sevens"—which he believed pointed to the Second Coming. Notably, Newton was unique in his interpretation. In fact, as was footnoted in this chapter, most popular interpretations completely miss the prediction of the Second Coming in this passage because they *add* the "sixty-two weeks" and the "seven weeks" instead of treating them as separate periods. Newton, who was mindful of the fact that most prophecies concerning the Messiah refer to both His first and second advent, believed that God separated these two periods of weeks for a reason—that reason, again, being to identify the timing of both the First *and* the Second Coming!

According to Newton, the final return to restore and rebuild Jerusalem would "precede Messiah the Prince 49 years." Assuming that this restoration was realized in 1967, or the Hebrew year 5727, we find that by adding forty-nine years we arrive at the Hebrew year 5776, or 2015!

Chapter 5, *The Feasts of the Lord*

Here, we learned that while largely ignored by the Modern Church, the feasts, or "appointed times," are a critical piece of the puzzle in regard to understanding the unfolding of key prophetic events. It is stunning to consider that when God gave Moses the feast dates He was looking millennia ahead into the future, identifying the precise times in which He would intersect human history through His Son, Jesus Christ.

Just as the Lord used His appointed feast days to mark the calendar days of events related to the First Coming, we can be certain that He will likewise use the fall feasts to fulfill the events related to the

Second Coming. Therefore, we can assume that the saints will be resurrected at the Feast of Trumpets and that Christ will return to Earth with them on the Day of Atonement. The year, or years, for now, remain a matter of less certainty.

Chapter 6, *Signs in the Heavens*

Here, we noted how God has gone to great lengths in the Bible to describe the Sun being "darkened" and the Moon being "turned to blood" as signs of Christ's return in the last days. This begs the question, what could He have been referring to if not the fact that He would place solar and lunar signs (or eclipses) in such a manner that they could be discovered in advance by those watching?

We also noted, interestingly enough, that the word "sign," as used in Genesis to describe God's purpose for the Sun and the Moon, is translated from the Hebrew, *oate*, which means "to come." The word "season" used in the same context is translated from the Hebrew, *mo'ed*, which means an "appointed time" (as in the Feasts of the Lord). It therefore makes perfect sense that God would *combine* the two—feast days and solar-lunar signs—to signal the timing of Christ's return.

Remarkably, just a few years away in 2015, the same year that Newton's interpretation of Daniel 9 seems to point to, we have an exceedingly rare occurrence of solar and lunar signs occurring on feast days. What is more, the feast and holy days in 2014-15 are "marked" in such a unique manner by solar and lunar phenomena that, according to NASA calculations, nothing like it will be seen for at least a millennia.

Chapter 7, *2012*

Here, we took a closer look at the ancient Maya and noted that they, like most other ancient cultures, claimed that their advanced knowledge was given to them by "gods" who came from the stars. We also noted that interlaced throughout Mayan lore are references that seem to corroborate the Bible's accounts of giants with six fingers and six toes, a great flood that destroyed the earth and its inhabitants, and demons being worshipped as gods.

We also identified and listed numerous points of congruence between the Mayan figures of worship and Satan, or his demons.

In connecting all of the dots, we concluded that the Mayan gods and the Bible's demons are most likely one and the same. With this insight, we noted how the mysterious begin and end dates of the Long Count calendar seem to harmonize with the date of the Flood as well as the six thousand year mark from biblical creation. We further concluded that the Mayan references to earth changes, or a coming period of "transition" circa 2012, are quite possibly an allusion to what is described in the Bible as the Tribulation, the time of God's wrath, and the subsequent beginning of the millennial reign.

Chapter 8, *Messages From the Dark Side: UFOs, Alien Visitations, and the New Age*

Here, we learned how a distinct set of teachings that are common to ancient religions as well as prevalent in the so-called New Age, Metaphysical, and UFO movements can be traced directly back to the Serpent in Eden. We also learned that, today, due to the mainstreaming of UFOs and the alien abduction phenomenon, there is an ever-growing fascination with the notion that aliens might be responsible for man's existence and/or evolution. Thus, many expect some type of alien involvement or "assistance" in the coming period of transition that is anticipated within certain UFO or New Age circles.

In looking at UFOs and the alien abduction phenomenon, we noted how respected scholars, many previously avowed skeptics, now accept these phenomena as real. Most of these scholars agree that similar phenomena appear to have been occurring since the dawn of civilization in the guise of faeries, dwarves, or elves. Moreover, a growing number of experts note that the more that is brought to light about these phenomena, the more they resemble the age-old stories of poltergeist visitations, or demonic possession.

Lastly, operating under the assumption that these UFO beings are in fact the same demonic entities who have roamed the earth since Noah's time, we profiled two victims of alien abduction, one of whom was shown a vision of a mass alien arrival and the other a vision of devastating natural disasters, both taking place in 2015 and beyond. We further noted that while these visions and timelines given by the "aliens" cannot be considered necessarily reliable, they do seem to corroborate the notion of major biblical events (resurrection, rapture, time of wrath, etc.) occurring during this timeframe.

FINAL SUMMARY

Again, the common thread that binds all of these elements is the fact that they each point, in one way or another, to a very narrow timeframe. For instance, God's seven thousand year plan (in the sense of a six thousandth year start date for the millennial reign) points to the present day; the ancient jubilee cycle seems to point to 2015; Isaac Newton's three hundred year old interpretation of Daniel's "seven sevens" points to 2015; an exceedingly rare combination of solar and lunar eclipses occurring on particular feast and holy days points to 2015; the millennia-ago established end date of the Long Count calendar cycle points to 2012; the alien/demonic visions received by two separate individuals who live continents apart point to biblically apocalyptic events occurring circa 2015.

Yet, even with all of that, the ultimate question, of course, remains: Does all of this point to the Second Coming as being but a few years away? At this point we will let the data amassed here speak for itself, knowing that as time passes things will become clearer.

FINAL THOUGHTS

As we close, I would like to take a moment to point out what is perhaps the most obvious aspect to all that has been covered in this book, yet nonetheless an aspect so important that it cannot be over-emphasized: the fact that the whole combination of anomalous data discussed here, ostensibly unrelated and derived from a broad array of sources, can so easily be reconciled by simply viewing it from a particular perspective. Some of this anomalous data includes:

- The obviously planned or *designed* ratios of size and distance that allow for total solar and lunar eclipses, or what the Bible calls "signs."
- The odds-defying instances of *feast day* solar and lunar eclipses (signs) occurring in conjunction with pivotal events related to Israel and the Jews.
- Worldwide legends of gods who came from the stars.
- Worldwide flood myths as well as supporting physical evidence for a global flood.
- Worldwide myths about giants as well as physical evidence for their existence.
- The abrupt appearance of advanced knowledge in the archeo-logical/anthropological records some five thousand years ago.
- The existence of advanced architecture now buried under oceans.
- The existence of monolithic structures and monuments that cannot be duplicated even with modern machinery.
- The apparent ongoing visitation of UFO craft and alien beings who are increasingly acknowledged to behave in a manner consistent with the demons of ancient lore.
- The mysterious begin and end dates (3114 BC and 2012 AD) of the millennia-ago established Long Count calendar, which seem to fall eerily in line with the timeline estimates for Noah's flood and the six thousandth year mark from biblical creation.

And the list goes on—and on.

Today, despite the fact that the Bible has already provided an answer to each and every one of these mysteries, the conventional response to most items on this list is predictable: Astronomers who do not believe that the Universe had a "designer" will discount the eclipse as a cosmic coincidence; others who read of solar and lunar "signs" occurring in conjunction with biblically prophetic events will dismiss the notion as superstition stemming from a religion that uses a lunisolar calendar; many mainstream archeologists and anthropologists will continue to shrug off or offer implausible explanations for the seemingly impossible ancient structures; various UFO clubs and organizations will continue to speculate endlessly about the origin and motives of the supposed "ETs" who come from other star systems—but who for some reason, after centuries, even millennia of contact, continue to conceal their identities and motives; certain evolutionists will admit that a flood would, in fact, account for many of the earth's strange features, but will nonetheless refuse to entertain the idea of "Noah's flood" because it is found in the Bible, a book they wish to discredit.

And so, for better or for worse, all of these mysteries will remain mysteries until something fundamental is acknowledged.

THE TRUTH

As the popular slogan from the hit series, *The X-Files*, proclaimed, "The Truth is Out There." It is indeed—for anyone who is willing to go where the evidence leads; it is contained in a book that speaks of fallen angels, giants, a great flood, and demons whose sole aim is to deceive. This single book provides the only cohesive explanation for all of the above. In this respect, somewhat ironically it could be said, we have what is perhaps the perfect illustration of a *scientific* principle known as "Occam's razor" in action.

Occam's razor is a principle commonly utilized by scientists and researchers in determining the most likely solution to a given puzzle.

This principle essentially states: When seeking to understand a phenomenon or combination of phenomena, what can be surmised with fewer assumptions or concepts is done in vain with more. Or, in layman's terms, *the simplest answer is almost always the correct one.*

Of course, many atheists and skeptics would reject the notion of using the biblical narrative to apply this principle on the basis that, "You cannot explain away mysteries by simply posing that 'God' is responsible, or that the 'Bible' explains it." These types of assertions, however, completely ignore the Bible's widely acknowledged bona fides as a reliable historical document and thus seem to be based not on sound logic but on an obvious bias against any biblically oriented explanation.* The intent of Occam's razor is, again, not to lead to the explanation that one is most comfortable with, but to the one that is most likely.

Then there are those who would concede a certain degree of biblical correlation, this on the basis that its storyline *does* appear to match the evidence, but who would qualify this concession by suggesting that this harmony exists only because the Bible texts were authored *after the fact*, in response to these very anomalies. The problem with this position, though, is that most of the texts are proven to have been recorded millennia ago, long before many of these "mysteries" became mysteries. In other words, the Scriptures explained them before they required explanations. The truth, it seems, has a funny way of doing that.

Other truths contained in the Bible include a promise of a returning Savior. This return, according to Scripture, will be heralded by unmistakable signs in the Sun and in the Moon.

---

* Indeed the Bible is very trustworthy as a historical document. If we were to look at a chart that compares the biblical documents with other widely accepted ancient documents, we would see that the Bible is in a class by itself with regard to the number of ancient copies, their consistency, and their reliability. Moreover, one can open almost any page of the Bible and find a name of a place and/or a person that can be verified by archaeology. In fact, so far there has not been a single archaeological discovery that disproves the Bible in any way.

Are we seeing these signs today? Are they pointing toward a definite window of time—a year even? While only God knows the day and the hour, we have learned here that there is nothing to prevent those who watch from knowing the season. And, by all accounts, the season is at hand.

As further confirmation in the years and months ahead, we should expect exponential increases in the following:

- False prophets (Matthew 24:5).
- Wars and rumors of wars (Matthew 24:6).
- Famine, food shortages, pestilences, pandemics, earthquakes, tornados, typhoons, tsunamis, cyclones, hurricanes, etc. (Matthew 24:7).
- Derision or persecution of anything Christian or Jewish (Matthew 24:9).
- Inexplicable supernatural activity (Matthew 24:24).
- False Christs who promulgate false teachings (Matthew 24:24).
- Moral decay, corruption, and brutality (2 Timothy 3:1-5, 7).
- Falling away from the faith (2 Timothy 4:3).

Finally, the Gospel will be preached to every nation; and then, the end will come (Matthew 24:14).

In closing, as we consider the virtual mountain of evidence that points to the soon return of Jesus Christ, one is reminded of a quote by author Jack Kinsella:

> "From where we sit on the timeline, if this isn't the generation the Bible describes, then when that generation does arrive, it will have no way to identify itself."

APPENDICES

APPENDIX A: INTERESTING FACTS ABOUT THE RUINS AT TIAHUANACO

Tiahuanaco (also Tiwanaku) is located in the Bolivian Andes. It sits some fifteen miles from the shores of Lake Titicaca at an altitude of 12,500 feet (over two miles) above sea level. Some have hypothesized that its modern name is a corruption of the Aymara term "*taypikala*," meaning "stone in the center." This location is thought to be the birthplace of civilization in the Americas.[1]

As with many other ancient sacred sites, Tiahuanaco remains an enigma. Part of the mystery stems from the fact that much of the construction is unfinished.

Gateway of the Sun:

One of the featured structures at Tiahuanaco is the ten-ton "Gateway of the Sun" (photo next page) which is carved from a single block of Andesite granite. This monolith, when first discovered, was broken in half and lying askew deep in silt until restored to its proper position in 1908.

Found directly in the center of the gate is the so-called "Sungod," Viracocha, who is depicted with rays shooting from his face in all directions. He is holding a stylized staff in each hand, which may represent thunder and lightning. On either side of Viracocha are beautifully and intricately carved figures, including condors, toxodons, elephants, and various other symbols. These carvings, interestingly enough, are unfinished, leading investigators to wonder what could have caused the craftsmen to abandon their work.

According to legend, Viracocha was the god of action, shaper of many worlds, and destroyer of many worlds. It is said that he created people, with two servants, on a great piece of rock. He then drew sections on the rock and sent his servants to name the tribes in those areas. The Tiahuanaco also believed that Viracocha *created giants* to move the massive stones that comprise much of their archaeology. *Legend holds that he eventually grew unhappy with the giants, however, and created a flood to destroy them.*[2] Later, he would create a new, better people, whom he would teach the rudiments of civilization.

Taking to his wanderings as a beggar, Viracocha eventually disappeared across the Pacific Ocean (by walking on the water), never to return. It was thought that this god would re-appear in times of trouble.[3]

The Gateway of the Sun

Kalasaya Mound:

Entrance to the Kalasaya Mound

Other structures at Tiahuanaco include the megalithic entrance to the Kalasaya mound, seen here from the Sunken Courtyard viewing west. The Kalasaya stairway is a well-worn megalith, a single block of carved sandstone. Like the Kalasaya mound, the Sunken Courtyard is walled by standing stones and masonry infill. In this case, the stones are smaller and sculptured heads are inset in the walls. Several stelae are placed in the center of the thirty meter square courtyard.[4]

Once Under Water:

Polish-born Bolivian archaeologist Arturo Posnansky has concluded that the Tiahuanaco culture began in the region about 1600 BC and flourished until at least 1200 AD. By studying the thin layer of lime deposits in the stone, it has been determined that they had to have been underwater for a considerable period of time. Also, certain parts of the ruins were deeply buried in sediments, which indicates that a stupendous wave of water once washed over the entire area. Posnansky suggested the biblical flood may have been the reason for these deposits.[5]

Shades of Quetzalcoatl?:

In 1934 the Peruvianist Wendell C. Bennett carried out several excavations at Tiahuanaco. Excavating in the Subterranean Temple, he found two large stone images. One was a bearded statue, depicted with large round eyes, a straight narrow nose, and an oval mouth. Rays of lightning are carved on the forehead. Strange animals are also carved up around the head. It stands over seven feet tall with arms crossed over an ankle-length tunic, which is decorated with pumas around the hem. *Serpents* ascend the figure on each side, reminding one of the Feathered Serpent, or Quetzalcoatl.[6]

Violent Sacrifice:

It is noted in *The Tiwanaku: Portrait of an Andean Civilization* that the inhabitants of Tiahuanaco were known to make dedications to the gods on top of a building known as the *Akipana*. Here, people were disemboweled and torn apart shortly after death, then laid out for all to see."[7]

A Monumental Effort:

Because nearby quarries are lacking, scholars marvel at the large blocks used to construct the stone structures at Tiahuanaco. The red sandstone used in the pyramid has been determined by petrographic analysis to come from a quarry ten kilometers away—a remarkable distance considering that one of the stones alone weighs over 130 tons. The green andesite stones that were used to create the most elaborate carvings and monoliths originate from the Copacabana peninsula, located across Lake Titicaca. One theory is that these giant andesite stones, which weigh up to forty tons, were transported some ninety kilometers across Lake Titicaca on reed boats, then laboriously dragged another ten kilometers to the city.[8]

APPENDIX B: OTHER INEXPLICABLE ANCIENT STRUCTURES

Sacsayhuamán:

A Portion of the Wall at Sacsayhuamán

Sacsayhuamán (also known as *Saksaq Waman, Saesahuaman*) is an Inca walled complex near the old city of Cuzco, which sits at an altitude of 3,701 meters. Some scholars believe the walls were a form of fortification. Others believe the complex was built specifically to represent the head of a puma, the effigy shape which *Sacsayhuamán* together with Cuzco forms when seen from above. There is much unknown about how the walls were constructed. The stones are so closely spaced that a single piece of paper will not fit between many of them. This precision, combined with the rounded corners of the limestone blocks, the variety of their interlocking shapes, and the way the walls lean inward, is thought to have helped the ruins survive devastating earthquakes in Cuzco. The longest of three walls is about 400 meters. They are about 6 meters tall. The estimated volume of stone is over 6,000 cubic meters. Estimates for the weight of the largest limestone block vary from 128 tons to almost 200 tons.[9, 10]

Baalbeck, Lebanon:

Approximately eighty-six kilometers northeast of the city of Beirut in eastern Lebanon stands the temple complex of Baalbek. According to theories stated by the mainstream archaeological community, the history of Baalbek reaches back approximately *five thousand years*. Excavations beneath the Great Court of the Temple of Jupiter have uncovered traces of settlements dating to the Middle Bronze Age (1900-1600 BC) built on top of an older level of human habitation dating to the Early Bronze Age (2900-2300 BC).

The great mystery of the ruins of Baalbek, and indeed one of the greatest mysteries of the ancient world, concerns the massive foundation stones beneath the Roman Temple of Jupiter. The courtyard of the Jupiter temple is situated upon a platform called the Grand Terrace, which consists of a huge outer wall and a filling of massive stones. The lower courses of the outer wall are formed of huge, finely crafted, and precisely positioned blocks. They range in size from thirty to thirty three feet in length, fourteen feet in height and ten feet in depth, and weigh approximately 450 tons each. Nine of these blocks are visible on the north side of the temple, nine on the south, and six on the west (others may exist but archaeological excavations have thus far not dug beneath all of the sections of the Grand Terrace). Above the six blocks on the western side are three even larger stones, called the Trilithon. These great stones vary in size between sixty-three and sixty-five feet in length, with a height of fourteen feet six inches and a depth of twelve feet.

Foundation stones beneath the Temple of Jupiter. To gain a sense of scale, note the *ant sized* human figures in each photo!

Another even larger stone lies in a limestone quarry a quarter of a mile from the Baalbek complex. Weighing an estimated 1200 tons, it is sixty-nine feet by sixteen feet by thirteen feet ten inches, making it the single largest piece of stonework ever crafted in the world. Known as the *Hajar el Hibla*, or the Stone of the South, it lays at a raised angle with the lowest part of its base still attached to the quarry rock as though it were almost ready to be cut free and transported to its presumed location next to the other stones of the Trilithon.

The Stone of the South, or the *Hajar el Hibla*. Note the size in relation to the human figures! Its presumed destination lies up the hill, a quarter of a mile away (see the six tiny upright columns in the upper left of the photo).

The reason these stones are such an enigma to contemporary scientists, both engineers and archaeologists alike, is that their method of quarrying, transportation, and precision placement is beyond the technological ability of any known ancient or modern builders. Various scholars, uncomfortable with the notion that ancient cultures may have had access to knowledge superior to modern science, have decided that the massive Baalbek stones were laboriously *dragged* from the nearby quarries to the temple site. While carved images in the temples of Egypt and Mesopotamia do indeed give evidence of this method of block transportation (using ropes, wooden rollers and thousands of laborers), the dragged blocks are known to have been only one tenth the size and weight of the Baalbek stones and to have been moved along *flat surfaces with wide movement paths*. The route to the site of Baalbek, however, is up hill, over rough and winding terrain, and there is no evidence whatsoever of a flat hauling surface having been created in ancient times.

Next, there is the problem of how the mammoth blocks, once they arrived at the site, were lifted and precisely placed in position. It has been theorized that the stones were raised using a complex array of scaffolding, ramps, and pulleys that were powered by large numbers of humans and animals working in unison. A historical example of this very method has been cited by those posing a solution to the Baalbek enigma: The Renaissance architect Domenico Fontana, when erecting a 327-ton Egyptian obelisk in front of St. Peter's Basilica in Rome, used forty huge pulleys, which necessitated a combined force of 800 men and 140 horses. The area where this obelisk was erected, however, was a great open space that could easily accommodate all the lifting apparatus and the men and horses pulling on the ropes. No such space is available in the area surrounding the Baalbek stones. Hills slope away from the only locations where lifting apparatus could have been placed, and no evidence has been found of a flat and structurally firm surface having been put in place and then removed. Furthermore, not just one obelisk was erected but rather a series of giant stones were precisely placed side-by-side. Due to the positioning of these stones, there is simply no conceivable place where a huge pulley apparatus could have been stationed.

Archaeologists, unable to resolve the mysteries of the transportation and lifting of the great blocks, rarely have the intellectual honesty to admit they are baffled and therefore tend to focus their attention on redundant measurements and discussions concerning the verifiable Roman-era temples at the site. Architects and construction engineers, however, not having any preconceived ideas of ancient history to uphold, will frankly state that there are no known lifting technologies, even in current times, that could raise and position the Baalbek stones given the amount of working space. The massive stones of the Grand Terrace of Baalbek are simply beyond the engineering abilities of any recognized ancient or contemporary builders.[11]

APPENDIX C: ANCIENT DEPICTIONS OF UNUSUALLY LARGE BEINGS, AND BEINGS WITH SIX FINGERS

On the left is the hero "Gilgamesh" from the Palace of Sargon II. Note his size relative to the lion that he has captured. At bottom right, note the relative size of the three figures standing before the seated Sumerian god-king. The petroglyph (upper right) showing a hand with six fingers is found at Three Rivers in New Mexico.

APPENDIX D: 47 INCH HUMAN FEMUR

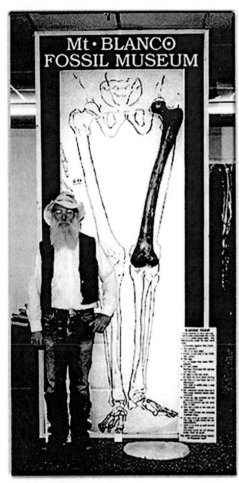

47 inch Human Femur

In the late 1950s, during road construction in south-east Turkey in the Euphrates Valley, many tombs containing the remains of Giants were uncovered.
At two sites the leg bones were measured to be about 120 cms "47.24 inches".
Joe Taylor, Director of the Mt. BLANCO FOSSIL MUSEUM in Crosbyton, Texas, was commissioned to sculpt this anatomically correct, and to scale, human femur.
This "Giant" stood some 14-16 feet tall, and had 20-22 inch long feet. His or Her finger tips, with arms to their sides, would be about 6 feet above the ground.
The Biblical record, in Deuteronomy 3:11 states that the Iron Bed of Og, King of Bashan was 9 cubits by 4 cubits or approximately 14 feet long by 6 feet wide!

GENESIS 6:4
There were Nephilim (Giants) in the earth in those days; and also after that when the sons of God (Angels?) came in unto the daughters of men, and they bare children to them, the same became mighty men which were of old, men of renown.

More Info & Replicas available at mtblanco1@aol.com or www.mtblanco.com
Mt. Blanco Fossil Museum • P.O. Box 559, Crosbyton, TX 79322 • 1-800-367-7454

APPENDIX E: TWO ALIEN ENCOUNTERS INVESTIGATED BY JACQUES VALLEE THAT CONTAIN INTERESTING/RELEVANT REFERENCES IN LIGHT OF THE "ALIENS EQUALS DEMONS" HYPOTHESIS

Transparent Gold:

In *Confrontations*, Vallee relates the abduction story of a couple who lives in an isolated Northern California lumber town. What makes this particular account interesting is a fairly obscure biblical reference used by one of the alien beings:

> "The main event took place five days later, on November 2, 1975, when the same principals (Steve, Stan and Helen) and two other people drove down a dirt trail into the canyon at the base of Cade Mountain. They were still trying to find an explanation for what they had seen earlier [a strange craft and two luminescent beings] and they had explored the area in more or less systematic fashion.
>
> In the canyon, however, they found an area of heavy fog that forced them to turn back, and they became very confused about subsequent events. They remember heavy boulders falling off the cliffs and bouncing around the truck. They remember the door locks being opened and a strange being telling Steve "you won't need that" when he reached for his gun. They believe they saw a hovering object. Helen recalls being lifted inside a room, but she is confused about the time sequence. *One [alien] occupant had a dialogue with her, in the course of which he described a transparent object as being made of gold. Helen answered that she knew what gold was like, and surely it was not transparent. The being answered simply, "There is such a thing as gold that you can look through. It's in your Bible."* Steve thinks he was

in the craft with a transparent window on top and bottom, through which he was able to see China Mountain (Vallee, 165, 166) (emphasis mine).

Apparently, Helen had never read the following passage from Revelation which refers to "transparent" gold. The supposed alien being she was conversing with, however, obviously had:

The wall was made of jasper, and *the city of pure gold, as pure as glass.* The foundations of the city walls were decorated with every kind of precious stone. The first foundation was jasper, the second sapphire, the third chalcedony, the fourth emerald, the fifth sardonyx, the sixth carnelian, the seventh chrysolite, the eighth beryl, the ninth topaz, the tenth chrysoprase, the eleventh jacinth, and the twelfth amethyst. The twelve gates were twelve pearls, each gate made of a single pearl. *The great street of the city was of pure gold, like transparent glass.*

—Revelation 21:18-21

The "Winged Serpent" Makes an Unlikely Appearance:

Another alien encounter detailed in *Confrontations* involves a police officer from Ashland, Nebraska who on December 3, 1967 encountered some strange red lights while on patrol. When he arrived at the location, he discovered that the lights came from a saucer-shaped object hovering above the highway. His next conscious recall is of the craft glowing brilliantly and rising with a siren-like sound as it left the scene. He purportedly had a feeling of paralysis at the time and was nervous, weak, and sick when he returned to the office (159).

Vallee relates part of his interview with the officer:

"During our meeting I asked Sergeant Schirmer directly about any health effects he might have suffered as a result of the UFO encounter.

At he time of the experience the witness felt a "tingling" in his body for a few seconds and local pain behind the base of the ear (he showed me the precise location), as if a needle had been inserted there. A red welt with tiny holes developed at the spot. For three years after the sighting he experienced throbbing headaches that lasted two hours and were not alleviated by aspirin. For the first three weeks following the sighting these headaches would actually wake him up.

I also inquired about his dreams, and I learned that they included a vision of a landscape with three mountain ranges, strange domes, and UFOs.

Dr. Sprinkle noted that after the sighting the witness drank two cups of hot, steaming coffee "like it was water"; he often experienced a "ringing, numbness and buzzing in his ears before going to sleep, and other violent disturbances during his sleep."

Sergeant Schirmer presented me with a detailed pencil drawing of one of the "operators" of the craft as he remembered him under hypnosis. It shows a stern-looking man with a piece of dark clothing covering his head. The opening for the face has an ogival shape that gives it a very Gothic appearance. The forehead is wrinkled. The eyes, nose, mouth and eyebrows are of normal size, although the pupils are enlarged and elongated, giving the eyes a penetrating, fascinated look. Over the left ear there is a small round device with a short antenna, less than two inches long. *And over the right shoulder is a patch insignia representing a winged serpent*" (Vallee, 160, 161) (emphasis mine).

The obvious question that arises here: Why would the operator of a highly advanced craft from another world be wearing a patch with a representation of an ancient Mesoamerican god?

APPENDIX F: NOTEWORTHY COMMONALITIES BETWEEN THE HINDU CALENDAR AND THE MAYAN LONG COUNT CALENDAR:

The Hindu calendar, similar to the Mayan calendar, is divided into stages or eras. These stages are called "Yugas." The last of the four Yugas, called the "Kali Yuga" began in 3102 BC. Interestingly, Kali Yuga literally means "age of (the male demon) Kali," or "age of vice." Again, like the current Mayan great cycle, which begins only twelve years earlier in 3114 BC, no one seems to know *why* the Kali Yuga, begins at this date.

Further, in the Hindu religious text known as the "Brahma-Vaivarta Purana," Lord Krishna tells Ganga Devi that a *Golden Age* will come five thousand years after the beginning of the Kali Yuga. At present, we are well over the five thousand year mark into this stage; thus the timing of Lord Krishna's Golden Age seems to corroborate the Mayan calendar in predicting the beginning of a new era at this point in history.

It is noteworthy that these two civilizations were separated by an ocean and are therefore believed to have had no contact. Is it nonetheless possible, despite this vast geographic separation, that the Maya and the Hindu derived their respective calendars from the same ultimate source?[12]

APPENDIX G: INTERESTING INSIGHTS INTO FOLKLORE, FABLES, AND GODS: EXCERPTED FROM AN ARTICLE ENTITLED "ENOCH AND THE NEPHILIM."

Another source of insight regarding the events of Genesis 6 is the abundance of legends, folklore and fables that speak of "giants" upon the Earth in ancient times, and how there was sexual union between demi-gods from Heaven and women from Earth. Many scholars be-lieve that [these] myths emerged from a kernel of historical fact.

According to Andrew Tomas, mythology and folklore are "thought-fossils depicting the story of vanished cultures in symbols and allegories." There are indeed numerous such traditions among many nations.

For instance, most people are acquainted with the mythologies of ancient Greece and Rome. The gods or semi-gods in these traditions go under different names, but their behavior has a common denominator. Whether these gods are called Zeus or Jupiter, Poseidon or Neptune, Aphrodite or Venus, Eros or Cupid...their sex orgies, promiscuities, cruelties and violence are all of the same cloth. And so are their offspring.

The Genesis story...[it is said] corresponds precisely to the Age of the Heroes in ancient Greece. These heroes were also spawned by divine fathers and human mothers. One of them was Hercules.

The story of Zeus also is well known. Promotheus was aware of the secret that Zeus had no control over his lusts, and aware also of the names of the women whom he would seduce. Because of this and other reasons, Zeus planned for Promotheus to be chained in the Caucasius, where an eagle would feed on his liver each day. But each night his liver would be renewed. In this way, the torture of Promotheus was endless. Eventually, however, he and Zeus were reconciled. But cruelty was not the only distinctive of Zeus. There seemed to be no boundaries or limits to his lust, and numerous women were seduced by him, including Thetis, Europa, Leda, Metis and Dione. Emile Gaverluk says:

> "Zeus' amorous victories illustrate the actions of uncontrolled spirit-beings lusting after human flesh. The whole story of Greek mythology is an expanded version of that astonishing verse in the Bible: 'The sons of God saw the daughters of men that they were fair, and took them wives of all they chose.' (Genesis 6:2)...The mythology of the past is a startling revelation of the uncontrolled behavior of both spirit-beings and rebellious man."

But the mythologies of Greece and Rome are not the only ones that relate such strange events....Ancient Sumerian records tell of gods descending from the stars and fertilizing their ancestors. This interbreeding of gods from heaven and women from Earth is supposed to have produced the first men upon Earth.

The native inhabitants of Malekula, in the New Hebrides believe that the first race of men were direct descendants of the sons of heaven.

The Incas held that they were the descendants of the "sons of the Sun."

The Teutons claimed that their ancestors came with the flying Wanen.

Some of the South Sea islanders trace their ancestry to one of the gods of heaven, who visited them in an enormous gleaming egg.

The Koreans believed that a heavenly king, "Hwanin," sent his son, "Hwanung," to Earth, married an earth woman who gave birth to Tangun Wanggom. It was he who was supposed to have welded all the primitive tribes together into one kingdom.

The ancient tradition Tango-Fudoki in Japan tells the story of the Island Child. The only difference here is that it was a man from Earth and a maiden from heaven that came together in marriage, and spent their time together in heaven and not on Earth.

From India comes the Mahabharata and other ancient Sanskrit-texts, which tell of "gods" begetting children with women of Earth, and how these children inherited the "supernatural" skills and learning of their fathers.

A similar mythology is found in the Epic of Gilgamesh, where we read of "watchers" from outer space coming to Planet Earth, and producing giants.

An early Persian myth tells that before the coming of Zoroaster, demons had corrupted the Earth, and allied themselves with women.

When these and many other accounts, are all tied together, they amaze us by their common core. Each one refers, with slight variations, to the traffic between "the sons of God" and "the daughters of men"; to the sexual activities in which they engaged; and to the unusual and abnormal offspring they produced. A further convincing element in this string of samples, is that these myths and legends belong to people so far removed from each other by time, space and language that collaboration or conspiracy is out of the question. How then does one explain this phenomenon?

Could it be that at some distant point in time these bizarre events actually did take place? Rather than being the fertile product of the imagination of primitive man, they were simply man's crude description of what actually happened? Beings from Heaven and beings from Earth did actually come together, did generate children, and did produce the Nephilim.

Later, of course, many of these myths and legends developed an overgrowth of fictional imagery and imaginative fantasy, which clung to them like moss to the mill. There can be little doubt, however, that beneath this dense overgrowth lies the plant of truth. What began history, ended up as legend.

Above all else, we are convinced that the Bible speaks of these things. The basic message of the apocryphal documents and the various mythologies find corroboration in God's Word. Spirit beings from outer space did arrive on Earth, and did produce these unnatural offspring. By this cross-breeding, man became more and more absorbed with evil and violence; the human race became tainted and corrupted; and soon the Earth was unsalvageable. These extraterrestrial beings, by means of genetic manipulation, had succeeded in contaminating God's special creation; so much so, that their destruction, as well as that of man became a moral necessity.[13]

Selected Bibliography

Brown, Walt, *In the Beginning: Compelling Evidence for Creation and the Flood, Seventh Edition*, (Walt Brown, 2001).

Charles, R.H. (translation), *The Book of Enoch*, (Dover Publications, Mineola, New York, 2007).

Chumney, Edward, *The Seven Festivals of the Messiah*, (e-book) http://www.mayimhayim.org/Festivals/Feast_index.htm

Cumbey, Constance, *The Hidden Dangers of the Rainbow: The New Age Movement and our Coming Age of Barbarism*, (Huntington House, Inc. Shreveport, Louisiana, 1983).

Jacobs, David, *The Threat: Revealing the Secret Alien Agenda*, (Simon & Schuster, 1998).

Marzulli, L. A., *Politics, Prophecy & the Supernatural: The Coming Great Deception and the Luciferian Endgame*, (Anomalos Publishing House, Crane, 2007).

Newton, *Isaac, Observations upon the Prophecies of Daniel, and the Apocalypse of St. John*, (the Echo Library, Middlesex TW, 2007).

Schoeman, Roy, *Salvation is From the Jews: The Role of Judaism in Salvation History From Abraham to the Second Coming*, (Roy Schoeman, 2003).

Thomas, I.D.E., *The Omega Conspiracy: Satan's Last Assault on God's kingdom*, (Anomolous Publishing House, Crane, 2008).

Vallee, Jacques, *Confrontations: A Scientist's Search for Alien Contact*, (Anomalist Books, San Antonio*New York 1990, 2008).

Vallee, Jacques, *Messengers of Deception: UFO Contacts and Cults*, (Daily Grail Publishing, Brisbane Australia, 1979).

NOTES

Introduction:

1. *Human Role in Climate Change Not in Doubt-UN's Ban*, Reuters, Dec 8 2009, http://www.alertnet.org/thenews/newsdesk/N08198995.htm (accessed December 11, 2009).

Chapter One: Can We Know?

1. For reasons that will be discussed in chapter 5, it is believed that this verse is a reference to "The Feast of Trumpets."

Chapter Two: God's Sevens

1. J.R. Church, *The Millennial Day Theory*, http://www.prophecyinthenews.com/articledetail.asp?Article_ID=223 (accessed December 6, 2009).
2. Claude Mariottini, *Of Making Many Books: Writing on the second coming of Christ*. http://www.claudemariottini.com/blog/2006/02/of-making-many-books-writing-on-second.html (accessed December 6, 2009).
3. George Foot Moore, *Judaism in the 1ˢᵗ Century Christian Era*, Volume I, Chapter I, http://www.hebroots.com/lul6.html (accessed December 6, 2009).

Chapter Three: The Jubilee

1. Bonnie Gaunt, *The Rebirth of Israel and its Amazing Timeline corresponding to the Jubilees and the Golden Proportion*,

http://www.fivedoves.com/letters/aug2006/Jubilee.pdf
(accessed December 6, 2009).

2. ibid.

3. ibid.

4. Hillel ben David (Greg Killian), *Yovel (Jubilee) Years*,
http://www.betemunah.org/yovel1.html (accessed December 6, 2009).

5. Nora Roth, *What Are the Dates of the 70 Jubilees?*
http://www.markbeast.com/70jubilees/jubileedates.htm
(accessed December 6, 2009).

6. Rebecca Redinger, *Middle East and West Asia Chronology: Balfour Decla-ration, November 2, 1917*, WebChron: The Web Chronology Project,
http://www.thenagain.info/webchron/middleeast/Balfour.html
(accessed December 6, 2009).

7. IsraCast, *Dec. 1917 - General Allenby Enters Jerusalem*,
http://www.isracast.com/article.aspx?ID=763 (accessed December 6, 2009).

8. The British defeated Ottoman Turkish forces in 1917 and occupied Palestine and Syria. The land was under British military administration for the remainder of the war. The British Mandate expired in 1948 and British forces departed Jerusalem. Israel proclaimed statehood on May 15, 1948 and was immediately attacked by Arab forces that on May 28, 1948 captured the Jewish quarter of the "Old City" which contained the holiest sites in the Jewish religion. Thus, the Jews lost control of East Jerusalem until regaining it in 1967.

9. Gerald M. Steinberg, *Jerusalem – 1948, 1967, 2000: Setting the Record Straight*, http://www.cdn-friends-icej.ca/straight.html
(accessed December 6, 2009).

10. In considering 1917-18 and 1966-67 as possible jubilee years, we should note that some would instinctively presume that 1948 (the year of Israel's rebirth as a nation) was a more pivotal date than either of these and is thus more likely to be a "jubilee" type of event. As noted, however, the determining factor is the nature of the events that transpired, in that each is seemingly linked to the "liberation" of Jerusalem. The same could not be said for the events of 1948. At this time, though Israel was indeed recognized as a sovereign state, during the ensuing war, East Jerusalem actually fell to the Jordanians and was subsequently divided between the two countries via the Israel-TransJordan Armistice Agreement. (http://jeru.huji.ac.il/jeru/timetable.html) Needless to say, not an ideal circumstance for the Holy City! It could thus be said that, rather than a time of liberation, 1948 was essentially about rebirth—and survival. The years 1917-18 and 1966-67, however, seem to fit the theme of jubilee more so than any other two years during the twentieth century.

11. Revelation: The Story of Redemption,
http://www.danielrevelation.com/sda/reference/70th_cycle.html

Chapter Four: Daniel's Seventy Weeks

1. International House of Prayer, *150 Chapters On the End Times*,
   http://www.fotb.com/Publisher/Article.aspx?ID=1000042099
   (accessed December 6, 2009).
2. Arthur B. Anderson, *Sir Isaac Newton and the Bible*,
   http://www.reformation.org/newton.html (accessed December 6, 2009).
3. ibid.
4. ibid.
5. Newton actually predicted the unique circumstances of the Jews' return to the
   land. He writes: "and that since the commandment to return and to build Jerusalem, precedes that Messiah the Prince 49 years; it may perhaps come forth not
   from the Jews themselves, but from some other kingdom friendly to them, and
   precede their return from captivity"
   The prophesied return of the Jews to Israel was something only imagined in
   Newton's day, yet he speculated that the orchestration of the final return of the
   Jews would not occur at their own hands, but at the hands of some other king-
   dom friendly to them. Because the event(s) were as of yet future, he stated,
   "The manner I know not. Let time be the interpreter" (Newton, 54).
   History records that after World War II, at the urging of, and, in concert with
   the political maneuvering of President Harry Truman of the United States of
   America, the United Nations voted to grant sovereign nation status to the Jews,
   allowing them to return to Palestine in 1948 in complete political autonomy.
   In May of 1948, individuals representing all twelve tribes of the nation of Israel
   returned and established the newly chartered country of Israel under the watch-
   ful eye of America, a Gentile nation "friendly" to the Jews. Thus, as was
   prophesied in Isaiah 49 (and in the manner predicted by Newton) Israel was
   reborn in 1948. Of course, the actual restoration of Jerusalem would not occur
   until 1967, thus presumably setting the clock ticking off the final forty-nine
   years until Messiah's return.
6. The Camp David Accords, *Annex to the Framework Agreements*,
   http://www.jimmycarterlibrary.gov/documents/campdavid/letters.phtml
   (accessed December 6, 2009).
7. The Jews lost Jerusalem in 605-606 BC when it was sacked by the Babylonians,
   followed by Medo-Persia, the Greeks, then the Romans in 65 BC. In 167 BC
   the Jews briefly self-ruled under the Maccabees, but since this time it had (until
   1967) remained under foreign control.
8. June 7, 1967 falls in the Hebrew year 5727, adding forty-nine prophetic years
   to this date we arrive in the Hebrew year 5776, which is 2015 on the Gregorian
   calendar. Interestingly, if one counts exactly forty-nine (360 day) prophetic
   years (17,640 days) from the June 7, 1967 date of Jerusalem's recapture, we ar-

rive at September 23, 2015—the Day of Atonement! Coincidence?

9. The "people of the ruler" are often assumed to be of European decent as they were led by a Roman leader, yet if one digs deeper, it becomes apparent that the legions who destroyed Jerusalem were mostly Eastern Roman citizens who were primarily Arabs, Syrians, and Turks (God's War on Terror, page 349). This lends credibility to those, including myself (see From Abraham to Armageddon), who argue that the Antichrist himself will emerge from the Muslim world rather than that of the West or Europe as is popularly taught today.

Chapter Five: The Feasts of the Lord

1. *Christ Our Passover,*
   http://elmersbro.bloghi.com/2006/04/13/christ-our-passover.html
   (accessed December 7, 2009).
2. ibid.
3. ibid.
4. Wil Pounds, *The Feast of First Fruits,*
   http://www.abideinchrist.com/messages/lev23v10.html
   (accessed July 2, 2008).

Chapter Six: Signs in the Heavens

1. Total Solar Eclipse, *Solar Eclipses in History and Mythology,*
   http://www.bibalex.org/eclipse2006/HistoricalObservationsofSolar
   Eclipses.htm (accessed December 7, 2009).
2. *Solar Eclipse,*
   http://en.wikipedia.org/wiki/Solar_eclipse (accessed December 7, 2009).
3. *Tests of General Relativity,*
   http://en.wikipedia.org/wiki/Tests_of_general_relativity
   (accessed December 7, 2009).
4. Joe Kovacs, *Blood Moon Eclipses: Second Coming in 2015?*
   WorldNetdaily, April 30, 2008,
   http://www.wnd.com/index.php?pageId=63076
   (accessed December 7, 2009).
5. *Hebrew and Greek Study Words for Biblical Holy Days: Moed,*
   http://www.biblestudy.org/bibleref/holy-days/hebrew-greek-words-for-holy-
   days.html (accessed December 7, 2009).
6. J.R. Church, *Solar and lunar Eclipses in 2014-2015,* Prophecy in the News
   magazine, May, 2008.
7. ibid.
8. ibid.

9. This determination was made by using data from the NASA eclipse website (http://eclipse.gsfc.nasa.gov/eclipse.html) and a Hebrew date converter (http://www.hebcal.com/converter/). Gregorian eclipse dates were plugged directly into the converter, and if an exact match was not found (Total lunar eclipse on Passover, 'Nisan 14' and first day of Tabernacles, 'Tishrei 15'), the tetrad was rejected as not being identical to the instances Biltz discovered.

It should be noted here that some have criticized the notion of using the Modern Hebrew calendar to link eclipse activity to feast days. These critics assert that the current version is not accurate because it is not the same calendar that God gave to Moses. The Hebrew calendar has, in fact, seen many changes, including going from an *observation based* calendar to a *mathematically calculated* one. Moreover, it is noted that there have been at least three or four different calendars officially employed in Israel throughout its long history.

In looking to resolve the various issues surrounding the Hebrew calendar, scholars have studied it for many centuries; yet the historical material is often fragmentary and incomplete. Nonetheless, in the course of my own research, I happened upon an extremely well-researched and heavily-sourced article (http://www.bnaiavraham.net/guest_articles/The%20Hebrew%20Calendar.pdf) whose author injects a dose of reality into the debate. He begins by stating that scholars "actually have very little information regarding the calendar of the ancient Hebrews" and that, "No one [even] knows when the Hebrew calendar of today reached its final form, adding that "There are as many dates as there are ideas. Scholars contradict themselves in the matter constantly."

As for the argument for the "original" calendar, he notes, "Those who tout the calendar God gave to Moses can go back for support only as far as the latter part of the Second Temple period and to the third and fourth centuries of the AD period." In other words, no one knows which calendar God gave to Moses. Thus it seems, as we found with researching the "true" jubilee cycle, the supposedly "true" Hebrew calendar has been lost to antiquity.

Of course, all of this begs the question: If God intended to use His feasts days as "signs" of His "appointed times," would He allow His plans to be thwarted by man's inability to maintain continuity in observing the feast days? It would seem that the Creator would have made provision for this.

To this point, Daniel seems to imply that God *does indeed* change things to suit His purpose: "And he changeth the times and the seasons..." (Daniel 2:21).

The bottom line to all of this is that the matter is in God's hands. If He has, as the Bible indicates, planned to use the feast days as signs to be recognized by the Church, He will no doubt ensure that the heavens "align" as they should.

10. Passover-Tabernacles lunar tetrads have occurred a total of seven times since 1 AD: 162-163 AD; 795-796 AD; 842-843 AD; 860-861 AD; 1493-1494 AD; 1949-1950 AD; and 1967-1968 AD. No one has yet linked the first four of

these occurrences to any specific events, yet some note that there was significant Jewish persecution in the eighth and ninth centuries. http://jesusmessiah.wordpress.com/2008/07/31/eclipses-of-2014-2015/

11. The dates of the three most recent lunar tetrads are as follows: Passover April 25, 1967, Tabernacles October 19, 1967, Passover April 13, 1968, Tabernacles October 7, 1968, Passover April 14, 1949, Tabernacles October 8, 1949, Passover April 2, 1950, Tabernacles September 26, 1950. Passover April 2, 1493, Tabernacles September 25, 1493, Passover March 22, 1494, Tabernacles September 15, 1494.

    http://www.watchmanbiblestudy.com/rticlesFeasts2014_15.HTM
    http://joybysurprise.com/Sign_of_Messiah_s_Return.html

12. Chuck Missler, *Was Columbus Jewish?*, Koinonia House, http://www.khouse.org/articles/1996/109/ (accessed December 7, 2009).

13. It is also interesting to speculate as to whether this tetrad may have had anything to do with the discovery of the New World by Columbus. Columbus, who many believe was a Jew himself, was convinced that it was his mission to take the light of the Gospel to the heathens of the undiscovered lands (Stephen Mansfield, dates and dead People, page 27). He was quoted as saying, "*God made me the messenger of the new heaven and the new earth of which He spoke in the Apocalypse of St. John after having spoken of it through the mouth of Isaiah; and He showed me the spot where to find it.*" (Quoted in Bryan F. LeBeau, Christopher Columbus and the Matter of Religion, Center for the Study of Religion and Society Vol 4, number 1). Columbus believed that the discovery of America was the climax of a great pilgrimage and the opening of a new millennial epoch in salvation history.

    (http://www.paulbarker.org/Christopher_columbus.html).

    In taking this a step further, many have believed that the establishment of America was divinely ordained by God. Illustrating this, in an article addressing America's role in God's overall plan of redemption, Stan Goodenough describes a view that is held by many Christians:

    "His [God's] reason for elevating America to this position was so that she would ally herself with the surviving remnant of the Jewish people, help them to take root again in their national homeland, and support them in their struggle against a hostile world." He continues, "America's God-ordained, glorious role and privilege...is to serve Israel by standing with her against the rest of the world, and enabling her to fulfill her mission."

    (http://www.jnewswire.com/article/681)

    Thus, while it could be argued that the fifteenth century tetrad may not have involved Israel directly, as the nation, of course, did not yet exist, the timing is interesting in light of the notion that God may have raised up America, at least in part, for the purpose of enabling Israel to fulfill her destiny.

14. J.R. Church, *Solar and lunar Eclipses in 2014-2015*, Prophecy in the News magazine, May, 2008.

15. Baruch S. Davidson, *When is the Next Sabbatical Year?* http://www.chabad.org/library/article_cdo/aid/538797/jewish/When-is-the-next-Sabbatical-Year.htm (accessed December 7, 2009).

16. J.R. Church, *Solar and lunar Eclipses in 2014-2015*, Prophecy in the News magazine, May, 2008.

17. *What Are the Three Weeks?*, Chabad.org http://www.chabad.org/library/article_cdo/aid/947558/jewish/What-are-the-Three-Weeks.htm (accessed December 7, 2009).

18. *Eclipses of 2014-2015*, The Beginning of Wisdom, http://jesusmessiah.wordpress.com/2008/07/31/eclipses-of-2014-2015/ (accessed December 7, 2009).

19. *Financial Crisis of 2007 – 2009*, http://en.wikipedia.org/wiki/Financial_crisis_of_ 2007%E2%80%932009#First_effects_of_the_bubble.27s_collapse (accessed December 7, 2009).

20. Stephen Foley, *Buffett Likens Financial Crisis to Pearl Harbor*, The Independent, September 25, 2008, http://www.independent.co.uk/news/business/news/buffet-likens-financial-crisis-to-pearl-harbor-941619.html (accessed December 7, 2009).

21. Noeleen Heyzer, *Natural Disasters in Asia and the Pacific Underscore The Urgency For A Meaningful Climate Change Agreement*, United Nations, ESCAP, http://www.unescap.org/unis/press/2009/oct/g63.asp (accessed December 7, 2009).

Chapter Seven: 2012

1. *Human Sacrifice in Aztec Culture*, http://en.wikipedia.org/wiki/Human_sacrifice_in_Aztec_culture (accessed December 7, 2009).

2. *Human Sacrifice Mesoamerica*, http://en.wikipedia.org/wiki/Human_sacrifice#Mesoamerica (accessed December 7, 2009).

3. Mark Stevenson, *A Fresh Look at Tales of Human Sacrifice: Mexican Digs Confirm Grisly Spanish-era Accounts*, Associated Press, January 24, 2005, http://www.msnbc.msn.com/id/6853177/ (accessed December 7, 2008).

4. Why is the 260-day cycle so important? Fore mostly, because it corresponds to the nine month gestation period of human beings, which has everything to do with growth and unfolding. It also corresponds to the interval between Venus emerging as evening star and its emergence as morning star (about 258 days),

the interval between the planting and harvesting of certain types of corn, and is related to planetary cycles. Thus, we have biological, agricultural, and astronomical references. http://alignment2012.com/fap4.html

5. In one sense, these two cycles (Tzolkin and Haab) represent the secular and sacred interests of the culture. The Haab is the obvious yearly cycle, while the Tzolkin structures a hidden dimension, closer to the sacred spirit realms. Together, the Tzolkin/Haab serves as a framework for predicting eclipses, timing festivals, and for scheduling visits to shrine sites. http://alignment2012.com/fap4.html

6. Remarkably, thousands of years ago, purportedly using nothing more than two sticks in the form of a cross through which to view astronomical objects at a right angle, they were able to calculate the length of the year to be 365.242 days (the modern value is 365.242198 days).

7. Keith Hunter, *The Long Count Mayan Calendar System*, Ancient World Mysteries, http://www.ancient-world-mysteries.com/long-count.html (accessed December 7, 2009).

8. *20 Questions on 2012*, 13 Moon.com http://www.13moon.com/prophecy%20page.htm (accessed December 7, 2009).

9. *Giants, Gods and the Bible*, http://www.drydeadfish.co.uk/junk/giants_gods__bible_similarities /index.php (accessed December 7, 2009).

10. John Major Jenkins, *What is the Galactic Alignment in 2012?* http://www.bibliotecapleyades.net/esp_2012_03.htm (accessed December 7, 2009).

11. Dr. Tony Phillips, *Severe Space Weather: Did you know a solar flare can make your toilet stop working?*, Science@NASA, January 21, 2009, http://science.nasa.gov/headlines/y2009/21jan_severespaceweather.htm (accessed December 7, 2009).

12. Interestingly, an early mention of a shifting of the Earth's axis can be found in an 1872 article entitled "Chronologie historique des Mexicains" by Charles Étienne Brasseur de Bourbourg, an eccentric expert on Mesoamerican codices who interpreted ancient Mexican myths as evidence for four periods of global cataclysms that had begun around 10,500 BC.

13. *Cataclysmic Pole Shift Hypothesis*, http://en.wikipedia.org/wiki/Pole_shift_theory#Scientific_research (accessed December 7, 2009).

14. ibid.

15. Keith Hunter, *Venus Conjunctions, the Pleiades & the Sheaf*, Ancient World Mysteries, http://www.ancient-world-mysteries.com/pleiades-venus-mayan-

calendar.html (accessed December 7, 2009).

16. Thomas H. Frederiksen, Aztec Religion – Major Deities,
    http://ambergriscaye.com/pages/mayan/aztecreligion-majordeities.html
    (accessed December 7, 2009).

17. Quetzalcoatl,
    http://www.crystalinks.com/quetzalcoatl.html (accessed December 7, 2009).

18. Armando Barraza, *Aztecs Beliefs Helped Conquer Mexico*, Borderlands,
    http://www.epcc.edu/nwlibrary/borderlands/17_aztec_beliefs.htm
    (accessed December 7, 2009).

19. Great Pyramid of Cholula,
    http://en.wikipedia.org/wiki/Great_Pyramid_of_Cholula
    (accessed December 7, 2009).

20. Thomas H. Frederiksen, Aztec Religion – Major Deities,
    http://ambergriscaye.com/pages/mayan/aztecreligion-majordeities.html
    (accessed December 7, 2009).

21. Diane E. Wirth, *Quetzalcoatl, the Maya Maize God, and Jesus Christ*, Neal
    A. Maxwell Institute for Religious Scholarship,
    http://mi.byu.edu/publications/jbms/?vol=11&num=1&id=298
    (accessed December 7, 2009).

22. ibid.

23. Quetzalcoatl,
    http://www.crystalinks.com/quetzalcoatl.html (accessed December 7, 2009).

24. Diane E. Wirth, *Quetzalcoatl, the Maya Maize God, and Jesus Christ*, Neal
    A. Maxwell Institute for Religious Scholarship,
    http://mi.byu.edu/publications/jbms/?vol=11&num=1&id=298
    (accessed December 7, 2009).

25. Was there an actual man named Quetzalcoatl? Likely so, the identities of the
    Mayan gods were often also attributed to rulers who were seen as the "earthly
    embodiment" of that god.

26. Dennis Crenshaw, *Plasma Guns & Sub-riders*,
    http://www.onelight.com/thei/pacal.html (accessed December 7, 2009).

27. *Pacal's Sarcophagus Lid*,
    http://en.wikipedia.org/wiki/Lord_Pacal (accessed December 7, 2009).

28. *Olmec Giant Stone Heads Mystery Solved?*,
    http://www.abovetopsecret.com/forum/thread445497/pg6
    (accessed December 7, 2009).

29. Dennis Crenshaw, *Plasma Guns & Sub-riders*,
    http://www.onelight.com/thei/pacal.html (accessed December 7, 2009).

30. Luke 3:38.

31. Romans 8:14

32. Introduction to the Book of Enoch, Heaven Net

http://www.heaven.net.nz/writings/enoch.htm
(accessed December 10, 2009).

33. *Giants, Gods and the Bible,*
    http://www.drydeadfish.co.uk/junk/giants_gods__bible_similarities
    /index.php (accessed December 7, 2009).

34. Ted Twietmeyer, *There Were Giants in The Earth in Those Days: Evidence of Giants who Walked the Earth,* http://s8int.com/phile/giants25.html
    (accessed December 7, 2009).

35. Cary Nelson, *Human Giants,* http://hubpages.com/hub/Human-Giants
    (accessed December 10, 2009).

36. It is also interesting that Josephus makes it clear that the Great Flood was *an actual world event which had certainly occurred and which was well-corroborated in his day.* Josephus wrote:
    "Now all the writers of barbarian histories make mention of this flood, and of this ark; among whom is Berosus the Chaldean. For when he is describing the circumstances of the flood, he goes on thus: 'It is said there is still some part of this ship in Armenia, at the mountain of the Cordyaeans; and that some people carry off pieces of the bitumen, which they take away, and use chiefly as amulets for the averting of mischiefs.'" Hieronymus the Egyptian also, who wrote the Phoenician Antiquities, and Mnaseas, and a great many more, make mention of the same. Nay, Nicolaus of Damascus, in his ninety-sixth book, hath a particular relation about them; where he speaks thus: "There is a great mountain in Armenia, over Minyas, called Baris, upon which it is reported that many who fled at the time of the Deluge were saved; and that one who was carried in an ark came on shore upon the top of it; and that the remains of the timber were a great while preserved. This might be the man about whom Moses the legislator of the Jews wrote."
    What Josephus writes must be regarded as highly significant, for here was an obviously very intelligent man who would not have been easily fooled. Not content to simply record the biblical description of the Great Flood, rather, he was able to cite other historical sources which were obviously available in his own day to authenticate the biblical account.
    http://www.ukapologetics.net/08/josephus.htm

37. Tim Lovett, *Dating the Flood,*
    http://www.worldwideflood.com/flood/dating_the_flood/dating_the_
    flood.htm (accessed December 10, 2009).

38. *Archaeology Dictionary: Maya,* Answers.com,
    http://www.answers.com/topic/maya (accessed December 10, 2009).

39. *Origin of the long Count Calendar,*
    http://en.wikipedia.org/wiki/Mesoamerican_Long_Count_calendar
    #Origin_of_the_Long_Count_calendar (accessed December 10, 2009).

40. *Underwater Cities, Monuments; Noah's Flood Proof?*
http://www.s8int.com/water6.html (accessed December 10, 2009).

41. Tom Housden, *Lost City Could Rewrite History*, BBC News, January 19, 2002,
http://news.bbc.co.uk/2/hi/south_asia/1768109.stm
(accessed December 10, 2009).

42. *Quetzalcoatl,*
http://weber.ucsd.edu/~anthclub/quetzalcoatl/que.htm
(accessed December 10, 2009).

43. It should be noted that there is some debate as to the precise origin of some of
the Mayan myths and legends, most specifically those that associate certain attributes of Quetzalcoatl with traits normally ascribed to Jesus Christ in the Bible. Chief among these is the notion that this Mayan god was "born of a
virgin." Some legends even describe him as having light skin and a beard. Thus,
the Aztec Emperor Moctezuma purportedly interpreted the appearance of Cor-
tes in November of 1519 as the "return" of Quetzalcoatl.
(http://en.wikipedia.org/wiki/Hern%C3%A1n_Cort%C3%A9s#Arriva)
Scholars note that sorting out the numerous parallels and even contradictions
surrounding Quetzalcoatl's character as viewed through the eyes of the ancient
Maya is an extremely complex if not impossible task. Nonetheless, looking at
the whole of the myths surrounding Quetzalcoatl we find many attributes that
can be interpreted as being linked to Satan, or Lucipher, but also some that
seem to cast a Christ-like cloak of virtue around this god. Perhaps this is part of
a demonic agenda that involves a degree of impersonation on the part of the
one who desires to be "like the Most High."
http://mi.byu.edu/publications/jbms/?vol=11&num=1&id=298

44. Collection of images of figures with six fingers and six toes,
http://www.sydhav.no/sixfingers/statues.htm
(accessed December 11, 2009).

45. Diane E. Wirth, *Quetzalcoatl, the Maya Maize God, and Jesus Christ*, Neal
A. Maxwell Institute for Religious Scholarship,
http://mi.byu.edu/publications/jbms/?vol=11&num=1&id=298
(accessed December 11, 2009).

46. ibid.

47. *Dresden Codex*, http://en.wikipedia.org/wiki/Dresden_codex
(accessed December 11, 2009).

48. Popol Vuh, http://en.wikipedia.org/wiki/Popol_vuh
(accessed December 11, 2009).

49. Diane E. Wirth, *Quetzalcoatl, the Maya Maize God, and Jesus Christ*, Neal
A. Maxwell Institute for Religious Scholarship,
http://mi.byu.edu/publications/jbms/?vol=11&num=1&id=298
(accessed December 11, 2009).

50. *13 Crystal Skulls: Legend and prophecy*, CrystalSkulls.com,
http://www.crystalskulls.com/13-crystal-skulls.html
(accessed December 11, 2009).
51. Carl Johan-Calleman, *Quetzalcoatl: The Venus Transit and the Return of the Energy of Christ and of Quetzalcoatl*,
http://www.experiencefestival.com/a/Quetzalcoatl/id/2327
(accessed December 11, 2009).

Chapter Eight: Messages From the Dark Side: UFOs, Alien Visitations, and the New Age

1. *Channeled Messages*,
http://www.angelfire.com/space2/light11/fc/ what1.html#eclipse10
(accessed December 11, 2009).
2. Kerby Anderson, *The New Age Movement*, Probe Ministries,
http://www.leaderu.com/orgs/probe/docs/newage.html
(accessed December 11, 2009).
3. ibid.
4. ibid.
5. ibid.
6. *The New Age is Condemned by the Vatican: It Teaches that We are All Gods*, http://www.michaeljournal.org/newage.htm
(accessed December 11, 2009).
7. *Jose Arguelles*,
http://en.wikipedia.org/wiki/Jos%C3%A9_Arg%C3%Bcelles
(accessed December 11, 2009).
8. *David Wilcock: Thoughts on the 2012 Prophecy, Coast to Coast Jan 2009*,
YouTube.com, http://www.youtube.com/watch?v=dSg_clr3gac&feature
=related (accessed December 11, 2009).
9. *George Hunt Williamson*,
http://en.wikipedia.org/wiki/George_Hunt_Williamson
(accessed December 11, 2009).
10. *Daniel Pinchbeck, 2012 Time for a Change*, Coast to Coast AM interview with George Noory, You Tube.com (accessed December 11, 2009).
11. *Daniel Pinchbeck*,
http://en.wikipedia.org/wiki/Daniel_Pinchbeck
(accessed December 11, 2009).
12. *Vision Serpent*,
http://en.wikipedia.org/wiki/Vision_Serpent (accessed December 11, 2009).
13. Patricia B. Corbett, *UFOs - A Challenge to Mainstream Science*, UFO Evidence.org, http://www.ufoevidence.org/documents/doc569.htm

(accessed December 11, 2009).

14. *Phoenix Lights*,
http://en.wikipedia.org/wiki/Phoenix_lights (accessed December 11, 2009).

15. String Theory,
http://en.wikipedia.org/wiki/String_theory#Dualities
(accessed December 11, 2009).

16. *Science-Fiction et Soucoupes Volantes* (Paris, 1978); *Soucoupes Volantes et Folklore* (Paris, 1985).

17. *Leading UFO Researchers Confirm Christian View*,
http://www.articlesbase.com/religion-articles/leading-ufo-researchers-confirm-christian-view-454373.html (accessed December 11, 2009).

18. Thomas Horn, *Is the Vatican Easing Humanity Toward Alien Disclosure?*
NewsWithViews.com., May 24, 2008,
http://www.newswithviews.com/Horn/thomas12.htm
(accessed December 11, 2009).

19. John Ankerberg and John Weldon, *The Facts on UFOs and other Supernatural Phenomena*, http://www.crossroad.to/Quotes/spirituality/aliens.html
(accessed December 11, 2009).

20. *Kelly-Hopkinsville Encounter*,
http://en.wikipedia.org/wiki/Kelly-Hopkinsville_encounter
(accessed December 11, 2009).

21. Exopolitics UK Talk to Jim Sparks,
http://www.exopolitics.org.uk/exopolitics-uk-talk-to-jim-sparks/#
(accessed December 11, 2009).

22. Susan A. Clancy, *Abducted: How People Come To Believe They Were Kidnapped By Aliens*, Cambridge: Harvard University Press. Pp. 146-155.

23. *The Abduction Narrative*,
http://en.wikipedia.org/wiki/Alien_abduction#The_abduction_narrative
(accessed December 11, 2009).

24. ibid.

25. ibid.

26. ibid.

27. ibid.

28. ibid.

29. ibid.

30. Angela Hind, *Alien Thinking*, BBC News, June 8, 2005,
http://news.bbc.co.uk/2/hi/uk_news/magazine/4071124.stm
(accessed December 11, 2009).

31. *John E. Mack*,
http://en.wikipedia.org/wiki/John_Edward_Mack#Abduction_phenomenon

(accessed December 11, 2009).

32. John Ankerberg and John Weldon, *The Facts on UFOs and other Supernatural Phenomena*, http://www.crossroad.to/Quotes/spirituality/aliens.html (accessed December 11, 2009).

33. David Bay, *Antichrist, Aliens and UFOs*, http://www.cuttingedge.org/ce1030.html (accessed December 11, 2009).

34. Alien Abductee Testimony, http://www.aliendoodles.com/mystory.htm (accessed December 11, 2009).

35. ibid.

36. *UFO Abductee Story*, http://profile.myspace.com/index.cfm?fuseaction=user.viewprofile &friendID=113298905 (accessed December 11, 2009).

37. ibid.

38. *Life After Life After Life & My Death (part 1)*, Abductee Video Narrative, http://www.youtube.com/watch?v=s6RWpWMVVFU&feature=related (accessed December 11, 2009).

39. *Life After Life After Life & My Death (part 2)*, Abductee Video Narrative, http://www.youtube.com/watch?v=s6RWpWMVVFU&feature=related (accessed December 11, 2009).

40. *Life After Life After Life & My Death (part 1)*, Abductee Video Narrative, http://www.youtube.com/watch?v=s6RWpWMVVFU&feature=related (accessed December 11, 2009).

41. *Life After Life After Life & My Death (part 2)*, Abductee Video Narrative, http://www.youtube.com/watch?v=s6RWpWMVVFU&feature=related (accessed December 11, 2009).

42. *Alien Abduction Story: 2015 – the Arrival!*, http://www.youtube.com/watch?v=hYb-PB6KNCA (accessed December 11, 2009).

43. *UFOs and Alien Abduction*, Christian Information Ministries, http://www.christianinformation.org/article.asp?artID=55 (accessed December 11, 2009).

44. *ET's Explanation of Soon to be Visible UFO's, 2012, & Earths Changes*, http://www.godlikeproductions.com/forum1/message638198/pg1 (accessed December 11, 2009).

45. *Coast to Coast AM: Bud Hopkins, David Jacobs – Abductions (part 5)*, YouTube.com, http://www.youtube.com/watch?v=uJT97OE36S4 (accessed December 11, 2009).

46. *John E. Mack*, http://en.wikipedia.org/wiki/John_Edward_Mack#Abduction_phenomenon (accessed December 11, 2009).

Appendices:

1. Tiahuanaco, Bolivia, *Christ Our Passover*,
http://www.crystalinks.com/tiahuanaco.html
(accessed December 12, 2009).

2. Tiwanaku,
http://en.wikipedia.org/wiki/Tiahuanacu (accessed December 12, 2009).

3. Tiahuanaco, Bolivia, *Christ Our Passover*,
http://www.crystalinks.com/tiahuanaco.html
(accessed December 12, 2009).

4. ibid.

5. ibid.

6. ibid

7. Alan Kolata, *The Tiwanaku: Portrait of an Andean Civilization*,
(Wiley-Blackwell, 1993).

8. Tiwanaku,
http://en.wikipedia.org/wiki/Tiahuanacu (accessed December 12, 2009).

9. *Seventy Wonders of the Ancient World*, edited by Chris Scarre 1999
p. 220-3.

10. *Mysteries of the Ancient Americas: The New World Before Columbus*, 1986,
Readers Digest, (p. 220-221).

11. *Baalbeck, Lebanon*, Places of Peace and Power,
http://www.sacredsites.com/middle_east/lebanon/baalbek.htm
(accessed December 12, 2009).

12. *Hindu Calendar*,
http://2012wiki.com/index.php?title=Hindu_Calendar
(accessed December 12, 2009).

13. *Enoch and the Nephilim*,
http://www.bibliotecapleyades.net/bb/enoch03.htm
(accessed December 15, 2009).

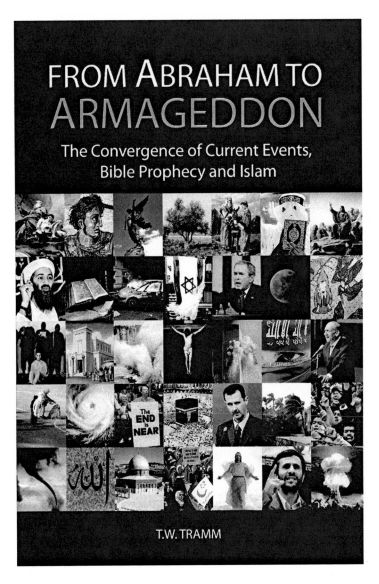

FROM ABRAHAM TO ARMAGEDDON

The Convergence of Current Events, Bible Prophecy and Islam

T.W. TRAMM

Many Christians today are either misinformed or blissfully unaware of what is presently taking shape in the Middle East. *From Abraham to Armageddon: The Convergence of Current Events, Bible Prophecy and Islam* interweaves history, Bible prophecy, and current events to illustrate how the religious and political ideology known as "Islam" perfectly fits the profile of the "antichrist" force that the Bible describes as coming to power in the last days.

Learn how the ten-horned "beast" of Revelation 17 is actually an ancient description of a revived Islamic Caliphate consisting of ten Muslim nations!

Also, the stunning truth about the origins of the Middle East conflict, the Mark of the Beast, and more!

Get your copy today from all major online booksellers.

For more information on this and other titles by T.W. Tramm, visit <u>www.theseasonofreturn.com</u>

CPSIA information can be obtained at www.ICGtesting.com
Printed in the USA
BVOW081436251012

303944BV00002B/25/P